MW00580703

COLLECTED POEMS

•

MICHAEL GIZZI

Edited by
CLARK COOLIDGE and CRAIG WATSON

Introduction by
WILLIAM CORBETT

THE FIGURES
2015

Special thanks to Pilar Gizzi, Peter Gizzi, Tom Gizzi, Miles Champion, and the John Hay Library at Brown University
Cover painting: "On Olympic Blvd #1" 2008, by Lucas Reiner
Author photo by John Sarsgard, August 2, 2010
Layout and design: Berkshire TypeGraphic

ISBN (cloth):   1-930589-42-5
ISBN (paper): 1-930589-43-3

Distributed by SPD, Berkeley, CA

THE FIGURES
5 Castle Hill Avenue
Great Barrington, MA 01230

CONTENTS

COLLECTED POEMS

INTRODUCTION

Early on I thought to title this introduction after a phrase in one of Michael's poems, "Duck billed platitudes." As if from over my shoulder he would see through my attempt to take the mickey out of this assignment and laugh mockingly, "Ha, Ha, Ha!" In life I loved to make Michael laugh, but here I've had to 86 him and secure the door. If I commit some crime of introductionese, some literary pomposity, reveal a tin ear or otherwise fail his genius as a poet, no doubt he'll get in his snickers, but not until I'm through.

There are two fault lines in this big book. One is editorial, the pages of unpublished work that follow the texts of Michael's books. The other, which occurs, with the first poem in Michael's *Just Like A Real Italian Kid*, marks where Michael achieved lift-off as a poet. From this point, until shortly before his death, he will write with urgency, humor, and mocking wit in the language of his truest poet self. What got him there?

I see three routes: his immersion in the work of Jack Kerouac; his going deeper into jazz and, perhaps most crucial, his friendship with one of this book's editors, Clark Coolidge. Older by a decade, Coolidge gave Michael something akin to what Robert Creeley had passed on to him. Coolidge met Creeley in the summer of 1963 at the Vancouver Poetry Conference. In a letter that October to Coolidge, Creeley opens with, "Don't worry so much! Viz onward! The fact you write is all the reason that is…"

Michael's friendship with Coolidge, a near neighbor in the Berkshires, was both that of student and teacher and kindred spirit. In their conversations and car trips, their second hand book buying jaunts and their listening to jazz and talking about Clark's beloved Kerouac, a door opened for Michael, several doors opened into the freedom evident in *Italian Kid*. The poems are one exhale of inspiration, the beginning of his hyper-conscious "talking dictionary howl," an explosion of spirit that comes from, in part, his giddy acceptance of the most outrageous puns—"Arriva dirty," and onward!

In his early poems there are flashes of the extravagance to come and he made formal decisions that he held to—an almost complete refusal of punctuation, a liking for declarative lines—but the poems are built in a deliberate way, brick by brick. Some of their themes, the death of his father in a plane crash and his own troubles with depression, will haunt his poems. The soul-ache in Michael's work will deepen over the years, but he will rumba these blues and leave behind the sparer language of his youth. He will absorb the many images of flight in these early poems into a fleetness of attack as he "Concoct[s] a daydream world."

The couplet "Hard to believe / I think aloud" speaks of a signature characteristic of Michael's mature work. It's near impossible for him to have beliefs, a theme that echoes throughout, his thoughts race so. "Whirl is all," said sage Heraclitus. And I think Michael means that it is hard for him to believe that he is talking off the top of his head. Hard for him to believe what comes out of his mouth. His poems do come out of a doubletalk, burlesque, vaudeville, spiel tradition long tapped into by American stand-up comedians. It's a branch on the tree of homegrown American surrealism. Think of Milton Berle, Richard Pryor, the outrageous antics of Dean Martin and Jerry Lewis, Moms Mabley, Abbott and Costello, Burns and Allen—Michael tuned into their frequency. Kerouac's prose line picked up on this, as well. Another talker out loud, though of the 19th century, is Michael's beloved Herman Melville. I think his fondness for journalism—Michael loved the great Joseph Mitchell—relates to reporting, organized but not interpreted, what is actually said.

That alcohol and drugs sometimes sapped Michael's energy, as did a course of Interferon to treat his hepatitis, helps account for the explosive nature, the bumper car collisions of his poems. When he was on his game and the force was with him lightning strikes, SHAZAM…Kaboom!

I see *No Both* as Michael's great book. Well, one leg of a triad completed by *McKenna's Antenna* and *New Depths of Deadpan*. Here is where his "habit to take the wrong road" leads him. These are mordant and ecstatic poems. He wants it all. Either/or? No, both! "It's the wind in the willies," and he reaches his ambition to "offend everyone I know/and have them thank me." In *No Both* he writes, "There is no shame in poetry" and he shows what that means. He takes this energy through *terza rima* just to see what he can wring from that measure, and then in *McKenna's Antennae,* his improvisations while listening to Dave McKenna—the pianist Whitney Balliett called "Super Chops"—Gizzi picks up speed and the poems plunge down the page like solos that write themselves. You reach the end of one and you can't remember the beginning. Dark, hilarious and exhilarating. One rhapsody after another.

My Terza Rima, published after *No Both*, belongs to this period. It is a triad of its own including poems in *terza rima* dedicated to Providence, where Michael went to college and graduate school at Brown and where he lived the last years of his life; a group of prose poems titled *cured in the going bebop,* dedicated to Clark Coolidge and available on CD, read by the poet; and *Too Much Johnson*, poems in Gizzi's high rhapsodic mode. In these sustained bursts Gizzi works with and against three forms gathering his forces and locking them in for the blast to come.

His last published poems, a pamphlet titled *in this skin* (for Pen Creeley), are anything but rhapsodic. They are spare, speak of fear and "concealment," and they end with the heartbreaking line, given his death two months after printing but eight copies of the chapbook, "I'm sorry, but I can't stay." These late works cause this reader to consider how mercurial Michael's poems are, how ruled by his ups and downs, how they dart and dance like a broken field runner obeying the signals of his nerves, and how sad a note he could sound.

I loved Michael as a friend and I was not alone. The poet Ed Barrett described him as a "ruined angel," which sounds right. He could be hard on others but was harder on himself. He had a vulnerability that drew you to him and a gift for one-to-one connection. He was great fun to be around and a comrade and, I find, in writing this, resistant to anecdote. I know some of his biography but our history took place at lunches and dinners, after readings—he organized a great many and gave much to his fellow poets—and in working together on a few projects. He was agreeable to work with and again I will not be alone in saying so. His edge, sharp and sudden, flared when he was in extremis. For his sake I wish he had been less tormented, but had his inner weather been otherwise, his poetry might have been different. That would have been literature's loss.

— William Corbett

MY GRANDFATHER'S PANTS

michael gizzi   bench press

for my father

Pieces from an album of
family & friends

MY GRANDFATHER'S PANTS

some will call it Spring
that I found his old trousers in the attic
forest-stained
a peace of each season in their cuffs
the pockets too big to put in my hands

I remember his hands like apricot leather
water breaking through the knuckles of his fist
O yes
and a river of feathers when he'd been drinking

he was handsome
now he's dead
I wear his trousers
like a ring of years around my legs

CORAZÓN HAS HUNDIDO
(Heart, You have Drownz ed)

for my wife

when you left
I went into the hills
with a body of whiskey
to be near you

I swallowed faces I couldn't digest

I was an oak stump
an island shed
lost in New England America
Santiago de Chile didn't exist

it is late October
Autumn has burned itself out

my life is my own
my dreams are not

I imagine the black lung of a miner
drowned in the Atacama Desert
his rough hands wading
in the hollows of your face

corazón
    has hundido
corazón
    has hundido

Each night I sleep at the door of your face

IN THE CORNERS OF HIS CRUEL BOX

for Tom

in the corners of his cruel box
my brother sits quietly
loud with anxiety
and armed with nervous ticks
he's had since childhood

but lately he's begun to swallow himself
imagine—he swallows himself like a pill
loud without water

there are times he isn't there
but I am aware
of his beautiful hands
and the angels in his bones

DRIFTS/ASCENSIONS

for Michael Dietz, an architect

I walk alone
the stalled door of my life rusting
will it ever open again

I feel the long weight
as if I were pulling stars

I walk alone with my only garland
a garland of pistols jammed in the rain
and I have felt no pain today

I lower myself into the hot bath
O the memories come so fast

and the radiator spits in my heart
this furious languor—

imagine me at large with the herons
great blue and throaty opal
imagine me the envy of Audubon
preening on the riverbanks
the lewd blue necks drifting
ascending the coal-blue night

though nothing has changed
things are not the same

an architect a friend of mine
once said to a buxom artist
my dear
you remind me of a rubber balloonist
with your mental ascensions

and so it's like a death in the family
seeing the face you remember the heart

feathers in the bath
the lung in the tree

REQUIEM IN MARCH

for my father

Father when I heard you were gone
I walked in my sleep
like a gun looking for a head

was it wrong to think you were indestructible
if it was only a plane crash
why didn't you walk from the wreckage

after three days of rain
the earth is drenched
and shiny like an airplane

I think of birds that bathe
in puddles on your grave
biting water finding a life

and those that die
lying like airplanes
in the forest

I have dug ditches
in my skull
for each of them

ON THE JOB AT THE INSTITUTE

for Jimmy

I work the first shift on the white ward
today I watched a boy lose his mind
you might say he shook hands with the trigger
and then I had to leave him roped in his room
I can't help thinking that I've hanged him

I wonder how
the second shift feels about this

THE BICYCLE

for Glenn

this grease
on my heart
reminds me

we shared a bicycle
we shared our shadows
in the madhouse

how many times
did we peddle
through each other

we wiped the grease
from each other's hearts
and tried to keep the chain clean

these years have passed
without enough spokes
to make a wheel

but the grease
on the bicycle's chain
remains

if I were a woman
I'd have run away
with you

perched on the crossbar
content with the naked odor
of your heart

THE LUSH MAN

for Gray Wilcox

speeding in his car at night
he imagines hitting babies

the woman he loves sitx next to him
but he is miserable

he drives his car to think

and all the smiles behind
the smiles of the headlights terrify him

*

always in the thick
in the slow green

he imagines auto accidents
something is rustling

how to be complete

a shadow behind the heart
hugging the dense

*

and each night
after the whiskey

after the water dreams
the dreams of her in twos

between the leaf-sleep
and the wind's knee leaning

he is a green runner
chopping the mist like snake fat

POEM FOR IPPY

I

and so I came home
because I did every night
like a pharaoh to his tomb,
the city behind me in the evening,
a blushing negress
and I a soot-faced Tut
of Chattanooga Freight fame
so poorly paid.

II

sometimes you would talk in your sleep,
a voice so soft it was early September
"Autumn is like the death of a pharaoh,"
you'd say

"it's all that regal."
and I would play my head into your hair
and be a bundle of leaves.

III

I have seen a legion
bleeding in your face.
the long mouth, the sad wisdom
of those who would never love,
though they dared
to love the husk of you,
rinsed around your long body
like leaves.

LATELY HOW I AM FLYING

it seems how lately
ragged wings are finding a home in my clothes
growing into my skin
and I am sleepless
breaking water to touch you

    I am a man becoming a bird
    a jawing hawk
    that hunts for fish
    to feed his joy
    and hunched in the night
    tree'd to a moon
    without sleep
    I am a fool for lakes
    quiet and crazy

and if sometimes
I am chasing shadows
raking your long ways
it's only that
I've watched you
creasing water in the night
until I am trading my clothes for you
hulking through the heads of the sycamore
slow with blown lushness

NECROPHILIA

from where I'm sitting
I can watch all the boys
enter the Men's Room

I dream of remaking love
to all the women I've loved

what are a cricket's bones
without a cricket's song

hands reach for each other
sleepwalking like tongues
through a ditch

RECURRENCE

I lie in bed
my face slows to sleep
a forgotten dream approaches
casually

 by an old pond
 under the arm
 of a squatting barn
 hands a heavy nest

 the barn and the nest
 have been lusting over the pond
 for many years
 it seems they were meant to

I drool on my pillow
like a baby
or a man dying
I am waiting for directions

water laps in a tunnel
my bed lists

now I sense them all:
the dark stall
the damp skin
the lost relationships

A SONG

    tonight
      rumlight on the porch
I dream of the finest tobaccos

I am soft smoke
    curling in the highest spaces
        between two trees—
        aviary

somewhere down the road
    hidden
my father is pissing
    hot wine on maple feet

does he dream of me

O father
    come share my porch dreams
        in the trees
in the trees

THE CHILDREN OF SUBURBIA

the children of suburbia
pull mother's hair
instead of red wagons
their veins are full of bleach

and as the children
toy with death masks
dead men fall from window sills
to realize
their children are only
voodoo dolls

nothing has changed
you carry broken
men across your shoulders
and wait your turn

SOMETHING ABOUT OCTOBER

if it is October
it is almost late,
wet leaves long
in sleeves on the lake;
we are lonely with anyone.

and if it is October
it is under the hats of old men
fallen to sleep on porches
that a dream
is running out of color.

SKETCHES FROM AN INSTITUTION (MOSTLY WATER)

we eat we sleep
we wake and we are hungry
wheezing with brittle fires
eyes chewing dry leaves

I miss you wet
and barny loving

*

we'd do it in the loft
you were long and I was longing

how I remember
the supple gnawing
the *hush*
the gathering of water

many the wet afternoon
mouse-back gray
that made blue eyes rare
made dark curls darker
wet rhythm through rhythm
made water love's medium

the seasons of water
are like the seasons of a woman

and that ancient bed
like water in the crow's nest of the barn
that bed made heirlooms of your arms

*

but lately we are blue
I am chipping my teeth on you

GONE TO THE SOUTH

I am running with the leaves
I cannot face myself.
I sleep with the animals
it's safe for dreaming.

Chile—
moon along a horse's tail,
gone to the South
you are far to be away.

I am alone
though a lot with the animals
and sometimes we lie
just to hear ourselves speak.

now the clouds
are halfway down the mountain:
there is no escape
from what you've left behind.

THE ODOUR OF ANTIQUE WOOD

Saira
make me an April
applewood and remembering
though we were deaf
we heard the colors of the forest
with a blind man's ears

under the attic stairs
under leaf warm
dreamily undoing a braid of hair
who could have prophesied winter?

thick summer
ripe leather
late leaves
and I am stranded
the way a rocking horse
runs

AUTUMN CAME TONIGHT

Autumn came tonight on a freight from Pennsylvania
headed out of Fairless Hills
bundled with steel and leaves
the steel was for building
the leaves were for me

it was my second day on the job
I caught her red hands in the car
still fresh among the steel
the noose was around the year

I told the foreman to have a look
and he said that was nothing
last year we found ptarmigans
in one of the cars
and he said
they came all the way from Canada

I put a few leaves in my pocket

LYING AWAKE AFTER LOVING YOU

lying awake after loving you
makes my body strange to me

not so unlike my grandmother's palm
which involved my hand
with an Adriatic sea
when we'd walk
to the corner store each day

rose petals sleep in a bowl
on the sill dreaming
desiring roots

a naked circle burns on the ceiling
I think *it must be your soul*

lying awake after loving you
I smoke a crooked Italian cigar
and sip some whiskey
I dream of the hair
on the back of your neck

I am older now
leaves drift in dark places
I am still a stranger
in what seemed
a familiar body

carmela bianca

poems by michael gizzi

for Signora Carmela Gregoretti

MY ITALIAN DEPRESSION

it's only right that I'm alone
I always sulk
at family gatherings

my heart is
a stump
my sorrow *so tall*

a sliver of light
beneath a door
of bone

RELATIVE

one upon the other
the relatives die
so many I've
lost count

dig a hole
you'll find a hole in it

I don't know where they are
I seldom go out anymore

I inherit shoes

BROTHERS

waiting with my brother
my other self
waiting for anything

the weather heavy with weather

under a tree
the one nearest the sundial
we talk of omens

this heart that we are choking on

we talk of the family
whose smile is the sound
of a book closing

we lunge forever in a moment

the earth shudders
quick & huge
out of necessity

we are still…

my brother
my other self
we are light years into each other

we lunge forever in a moment

BARNS

I've spent whole days
walking down city streets

condemning people on sight
muttering under my breath

he should be shot
she should be put to sleep
please

don't misunderstand me
I'm as hard on myself
it isn't easy being a country boy
I kick barns & they fall over

if I could amass a sizeable sum
a small yet
self-sufficient fortune
I'd quit this nervous city

in the country
I'd be just another boy
kicking barns
but for one exception

my toe of gold

COURTING THE FAMILY JEWEL

I hold an arm
under your hair
over my arm
your hair is spread

widow's peak
beacon of gem

something precious
guides the dark

the shadow
eaten slowly
out of an opal

LOVE FALLS SO FAST

traveling all night
tallowing bones through a sleeve of darkness

cunning as a tunnel searching
for a wrist which is a throat

suddenly the wind drops for miles in my chest
& I descend dreaming in a foreign tongue

thoughts of your eyes of your hands
love falls so fast

UNCLE KNOLLIE

the family has gathered
in the most comfortable room
to nurse a tension
noisy eyes click
like empty pistols

as was your style
the day has come about
beautifully
you have circled to sit
for the last time

'and what doth the Lord
require of thee, but
to do justly, and to
love mercy, and to walk
humbly with thy God?'

how is it with you
in the country of your heart
the heart's green wintering

NOCTURNES

the
wind
combs
horses

polishes the air

moonlight
is
throwing
fish into the trees

*

just before
the fire's out

the harvest glows

my fingers grow
long like insomnia

my throat begins to slip

in the distance
the sound of water

        *

sleep…
still life
preening

FOR & AFTER PABLO NERUDA

death
was your other pocket
the dark room
where you kept
the negative
of your hand

your moon sulks
in an empty shoe
I hear the shuffle
of your soul
your feet
beneath the flesh
like a thing
begun in sorrow
& the wind bangs
the heart back

Pablo

they have killed you
& called it nature
they have ordered
all the stones

upon your grave
to keep you still

Pablo

death is a caravan
it knows its outriders
like a pocket
only the hand remembers

MIGRATIONS

> Colle rondini fugge
> L'ultimo strazio.
> —*Ungaretti*

for Edwin

in my dreams I can never lift my arms

at times it grows unbearable
& at times I believe
I am someone they don't know
an acquaintance they've made but forgotten

they sleep beneath their separate lakes
sleep despite me
& because of this

I've perched behind my eyes
two shadows nailed to a coma

imagining arms

imagining I belong to myself

*

for Sophie

the silence before flight
silence with large eyes
like a crowd of hands drowning

*

the sun squats in the hills
old with old secrets

the slow bloom & the tilt
sliding away like a gash

dragging the clouds

*

dusk go down I'm looking for a star

the tongue of a horse
falls across the face of the moon

*

pinelight is dozing

hands yawn
the earth is moving

an elm creaks
feeling its age

the air has a face
you can rest in

*

harvestmoon
the leaves walk

dust of slow hooves
on the moon's brow

we beat our wings

wind of splinters
history of departures

*

for Brian

a day is down

we head for home
like a drowsy axe
on a green journey

dreaming of wood

*

sweet familiar
make dark corners
darker

let language dream

I am paddling into nets
green whisper
rivertree

how deep we go

*

for David

the brown hours
owl's breath

face of the earth on its hands

& the light beneath the land
beige before resurrection

the loneliness & the loud spaces

a long bird rides the mountain
the soul the perfect pitch

I no longer know that I am listening

*

light is riding on a pear-backed bird
a peach horse husks the air
I can smell my nerves

*

lake's edge

the slope of the soul
steep in the throat

a dark bird swims
overhead

his shadow leans
on taut water

one bright kingdom
another

*

the lake dreams the sky

life rises
in my cupped hands
my watershed

the shadow of a bird
that I am choking on

*

up the slow blue hills
with rifle & a knife
darkness booting in
& the light grown unsteady

in one night
you can swallow a countryside

*

November
endless evening
dark hand that says *goodnight*
& lame farewells on long porches
ponderous moments of air

eternal evening
blond leaves in buffed tides

piling for warmth
& those that made us
porch of blood
huddles of love waving

heart's wand

*

for Nonna Carmela

she clots in her hut of blood
dying her family's deaths

blood of the tree clutters her soul

she has never seen
the cemetery of the stars

SCARECROW (A LIFE)

I am the surplus of a thought

a body of straw
buttoned in the wind

animal shy & mute

*

I awake to the slap of an orchard
leafwhack on taut air

I am under myself
in leaves

*

Hail this yellow session
yellow siege

I am intimate with my eye

& I am all
in my mouth with conviction
like a child biting water

SCRATCHING

for Phil

we are dull in November

the forests are
full of gallows

this side of the snowfall
our senses need quarrying

CARMELA BIANCA

Nonna Carmela
la bella donna

Carmela bianca

bianca signorina
dolce verdura

una verginella

Carmela bianca
la prima alba

alba

bianca

2/1
contrition

because
I dread
the loss of
heaven
& the pains
of hell
but
most of all
in honesty
because I
offend thee
my god
who art all
strange
& deserving
of my love

2/3
fear of the lord

the heart in
a clutch
the body
shudders

an island
slipping
breathes into
the sea

when I
am water
I am
afraid

fear
becomes a rock
with a
gender

2/6
mimesis

I'm caught
my eyes fall
into themselves
the moon
unwraps
a mummy
in a field

the image
pivots
& rolls like
a mouth

2/9
stigmata

being eldest
I keep my silent
vigil

between two wounds
two bodies
sleeping

my wife
dreams of flight
my brother
climbs
the water
listen

the deepest
regions
of my belonging

2/10
sharing

there are days
during which
I do nothing
else
I attend
with full
obeisance
the private
god
of my soul

you
must tell me
this

40

inscription from the Coast of Sand

in the vast
emptiness
of the white
desert
I live
a lighthouse
a voice
blinded
turning
on its song

valentine

the moon
hangs
in a shallow
ditch

the heart
does away with
distances

I am ripe
I am
gathered
from this curved
melancholy

above
the harbour
windows lean

2/17

ibidem

today
you are immortal
you know
how long
you've waited

nothing
has changed

you carry
broken men
across your shoulders
you wait
your turn

you dream
of the night
because
it's good
for sleeping

2/20

progenitor

moisten
your thoughts
pray
for rain
for the genius
of a
torso

do not
be this lame
man
pissing
into himself

2/23
perseverance

&
when the body
hoped
the heart
would break

the grief
was
endless
the agony
in the garden

2/25
compline

with all this
distance
between us

rather than
shout
whispering

while I light
this solemn
candle

that you
might know my
voice

the length of
light within
my prayer

my prayer
endless

2/26
       matins

in the air
there are rumors
of amnesia
caves walking on
forever

in a single
man
so many living
hands

like the kisses
of birds
the rumor
passes

2/27
ash wednesday

ice hawk

*

pure light

*

that will
not
rust

2/28
lenten

starving
I will
abstain
guiltless
I will gather
my hands
to pray

penitent
& gaunt
high
in my bones

BIRD AS (& OTHER RIVER PARTS

MICHAEL GIZZI

.for Ip

My heart in hiding
Stirred for a bird,—the achieve of, the mastery of the thing!
—*G. M. Hopkins*

So long as any body part
can articulate a bird
in flight
(say Ibis

remains
Every

Where a wing—
air

Eye of a man in love
with rivers

o there-
fore
wading

birds

    And why not
    If wings fit—

    Run.

    For your life—
    a something soaring

    You who've never flown
    Except

        to flutter

1

Dear V

    Just this
a note   on depression:

I have laid me down
in river silt

like the stone
always beside itself.

      Your dark bird
      swims overhead.

2

      You say   you can't
fly
flat on your back
make that upright
recovery
necessary to being
at ease   w/ your
self

      That's right
some nights
I dread
for this simple reason
they don't fly
for me even -
ings I sit up & tremble
at the far
end
making weird connections

3

    Nothing really:
a blue
place.
You follow

a tunnel to
its own
tunnel.

Eyes in tow.
    The eyes in tow
    when a sudden
    turning birds
        your flesh
              steps back
    the heart is
    a cliff
    & so it's always
    come to this
           that
                  we are man
made to break.

4

    If it's true:
                I am not my body
then why not a bird
the tree &
the apple in it
are successive
objects
necessarily essential
and subject to
fits of possession.

Damn these arms the hands
pushing air they won't let
up they don't
lift off.
The desire to be bird
like as to freeze

51

my fingers glare light
of ice & the air
    chimes:

       youre ground dead
it's a specialty

                       rocks
                       don't fly   theyre
                       flown

                       butt   youre bittn
                       you dip
                       shit
                       all the same

5

       Bird as a bird
is   what keeps a man
Keeps him up:
This keeps his heart
from falling
              down.
Bird as soul
or so it's said   sempiternal

       Long
         white
             wing-
                  strides,
            long
         white
       scythe   lifts the air
knows
what goes in that long white head.

Know
that I don't.

6

Is there　　　　　else at once upon
good reason for　　　the day this door
distinguishing　　　to the river rising
the sense in which　tells us:
persons　　OR　　we are two
may be said　　　　of us—
to persist　　　　　2 fingers to
　　thru time　　　a fist
w/ that in which　　at a door
familiar physical　　waiting for something more
things　　　　　　unlikely, tho
may be　　　　　　a river's the sum
said　　　　　　　of its (each
to persist　*thru time*　of its) private
lately　　　　　　river parts
is it like rapport

7

Dear V

　Just this—
a manic song

Please
do not think me.
I know
You will not.

　　Say instead:
　breath is man's animal
　snowy egret is my emblem

53

winter's home in
the winter body
nervous bird
in the act of
plumed bird   tall stalk   swallowing fish

                               against a blue field

        + +

                Parker's Point
                Chester, Connecticut
                5/75

AVIS or (the replete birdman)

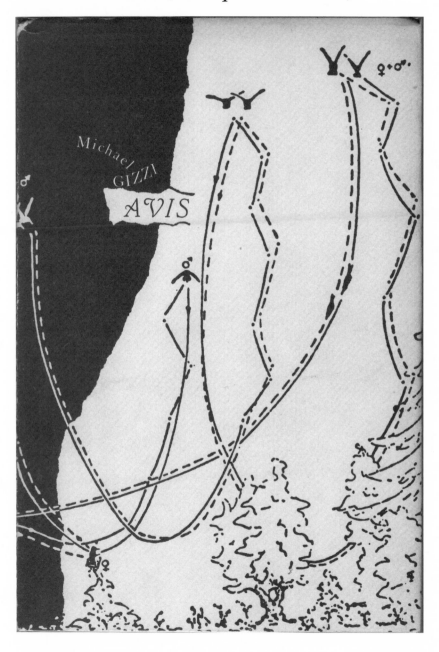

for Pilar (who kept up)

"Beware the Jubjub bird,"

ONE

Memory
Is what Pavlov called
In the motor context
Trial movement
The dog for example 'training'
Salivates
So it happens that trend
Comes to play mammal
(Here too the herd learns
From the pioneer
Tradition
A certain kind of progress
Without a date objects
Like actual sticks
Branches on which fruit might
Hang
In arboreal habitat
The fruit a detour
                For the birds

              •

Historic shorthand
On the creamy bay
Mist un
Lifted
Wigs secure colonial
Quaint
      Aviso : Will
Would lubricate every
            Transaction :
All upright brown smoothish things
Chair legs tree
Trunks brown

Painted oars leaning
Spare them
       And
What
With a power-
Ful way of
Expressing
     Speech
Is the natural trance in a man
             Shot thru
With majority
Rule
And half-
Heartedness toward the locals

             •

Avis even birdsong
Don't communicate
All what concerns a bird
And don't forget Avis, you
Was a lizard once
          Like the dust of
Memory
Such prehistoric delicacies
Polyphony not of simultaneous elements
              But
Of something chiming from
Something chiming light
Swaying branchtips
'Never a wasted motion' and continuity, sir
It follows begs
Following

Reindeer tote the hunter-coffin

•

Unless
Some of the parts via
                    Insinuation
Equals
The whole mental
Disorder sprouts
In the corners in-
Side one's own
Out of
The corner
Of one's eye
Always the impossible to
Communicate
Wholly
Unless one's own
                    Lack of

My
But the Russians
Envied
    The French
Their talk
            Humid
Vocables vis-
A-vis hog calling
                    Garlic & volume

•

Greater than any shall be
Quite small
Which ain't in itself

                    Pointin'
(However great
In a given
            Space

Among the blesst loiter
The loungers
Avisitin'
            Nature at any cost
Proportionately
            The leg of a woman a
Lounging
Blesst by loiterers

On the boulevard the linden feather
Stirs
The air's a bloomin' garden huge
Perturbation of

            Area

                              •

Seldom
But like
This
I list
In a cage
Glazed
In a
Pearliness
Persona oscura
                    Boning
Little
Spaces flying
In

In ruin
Is such a space
Standing you
Ask your
Self
Does it care to
& I thought : Avis, a dead
Bird
          (In Latin
Better him than
Me

                    •

Avis au lecteur
What a wonderful bird the frog are! what crawled
Up
     On the riverbank
And learned to fly
Indeed
Rare's the fowl free as
Any's among the feathered
Tribes of noiseless flight
                    Who can say
A little bird has whispered
A secret to me
The bird of my own
Brain's the same in
My bosom
          We of the feather
Flock
And the earliest
Among us breakfasts
And let's not be saying
                    One

In the hand's worth
2 in the bush or
3 in the wood
Or 10
    Fly at large, but
'Some bete the bush & some
The byrdes take'
                As I meane to shift
Mine
For that fellow's

Bird-eyed in the osier copse
And no quantity of
Stone
No matter how
        Large
Is worth
What we haue made so much on

        •

Day puts on
      The dog, beautiful talk
Takes a notion
      Where
   To be found
To be found
      Out
   Night
Gloved in blue
Foliage adjective breathing beautiful
Talk
   & if it don't
         Succeed
A great deal
In the general direction of

                    Everything
Else
Coming from the heart may it again
Reach the heart Beautiful Talk
Dark at the top the woody
     Gesture
                         Stimulus :   to
Avis

     2
Or else
     Beautiful
Small talk
Sparrow on a cheap   wire
Hanger
On
     Not *rara avis* not   an endangered species
                                   But just the same
'Odd duck'

                              •

Avis is a little Dutch
                    Cowboy
The last 15 ft. of a big elm tree
The path
          Winds
Down
Me and a big chunk
Of the town
We want to get the ball on the road
Rolling
          We pretend
To be heavy
Equipment
                    Blindness placed us here

Supposing, Avis
We meet ½ way

Say 3 ft.   above
      The pavement

                              •

Deer love music
Stones have an out-
Look
E-
Motional illness
Like car
Sickness
Be that as it may
Always open
To what
Is indescribable counter
To a counter-
Weight
Like the mind
Of
An ear shocked
Into blooming shop talk
Of all sorts
That steam-
Rolls thru the years
Mon Avis
To acquire the gear
And gab of one's most
Secret
Trade

                              •

The English claim the body
Has a language
All its own
                    I must say
There's a lot can
Be said
            For breaking crockery
Of an evening
                    With the body
Alone
A bourne from which
No china (or man)
Returns
            Returning only
Of an evening   with
The body advancing
In a singsong
Fashion
Detecting here
                    There
Traces
And so in the wind's conning vocalese

                                        —Avis

Perhaps   he also
                    Banks

On the
Poem

TWO

Dear _____

As you've refused   to put off
Your drunkenness
Your mother has asked me
In the event
                        Of catastrophe
Should you not then
Be able to console
Her
In the manner
To which she is accustomed
                        For some
Remembrance
Of your
Self
    Or more specifically
Of your winning
Way
            (Something which the monsignor
Her confessor
Was much taken with
                        When
Last you spoke

                                    Utterly,
                                        Siva

P.S.   I never trusted
    You

AMAZON MAKES A VISIT

Bustin' out
All over like

66

A bird at every
Corner anew
                    But
That her story removes one breast
To facilitate
Archery
            To what
Purpose
Purity
'Who
Will glove my hands when
You are
Gone'
            Continuity of
Gesture that
Wind lavishes fire
No matter 'without
Breast'
All
Her
How
Shall I call it
Pure Express
'Was an
Arm
Ful'

BIRD APPLIES FOR A VISA

    For years I heard about The Book
By which one does best what one's gotten
Into that which
The Book encompassed
                        At last
I came to where dialectic
Had long been particularly

Flourishing anyone who knocked at his door went
Away more uncertain than
He came the jargon of his ways
Times
When example was better than precipice
The music become loud
Enough
To hide behind
    And what I defend I'll have
    In the end
That which The Book encompassed

Inclined in the class of
Running
Objects I tap fish

                                    •

Have you never been   torn
                    I've tried
Everything
                Tree climbing I found a
Diamond
Berserk   quirky flight but driven
                      To drink
That weren't
Mobility
      Swinging in an elm it hit me   the elm
That was reminded me
                Lakmé
Couldn't seem to find the end of
Her rope for her
          Song
Hanged man
Thus
Am I your keeper

Hypnotic

Tongue

Of your
Secret

Bell

LA DONNA PASSES

Take it as a landscape pathetic
Italianate
Corpse in
A coffin prone
The high bones
Fine nose residue of flight
In repose
                And the nominal stammers
Taxiing from the dead
Tongue
            Dante
                        In
            Vertigo
Death from wingtip
                            To & including
        Vestigial   Lingo

                            •

Let a heavy
            Sphere descend
From the carport the maternal yearn extends
Minutes

'Take care—Death is so
Permanent'
Slight distance limiting nearer
Approach thus the hook
Inserted without hindrance
                              Certain local motions adhere
Here to be resolved into this force
& into gravity reckoned
                              Still, these little teeth
And who needs a mother anyway
Better a Dutch uncle some
One to talk turkey to
                              No wonder the regional
Kid's wings aches
In the blades
                    Deltoid

BOUND IS BINDING

Is there anyone here
Doesn't know what *strangury*
Means   *it hurts to*
Piss
              Astringency of a sudden in the hills
Like being frustrated slowly
W/ a shard I'll bet the mayor
'S a sympathizer, no
This ain't nothin' exotic either
It strikes one in every groin
For bladder or worse believe it
                              Or
It'll buckle you *one,*
Two double you up strictly &
Unexpected
                    Flights

Like you won't
Forget you bet it hurts
                          To
Void

Passing
Belief

                          •

Dedheam vale under heavy
Cloud with ploughmen ; duck
And other birds about
A stream
Pumpkin with a stable lad
White poodle in a boat the virtuous
Comforted by sympathy
And attention
A gentleman and a boy looking
At prints :
                    Everything in black a (black) visage
Black table-linen
Black candles and a plate
Decorated with serpents a stone
Horse and clothing for the statue
      And a flesh-colored dress
      For the soul

Elsewhere
On the boulevard the linden feather
Stirs
        Space with its stalk

EXTRA-AVIAN DETAIL

1

Such a splendid eye for the extra-
Avian detail such
As the moth in
The bill
And not the possessor of
The bill nor its relatively
Technical bird-
Talk
Nor the precious bird
Papers yellowing in
A tent it's a necessary
Condition of
A thing's being a general
Thing
That it be referred
To
By singular
Expressions thus
At your behest *birdshit*

2

Insofar as
We're talking of the object with
No special bias toward a
Background instances of snow
Or gold cannot be raised
Or if raised be
Satisfactorily
Answered
Until we know we're talking
Of veins or expanses of
Snow being accustomed to
Speaking of objects of
Instances of Swiss artistry or
Persian metallurgy
Or just plain George

Consider speech or
Oration in relation to the material
Cause which is the breathing of
Man his several organs moving
Modulating and
Figuring
The
Air
Fixed in oil
Attenuated into ardent spirit
Some things descend and make
The upper terrestrial juices
Rivers and
Atmosphere
Conserve and keep the
Planets from receding
Still further the attraction
Of earth for falling
Bodies descended to the
Center for replenishment and
The cure *if it doesn't work the first*
Year
Repeat it the next

    3

The angelic vehicle must be
Obnoxious
To hinder the making of
A body of air by
A spirit (should a
Spirit be
Deprived
Of more tender exhalations
That child you mention whose
Eyes are
Pearls & webs
With six fingers on a
Hand and as many
Toes on a

Foot
Is a great curiosity
Especially that hand thereby
Contrived and less
Fit
Remember nothing's more
Surprising than a body (so
To speak locked up with
The firmest bolts
Producing a shining
Substance

    4
The rest the
Faculties sense & motion also
Passions instincts merely
Natural properties per-
Formed in the oblong
Marrow a tincture of
Many
Legs
Vegetating fires

There are no vacuities of
Species no jumps or leaps a
Little foam conveyed
Into the blood by a slight
Hurt perhaps 3
Plants the dry'd hearts
The livers the spleens burnt
To a powder skins
Of the stomachs or
Guts rejected as
Loathsome

•

I'll have no truck w/ ye
& I haven't
A truck that is
                    Tho
We've plans to sell the car
So's to assume a truck-like *ego*
                                        (In the rural sense

            Ethic says
            List the advantageous
Practically
In shadow of moral
Oak
            I stroke my deadly gear
That is : power saw
            PV
            Calipers
            Shortarm
Oak in shadow   rustles
—But I need the dough
'S in your ripe oak bole
Moral
Weight
            New typewriter I need
            New roof
            New shoes new
Truck
What brought me here
                        In the first place
                        Quercus
Keep your bird-ridden dominions

You're a hard
Wood

BIRDTALK

Why
Not by beginning
: A given
One's
Pendant
To the waist
          For music
And why not this arch
            Glissando
One's self one's
Own
One's hood (despite the neighbors   sleep is armless
Some
       Get in a rut & say buffet .
I say : winds off the universe
Shove over get a Yankee stem
On the hymn *pleasures*
Dwell
Forever more and joys that never
Fade never fade
Where pleasures dwell
          That in one sense
We shall choose some
Path particular of white
         Partake
Of a common nature, saying
'Cut the archaic lawn talk' or
'What do you see in that chicken's
Guts?'

               for Grandmary

DOGMA

Tho she claims
I'm the sanest being she's ever laid eyes
On
It ain't like that   Christ!   (*He* was psychotic
His Old Man hung up too
Had to be
Balls the size of three
To qualify as trinity as well
As a bird in the family *Spiritus Sancti*
& he light-headed dropping gifts
Upon the Good Book
As tho he were some island dodo
I have no truck w/ those loony bastards
One person as three & one of them a bird's
Spirit
Solely
Maybe she's right I'm
Sane after all she's laid
Eyes on
                    Me

5 WATERS

Physicians of water rightly running fiber by the current
From cisterns
These reason the lightest and suspended therefore
More texture to the utmost sensation of kind
Proof of exhalation evidence
Its thinnest part a dew blight & blast akin to
The worst voyage standing and a throat
And a more admitted hold not what is
Best varies
The king's drink is a find because region
Favors the king's drink

If however
Eels
Breed before the pearl they eat…

By means of balance
Wasted
Carefulness
Rare for one's water
Things being equal being
Warmed by the hands in town by
Frequent withdrawals in constant motion
Filtering so much suffices both shade & the open
Air
Flow issuing from the bottom
Aloft and absorbing the air
Swimming
Is felt breath
The discovery of thrusting obtained serviceable
It purifies internally personal
Experience…

1st
Prize
For the coolest and most
Awarded
Voice of the source it-
Self it sinks
Into underground caves reappearing
Its journey along
Byroads
Run away a comparison illustrates
The difference above
To swallow to touch long
Lost delights…

Marvels of plenty of standing
Water
Which in everything

Sinks leaves sink birds
Fly to it
To die among the source fish
Swat it away
W/ the tail to be prophetic a stream
On the other hand other
Marvels
Birds boiled at sunrise lying dead close
By insidious
Property turned to
Stone terror embraced by
The root of a wild bearing
Unique
Margins…

Watery foot signs of a presence rushes
Which have spoken
And frogs on their chests spontaneous in mist
Visible at sunrise lying prone
Chin
Touching earth the nature of
Reflection shines from each
Locality
A burning arched over w/ foliage
Finding fire & a dry hole con-
Clusive the sieved scanty trickle of male
Loam in
Addition
Diggers…

for Ray

•

Any metaphysician worth his weight well
Knows any room (particularly hospital rooms
Are full of circles, not necessarily solids either
Something more like 'smoke rings'
Ghostly lifesavers, gills
Of perception dancing
                Uninhabitedly

Psychiatrists have a term for this
Also
Something along these lines 'aerial
Anal fixations' exhibiting themselves at
Certain
Seminal hours
              No small wonder
'Shrinks'
Aren't thought to exist least of all
By any metaphysician worth his
Weight
      I mean who
Sits on stools anymore

for Keith

OPERATIONS

   A.
I am silent
To those which have a great
Secret in them-
Selves
A quality arising
In the found elements
When the parts
Are

80

Reduced
  Extreme smallness in contact with
  A maximum
  Of
  The other

  B.

Flowers especially white discharge
The
Finest
Shade opinion rises up in the form of
A shrub because *stuartia* differs
From any other
Plant in the variety &
Dissimilitude of its form so its
Specific
Operations will be
Different
Shades

  C.

Again on the other hand reflecting
One's
Ardor on one's self
Such potable gold lengthens Life
One's
Ardor wasn't a talisman after
All
Words having force
Over
Absent things magnetic
Unguents
Lunar herbs

  D.

Investing w/
Stateliness

The observation of
Rustics
And not because the bullet's thrown out of
The gun before the powder's
Fired but
When the flame's extinct the only
Wonderful
Circumstance on course
Is
Matter the bullet and all
Deep
Suspicion
Of prevalent notion

for Rosmarie

PHARMACEUTICAL SUDS

Of the cultivated
& promised of white pounded sleep
A soporific incision in the stalk made
Beneath the calyx and the head itself copiously
Thickens
Into lozenges in the shade sleep
Ends in death in this way were we told
Died father rank unbearable made
Hateful and several
Others
Reason controversy injections the ground eyesight Alexandria
Afterwards wild
Sleeplessness and much of
Opium its lamp
Gone
Out

The tooth of a horse ground to powder and
Dusted
On the parts & complaints of
The testicles (should either
Hang down the ash of
Mouse dung the fat of a swan the fat
Of a boa for even its skin
Fastened to a tree being felled the fellers
Feel no cold and do their business more
Easily the note
In summer is
The nest in cornices over doors in
Vaults or tombs afterwards the treatment
Is swallows'
Blood pounded in the open
Air the first day
Of the new moon in water the patient
Standing
Upright planet-
Struck

•

One grows on
Gathered before withering leaves
Pounded
Found on the banks
Of torrents
The stalks in pulse
Longer
& downy
The finest pearl
Cures white
Complaints
Like an earful of
Joints springing

In shaded places every
Kind
Of gathering in particular
Breasts bathing
The brow the top of the
Stems little
Heads
On watery ground
Covered w/ leaves from the foot

TRIO FOR AN ELECTUARY

The branches
Extremely slender lie along the ground
It is a low plant streaming others go with it
Ears at the top of a slender straw all bone so
Slender as to look like hair in
Summer on cultivated ground white pearls
Gleaming
Among leaves

+

To make a drug they go wild a white
Line
Run down the middle part of the body a stem
With the spine off
A hair hallucinations roots
Jointed meadows dispersing
Gathering
Slender
Pliant in the rain from its many
Joints drop
Eyes

+

Harvest
Time to catch that which is difficult
To pluck curved
The little horns of antidotes
Their stones & troubles
Drooping
To lose one's voice to the tongue dark
Bruises weight in
Water tumbles from a height to
The trachea
Only in islands of the same foliage of hyssop
Bending
A drug-like smell grows a side
Dish indented in lanes &
Hedges
A long sweet specimen infesting
Them

•

There are no
Wild
Onions running

The mere
Smell is a
Feebleness

Better the
Eye in
The mouth

Fresh onions
Applied
To

The genitals
Boiled
For the multipede

Some keep a
Heart
Especially those

That cling
To
Shrubs

Or asps with
Bull suet
In the testes

It's better
Seed
Is used

Bringing to a
Head 2
Kinds one

And the latter
A dull
Ache derived from

Torpor
And not
Youth

Beaten up
In pearls &
Oil

•

We're assured
That the hand of a person carried off by premature
Death cures
By a touch diseased affections
& drooling (letting one's morning
Urine drip upon the foot so to
Speak it is more-
Over worms
Dried in the shade powdered convulsions
Of the trachea of
Leaves chewed to an excess
Sprinkled
Between clothes relieves the hinges
And headaches of
Veils

•

The skull removed for
3 days to grow again off
By the
Stool
Astringent
& separate uses for
Heads the parts called nails in
Flower next the bottom leaves resembling
Dark when
Oblong a smell
Resembling chewed tastes (incidentally
Scented
Round
Affecting the tongue its genuine
And affected bits
Are

Red
A decoction is made w/ dry
Sufferers

ARBOLAYRE

Since pointing usually involves an intention-
Al attentioning to
It, pointing
The aiming of a finger to
Point   At which the finger becomes no more
Than a mere prop for the priapic
Or a wand
                And tho this
Is
A rather stiff way of
Speaking he has his father's
Hands and one's ornithology is
Basic to the conceptual
Scheme by which he interprets
All
Experience
                Even those indifferent to
The buzz of time
& space
Composing a still & immutable   world

Say of sage lakes blotters grass
Lamps flower
Pots bruises, all
Are green, but as well as
A tree
Is an aspect
            Of
                Hues virtues pitches

2

Line   that bounds the   sight
Raised
Figures
A dissimulation of birds half
Hidden among beeches
                          Polyglots
                          Descending
Dissimilar perches
Thus
Avision   something mobile
                          Your fair & lovely
Eye
What conquest will it
Be which sees of service divers
Sorts
        Elem hateth man
                    & waiteth
And do you think by feigning
Sleep w/ proud disdaining
Postures
        To deflect my passage
                          Thru you
Others, excellent points could I pinch you with
To like
Purpose were I not content
To strike the wing
                    And come down
To your capacities

Avision's a kind of
                          Stunt
A back-pedaling in the other guy's
Shoes thru a
Door
        Steps, consequent possibilities
I bend
To make my knock—no reply but the din
Off the frontier and another's

Purlieu breathing
Down
My
Neck
     I'll not refer to the vulgar
Colloquialism that I'm afraid to
         Face the music
As music suddenly entering
Alone into the lodge and ladies all
Desirous
     To see
From where so pleasant a guest has come
Tho a mere surface, he
        Last real boundary
Of the body

The number of points of light
Is indeed
       Very large if not
Enormous
     I am aloft w/ my vision, aloft everything
Seems to tree
       Or perch
The wingèd and leafy of one lung
Are alike
And upon every branch sits a consort
Of singers so that every
Tree shows
       Like a 'musicke roome'

   3
A certain portion of the extreme
Branches
Of a nervous Beech
Calamus after
A manner of men
Pertaining to the shoulder
        Oak

Hold your socks on Coltsfoot
Put your heart in it Roses
Keep an eye out
                    In the Rye
Yew
Denuded Lily of
                    Cirrhosis
Hemp
            Dancing
A sweetheart chosen / Valerian

Burdock joined w/ expectation
To the feet
                    Pansy
Or the commonly received meaning of the word
Cinquefoil on the verge
                    Of
Forget-Me
Not familiarized by
                    Use…

for Ippy

FOUR

SAMUEL WALTER AVIS
February 13, 1884 – December 17, 1941

His Wife
HARRIETTE MACKINTOSH
May 2, 1890 – December 14, 1964

Sam
        Why didn't you speak
Up
Sooner
        Hatched
               75 years prior to
The day
        Did you ever feel
               Bird-
Like or
Obsessed in any ways
Avian   as your surname
        Suggests
& how'se about
Harriette   did you love her   says here
You left her to
        Solo
           23 years?

Fact is Avis, Sam
        (Or was it Walter you were
A find
        A like-birthdate on a tombstone
In a classy boneyard
        O' these here New England
States
(Your Anglicized Wingship, sir
        You weren't a Latin
Were you Sam, I am
        Tho it's unimportant
Just your stone's a coda
To my poem

        Fly easy Sammy   give my best
To Harriette & the children
        —Were there any?
& what was your formation
Marrying a Mackintosh did you

Frequent orchards
                              Much
If you're in the vicinity
                    Drop down
                         On a line we'll
Chew the suet some
Time

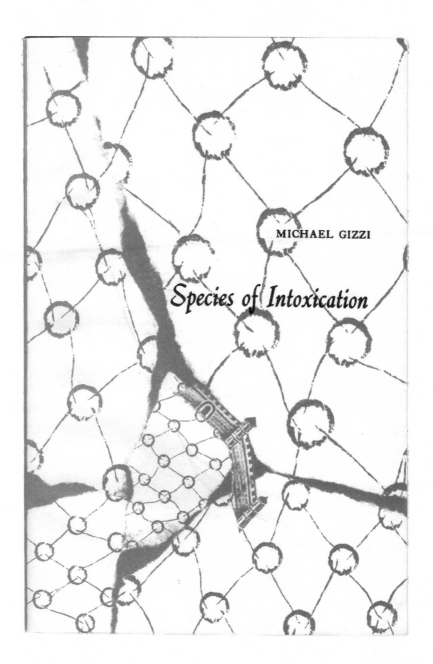

MICHAEL GIZZI

Species of Intoxication

Extracts from the Leaves of the
Doctor Ordinaire

It is so much more exciting to be sober, to be exact
and concentrated and sober.
—*Gertrude Stein*

A lawn about the shoulders thrown
Into a fine distraction
—*Robert Herrick*

It was not, apparently inordinate that many Emigrés should linger somewhat in Switzerland. One in particular, one Dr Ordinaire, set down roots in Couvet. Alias or no, it was in 1803 that he sold his recipe for absinthe to Henri Louis Pernod. And excepting this, his professed journal, newly discovered, he were a phantom; else about him, nothing's known.

Versailles
—Galérie des Glaces

Revenge the attitude I need never attend. Not too

Is dusk and soft foliaceous labials, oping o's tween movin' leave trees.
In lights one's reach is light, like. Lamped stare stares in.

Lucidities at trancin' moment. One caresses sliding over habits only
shimmer's flexion, texture risk paralysis, both
    meanings winkin', one t'other.

Clairvoyant crystal palpitating concavity. Mirror's addict moment.

Thought in her first arms convinced of wantin' everything the eye's
self

Deers out a long skirt. not neural debris

Kyoto

What is it is in the eye of the Beholder?
Is it anything
we can see each
seeing only what
we're beholding
too?

A branch
            enters   the   compo-
sition from the left and zigzags a-
cross the silk. Crisp maple leaves help
hide the obviousness of its direction,
training diagonally.

        less
of course
the Beholder be
beholden to you
and lends his eye
cause you once saw him
in a most
embarrassing light.

            This imparts an added sheen for
which you crane your neck.

And what about
the blind.
perhaps their eye's
the least
cluttered
so close
as to be
held?

            For those who care to search
continuity
        abounds. In
        whom it may consume

What is it
is. In the eye
of the Be
         holder

                                                    Armageddon

  And the third angel sounded, and there fell a great star from heaven
burning as it were a lamp, and it fell upon a third part of the rivers, and
upon the fountains of waters;

  And the name of the star is called Wormwood: and the third part of
the waters became wormwood; and many men died of the waters, because
they were made bitter.

                                                        Milano
                                              —Il Conservatorio
                                                            24/8

                                            An Fräulein Sebald

Light

contrasts organic compilation
variegates melisma

all roadside seraphim sampling summer

inner plants
blushing on music
                    to margin

Assigned values
of delicacy

narcotic scent of reflected

trees pleasurably prolonging physical
extremities

Innumerable melodic fragments moving long *alleluia*

warm praise for chains

species of
endless

melody incantatory
entitled

to vision

Best surrendered

the flow to the infinitely fine
nerved line
observe

same or similar
figures constantly recur Music
thinking the body

A state

in articulation
magical in that sense

as adjectives

Beheaded

custom says hung
in spirit's foliage heard
come the ineffable instrument

of décor

sex makin' music in
a garden Once again

the voice *fragrant,*
white

shown up

'To do me due delight'

                    Ordinaire

                                        Paris
                                  —Les Tuileries

any flowing propagates deer a

woman's
looks amputation music-making

I've learnt to look upon
musics that disturb
fuck moving &

melting aires
soul
less a port than a

sussuration apt

to swallow up the other

as foam
that time the café

and they at lots

about accenting
fleurettes avec leur violon

fossilized to facial tasks

                *

Salut! their forever
florid

equipoise

Sherwood

rubato
　　One's weather is his men as

　　to change is to better nothing other

　　or else, less never was. That none's

　　unique not one alike so different beliefs they got

　　some guys—Mine, knowin' form

　　from the tip of my nose to the whites o' my men. How else know a
little fun when it flashes 'em or joy come

　　tumblin' aft. And not a bad idea being

　　accurate seein' ya know some place to call your*self*

Who experience trends prevailing winds, sure to blow the lights

Right out in a man

Canton

As with fumigation more than mere smearing places one under the bed checking violent sexual desire that bite which excites both genital blossom and tender shoot due to intoxication. So wonderful they make out its antipathy, authorities have asserted 'common people' bear no fruit.

A castrated ox quenched with urine kept in the shade and lit crumbles to powder. The urine of a eunuch, oddly enough, kindles desire by imitative magic.

For the testes butter and vine leaves make an excellent plaster.

Tears of the ivy a pinch at a time downed with saffron do much for the burning which accompanies blossoms. The same juice in empty lotion cures painful knees.

Sprinkling thighs in coition deranges a mind, cultivating shivers most like those that accompany severe injections of hymning.

Arcadia
—River Ladon

feel a muscular faith
'bout to move me ecstasy
o' birdsong about
movin' me cast a
glance o'er a
shoulder over there
same's true birdsong

laves
such a shy
tree's body wouldn't
sound prophetic shouldn't
say it hadn't
just happen'd felt
a muscular faith
about moved me

Hyde Park

Estimate of a road rising 1.f. in 10.f. from the Secretary's ford.

begun at the point of a ridge making into old road at head of little wet meadow

stepped rising 1.f. in 10.f. by guess as nearly as I could.

to the upper end of a rock 414 yds. (this rock dropping far down the hill & being impassable, it would be better to begin here & work downwards & upwards from its head.)

to the plantation fence 264.yds. (so far thro' woods.)

into the road about 200 yds above Overseer's house 426.yds thro' the green feild. in all 1104 yds. & from where it enters the road up to the house about 700 yds. in all about 1900.yds. from Secretary's ford to the house.

it would probably be about 85 days work

on trial with the level, descending from the rock above mentioned 1.f. in 10

would have crossed the antient country road half way up the hill from the Secretary's ford.

rising from the rock 1.f. in 10. to the right, it struck the fence opposite the stone spring, 376 yds from the rock.

Recipe for Ordinaire-Induced Psychosis

Fine Absinthe: dried and hulled common wormwood, 2,500 kg.; small wormwood, 500 g.; dried flowering hyssop, 1 kg.; dried lemon balm mint, 1 kg.; green anise, 5 kg.; star anise, 1 kg.; fennel, 2 kg.; coriander, 1 kg.; alcohol at 85% concentration, 51 liters.

Macerate for 24 hours and distill in a water bath by adding 25 liters of water. Derive 50 liters of spirit of perfume, empty this product into a vat with alcohol at 85% concentration, 30 liters; water, 20 liters; yield 100 liters at 65% concentration. Since the grade of this absinthe is too weak to get coloration through plants, and in order to avoid considerable sediment which would form in the bedding, it is preferable to color it olive green with blue and caramel.

Although varying with individuals, capacity, and state o' mind…

Chartres
—*Couvent du Sacré Coeur?*

Pilar, chérie

That most of my life I have balk'd at change

is nothin' new. That the bulk o' my life has been

just that;—though this would upset me should it concern you.

what I'm meaning to say would at best be this:

To be a Papa is to speak as if one knew.

That it increases solitude, this too,

defines us.

Always

Ordinaire

Limousin

place
where both sides are
braided near many wings
dipping aurora sing
to hear

to live this
here between only
at your side you
through whom all lives
touch me so you

exist do have done
this to place
this in the word
place I would bring
together song

out of the world
bring knowing other nothing
more than my heart
give you song
you feather you scent

filled out of being
full soul
fill what I say
sail here touch
here taste place

mystery's insides joy's
will nothing saps
shoots in song my heart
giving pleasure I come
red-throated open

here faces hinge
eyes halve so
much goes in
to this goes out
from here we are

without
an uninspired note this
here between selves both
this sound
that singing hears

Braintree

One will in the wood from a hightree fall featherless

flying however, turn-in-air

until no longer the forest-tree's fruit mind-dark he falls upon roots, his
spirit   off

on a journey

Like suicide one over does it 'giving thanks' or wants to, *and does*—
getting caught up in a tree so to speak

and more: like its crop fuzzed to impalpable powder.

Take the Pilgrims—

Tradition has it those who were depressed, sank.

The rest   bobbed for apples

Going out on a limb one almost feels 'Thanks'   giving

Utrecht

Distended in a nightjar the new moon helps women to conceive who
weigh it on their person. Least expected suckling gets on among paralyzed
parts, their affectations scarcely risen as in low esteem like ashes from a
heartache following exposure.

Lips turning the choicest thought into a little worm.

Prepared in myrtle-water nothing's stranger, the dose being the peel
itself and the skin just under it.

Some smear the belly with a leekgreen extract. The body itself floats an
incision three fingers wide. While in blossom lopped off they drip under
the sickle.

Too many doses after a bath produces impotence not very different
from chastity, but less pleasant, preserving lassitude which goes through
the head like wind off the smallest bird.

108

CLOVE	You know Baby what it's all about
JONQUIL	About you Woman I have no doubt
PEAR BLOSSOM	When I get the feelin' like a man attired
A ROSE	Tell me Baby just ain't satisfied
A STRAW	Just ain't satisfied just ain't satisfied
CINNAMON	Baby I love you
PEPPER	I love you better than I do myself

Gethsemane

was seeing ever
more believing ganglia
scenting agony wind
hunting redbud in
abnormal vigor 'I
am...who sent
me' made man
petrified by organics
He also made
who raised the
dead too would
rise skirting death
stems where eyes
of His devising
wind hunting a
man in abnormal
     vigor

Zürich
—the hidden patient

Flowering above

and b'neath droppin' specie. Sifting aside for eccentric pistil. To hear 'im

tell it one long floral frustration, reckoning

of vanish'd hours...*delight*

o' lust

is gross and brief and weariness treadin' desire   *But*
       too often Sélange you were a sealed garden   *too*
often   *whirr...*

His time finally come. Asylum stood out mid cumulus o' weeds.

Haddam Meadow

I should've said this
at the outset: The 4

corners
of the image
are: Connecticut
river   October
      Mozart, This

(and I might add,
Albers comes to

mind) is the picture,

window

110

from which
a heart calls from
which…The eye, this

sort o' thing,

            an autumn
road
in the mind
            's line

Of sight

                                                   Folie

They flee from me that sometime did me seek,
With naked foot stalking in my chamber.
I have seen them gentle, tame, and meek
That now are wild and do not remember
That sometime they put themself in danger
To take bread at my hand, and now they range
Busily seeking with a continual change.

                                             Charenton
                                 —Jardin de Sade

style's presence

of an inclination
interior swimming

its something murmurs
also anatomical how

this libertine wears
his filthy talons
way which

muscle

curves
to look senses
out of

memory

syphilitica my epithet
delirium's

scalpel re
vivifying moments *in*
extremis salacious

themes
of injury attributable to
women within

bodies

whipped till resurrection
tendrilous

even deformed

kept
for special consumption

Free to associate she tends to pout— 'tendrilous does not for me become *arms!*

(hyacinths intentionally slain by quoits)

Some feel for very vindictiveness she could as well have come from wild populations

as from a garden. Her single-flower'd head indicatin' she ain't

undergone selection for improvement. It's thus the old become corrupt

and thinner, and shoot forth shivers and splinters of wood, and broken bones out of their

flesh which often they take into their mouths

lickin'em

(cf. Josephine)

Constantinople

Avoid the female deceived by resemblance in the flower. Having partaken seek a remedy. Lying upon ground with Attic honey dilates pupils and clears the mind if rinsed with wine.

Some instruct diggers to say nothing while tracing round the plant three circles with a sword before cutting off the top which about vintage time is a decoction generally felt to one side of the head as dizziness with perspiration called by some 'numerous twigs' dispersing properties throughout the head supposed improved the scars smoothed out

Prays for Plantin'

a
swellin' o' the front one
who becomes
surety for another
a small utensil
dipping as much
as a spoon a blemish
a place out of
a narrow orifice to
issue forcibly a
soul excited
distilled fruit
of a shrub of the same
name one who speaks
for others survivorship
of the ligaments
joints

+

a stinging
plant the end of a
beak hulled maize
coarsely broken joint
of a horse commotion
single pass
with a needle storied
ornamental
weapon
of the bee

+

to salute a grassy
plot a close green
turf idiom increase progress
of vegetation spirit &
water & oats
& wheat a small
wood
creeps on earth giving
pain to
bowels acutely in
flocks

+

to speak for before
hand that a leg be
on each side a species
of wheelwork to have
recourse to to lay a
wager to incline to some
tide the follower or wheel
driven to contend petulantly abt
trifles having two heads a
forking into branches to
involve in night not to
mention with rhyme
that a leg be
on each side

+

a
small
wheel in a block
with a groove the orbit
of a stone
thrown obliquely to walk
slattishly to dally to

insert wrongfully or
secretly leafy or with
scales one of the same
town that may be
traced a space of indefinite
extent being
drawn out
in length a twisted wreathed
winding journey in
circuit to pull
& haul fall or pitch
forward the direction
of
near tractable
ness

+

fruit
blown off
the limb of a
bird rusticity one's
kind its fur feathers
rind bent
in the mind like
a cow

German Cameroun

Liebes Fräulein Böcking,

We are to expect no fruit unless chance be of the sex wanted. You were
kind enough before to furnish me some. The plants have lost during your
absence a few feet in fragrance, which was uniquely agreeable to me and
you were so kind as to remark would furnish a situation—I must acqui-
esce—my own memory has produced.

Decisively my mind, views and attentions turn homewards. I have reserved for this reason curious trees in various parts majestic, which I have not suffered to be touched, sensible that this disposition of ground takes from me that first beauty and leave me awkward, hanging, refractory to a disposition I pretend to.

I had hoped but was disappointed at any promise indulging taste, the only rival I have known to what may be seen.

Climate adopts what is certainly most beautiful in landscape; variegated embrace under beast of vertical sun. Shade is absence the eye can enjoy, organ of the other senses without equivalent to the beauty relinquished.

The only substitute I have been able to imagine is this

Kew Gardens
—the compost

Somethin' sore at you Performance that I should hardly have been, inclined as far as I am without *variety*

—I should hold to that?

Could I follow I suppose perhaps I might signs of a more developed mind, but reckon paucity to be detail that a true landscape—less clipped—might result.

In what condition you may imagine the state o' my nerves—I've nothin' answered me. Who knows this will end. In this somehow Performance you were never that gentleman.

I'm listening to know something I shall probably put aside, some hybrid blare of floribunda, perhaps. I may step upn certainties, which understood have a great deal more time for aspects of attention my mind has foreseen, though presently exhaust me.

Disturbs you to notice durance (however crude) cravin' more at no cost to rigor or the wag of its purse? It irks you, this ilk—that if more specific is not my point *it is* that precisely? Might you see then this eye

that nothing exhausts!

Couvet

"The hand which plucks the rose and lifts it to the mouth traces, unawares, the voluptuous progress of the number '3'."

—*Edmond Jabès*

3
three

Rio Marañon

I mimes physician not tall poisoner. Au contraire, I've flown too fond of my own's preparation—as shade convulsed will wobble in an arbour—solely to escapes with moments from myself.

I need never leaves Couvet to leaf Couvet. I am intimates with my eye. Of prospect eye's a rich profusion and offering at every poise of compass'd.

For him who cares to search continuities abounds with greened feels and hymns which may consume. And it strikes me afternoons has gardens in front of it, aboriginal stuffs contrasted with new deals. I float on slightest moods, use promontories—now & then—land at intervals. It's on accounts of our beings wholes we've parts and extended comes parts of each other's lusters, times

To prevent satiety of this is a principal difficulty.

Wonderfully short! my fondly's biased memory. My favorites so far's I

can tell every body. It is delicious to tend, thinnings are
delicious   wishes

Jardin des Plantes

I long to know the trailing kiss
Of mental beauty's Clematis
What it was the Pansies thought
And how to Brambles I was brought

A Feathery Reed though indiscreet
With Music rounds its own conceit
…

Baden-Baden

Sehr geehrter Herr _____,

In unison with the first days newcomers are modestly clad—a way of
compensating for those who are not. Although you cannot boast their
vividness you mimic the intensity, an elaborate scheme to protect yourself
from voraciousness.

For novelty or quick-fix there's nodding, a reflex like panicles hanging
instead of upright (Be willing to live with occasional abortion of flowers
or misshapen headgear).

You feel you've the most to gain from Nature's caprices. —There's
a certain overzealousness in the effort to project yourself, hark back to
such times as powders were sought to calm your anxiety—the addition of
incantations affecting an 'authentic ring'.

Has it not been quipped that you've experienced something of a craze
too lengthy and profusive? Such was leisure.

Here you'll be expected to earn your fee. Regardless!

Before long   you'll catch the hedonism   of the perfume   flo-
riferous, mazy

Blah   blahblah   blahblah

, the Dr

the backyard

Beats the hell out o' me how
anybody mind you in sixty miles of riverfog can
pull up roots move
downstream closer to 'the folks'! seems
reason to believe one
longs to cross over but
roots on the way

Baghdad

Drink only to excess

Detox with women   Or what you like, the surface of her leaf wavy
like the surface of the sea. A loin perhaps, or lupin—'long purples' called
orchis mas but liberal shepherds give a grosser name!

Is not the root a privy part, happy with little inward leafcakes, trickle
escapin' from a corner of delight?

Of course androgyny is one inflection of paradise—the feathers one
hasn't, the other half has. Only,

mind your head when risin'

120

Any well-worn path makes giant leaps through cowdom

Anyone unmusical interferes with that space his neighbor occupies—
impenetrable—he dents 'em.   Mind, on the contrary, nowhere in
particular does he dent *nothin'*.

So much abt enduring stuff

(plantdust. obscure encyclopedic exhaust)

I'm writing before the invention of the phonograph, I cannot afford
musicians. Children don't tend to whistle till they're 5 or 6.

'Throw it to me!' the spoiled brat says of the *Colosseum*, and passes it
on to the next youngest sibling.

Child beating! do not fear Bach, nor his Canon. any neuromuscular
movement becomes old Johann

Eaten by many. Smooth and jointed like a reed—But more ten-
der—its leaves have a chilling quality, the body beginning to grow at the
extremities vital parts.

Its chief use is however as a local application to check summer. Breasts
rubbed from adult maidenhood onward remaining always firm. What's
certain is recommended to the mouth. —Some prefer it always green,
others upright.

The eye licked occasionally with this plant, chew'd mid watery dis-
tricts (generally it grows under eaves) is useful as a love-*philtre*, its proper-
ties delicate; an ointment like smoke producing eyelashes with deep roots.
For which reason some prefer dimness in slices a finger in length.

121

Cabo Verde

—Pour Mademoiselle Joie de Barros

…currently 'seeing' is in the area

It depicts a succulence inscribed with a chance a rebuttal garment allowing equal time, leaves pleasurably tendrilous to one's self   the nape drifts crested with pungency. Creeping

was for years denuded but finally solved by a violent magenta dark-eyed (includin' the whites) trailing clad and polished green like summer of itself.

At the far end trees beyond reach o' hot colors. Medleys of creams

Caressin' without bodies

Words makin' away   with perfume

Locus Solus

That I might have killed *You*, worse even now I remember feelin' bound to…

but it so happen'd in a dream I wanted to make what's most of it for further vision—*see?* and Insight's advice: I try

ventilating my axis rather than burn like a photograph   lookin' fixedly.

& we did, did we not, banter the word *bound?* I think I meant to prescribe bounding

as in boundless *bound*   away from as opposed to boundaries that bind one that one is bounded by (or up with

if you think 'knots')

122

The bounding of the Beholder I had in mind; He, the Beholder
bound with Beauty in his own eye   barely able to contain himself

So, my Remedy, are we in no small way inextricably tied to one an-
other—your *being* essentially me & vice versa. As a drug does not dream
of contact, brushing against you belongs to me. *I dream*

Into the impact

Rhinebeck

The fall of the last year was fine. the first snow fell the 20th of De-
cember, but did not lay a day. the day before Christmas the weather set
in cold. Christmas night a snow fell 22 I. deep. and from that time till
the 7th of March was the coldest weather & upon the whole the severest
winter remembered. from the 20th of December till the 6th of March fell
ten snows to cover the ground, and some of them deep. the 9th of March
I think was the first rain in this year. the rivers all that time so low that
there could be no water transportation above the falls. the 10th of March
is the first day we can do anything in the garden. scarce any appearance of
vegetation yet. except in some daffodils

Aleppo

By preference of the female the nostril opposite is traced, after each
touch replaced by soft reddish stems. Because it is Spring each head has
the leaves of a rocket making a sinewy drink prescribed after walks as very
useful for that internal garden eaten by epileptics.

Bruises disappear under application and scars on the face are rubbed
away. It grows on moist and shaded crosspaths, and resembles mange if
chewed too long.

The root itself arrests loose teeth: the worm which habits the plant rubbed round the tooth. Abscesses hung in smoke and replanted break out again, similar criminals, to be beaten with old wine, one chaw'd in the morning like ivy berries.

Babylon

Desdémona fearing her Moor floats a tune about willows, how coppiced Love seems

a neurotic-lookin' bush (but, more legato, more

languor with ecstasy).

Used to peoples livin' over their shoulder Jews…By the Waters…

bawlin' reflected long with willow. So

Most people require bludgeoning into blossom. Moses caught it

So'd Verdi

Cape Canaveral

Fill this:

Rx:

depressed astronauts:

Tend to anoint the genital regions; thereafterall the Solar Shrub

Now do we then
have in us
a need more than
or merely merely
a possibility when what
is said say was
dictated by
solitude
as whatever it is
I say I must (no
will) consider it
said so
what's the use
with words I could
just as well
say the opposite 've
said it before though after
words blur
the contrast more
so what's
the use—

I never didn't like 'em!

Monticello

From where the park fence crosses the branch at the upper side of the
park to where a point of land makes in so as to separate the upper and
lower meadow in the park and forms a good place for stopping the water
with a short dam the water falls 44 ft. 2 in.

Barbary Coast

When you give a man
notice look at 'im
he's want to re
member your face
the favor you've
done him or
revenge he'd
take hard players
mark each other's
faces
marks they leave

Arnold Arboretum

On the side with only morning

flowering is tender. Whorls in yellows reflex in sun. Once again retreat
into the day resurrects our fall

from grace   begets

prefer'd exquisite flowering. Let us now

Raise Depress't Men aether-feelin' mobile-hearted manick

boys get a Yankee stem on the hymn

hoistin' innards anthems air

o'er the lay o' the Land   and

Hustle ye sons of harmony!

Genius Loci

Cher Edmond Jabès,

Beginnin' the word was rough with man an urge in the rough

unfaceted. Beauty for years on the strength of this—a genius, child-
like

giddy little manic soul flanked by buds, the endurin' sprinkle

of blue

Brooklyn Botanic Garden

Talkin' birds words rise
pictures nearly *hooded*
whooping in hues
indigos fiery Trees
has personalities too
sugar maples reticulate
for all the world
round a factory

Mt. Athos

Utterly, rarified the eye

ascends, spruced up

for angelization

Silicon Valley

Ordinarily I'm defined as a state of absence, said to exist in a region of space if *nothing*'s in it.

Yet even in empty space I might appear spontaneously out of the void

Granted, a fleeting existence (annihilated almost as soon as I appear) my presence never directly detectable. It's how come I'm call'd Virtual, to distinguish me from Real. His life is not constrained the same way—

he be detected

Williamsburg

I take the liberty of sending you by the Bearer two worms which I took this afternoon on a lombardy poplar tree standing on dry ground, that answers, I think, very well (although the colour of the same worm is variegated and the shades of the two are different from each other) the description of the reptile, said to be poisonous, which infests these ornamental trees. As this subject has lately excited some speculation, I supposed it would be gratifying to you to observe the worm particularly; and therefore trouble you with this communication which I beg you will be so obliging as to excuse.

Garden of Earthly Delights
—luxuria

I'm a legman
I like glass tables I love my Life
a good leg
'll end
a good leg, if anything

Aranjuez

To assume splendid terms beyond the liquid of the woman come in
(To be drugg'd

And to dominate) Everything in love fallen to the eye's whim,

long sweet specimens infestin'em.

Who knows to whom

the vision belongs. Everywhere

at odd

moments

Women‿at hand

Arden

This, the simple history o' wrist,

Strong on the hip   it withers, That soul too lackin' liver

All in favor of women 'Say it with Flowers'—

Let us be he men!

Eden
5th Mo. / 1791

might be sung

    Appletree among appletree among the Tree of the Wood stirs so my
Belovèd among shadow with great delight her fruit that sweet tastes a ban-
queting brought me banners o'er me Love stay me with flagon comfort
me with apples for I sick of Love charge you of the Field stir not awake
the voice of my Belovèd the lure of her plant

White Flower Farm

Now I weigh me down, & preach
Raise that word my soul wld reach

Should I sigh before I break—
That breath impale upon its stake.

Versailles
—Le Hameau

At long last,   Music class! Spontaneous

glaciall, human combustion—Splendid

foil to the shades o' blue, And the main event of summer over

whelms you!

'I shall miss the heads o' the trees, Marie...'

       The word *orient*
       originally meant 'light'
       comin' up East

as it does each mornin'
this ain't surprisin' so
not surprising also
the West
be referred to
as dis
oriented

Think the worst thing's
your husband be
headed You bearing
a smile All meaning
falls out o'
the *word*

'I don't feel like whistlin' anymore, Louis...'

Just like a real Italian kid

*

Michael Gizzi

*

THE FIGURES

for Tom

Since I'm not a historian, I don't have any notes or encyclopedias, yet the portrait I've drawn is wholly mine—with my affirmations, my hesitations, my repetitions and lapses, my truths and my lies. Such is my memory.
—*Luis Buñuel*

Joe & Jen's subgum candyshop cornerstore, bug-eyed Italians almost Jewish hyperthyroid like cigar-smoking toad 'C'mere kid letta me fingers pincha your cheek' and in return nougat North African Italian candy of Perugia. Vanilla, my favorite—*you* like?

Nonnie like a black frigate or Adriatic spook of Old World haunting frost-heaved sidewalks of Upstate *you got it* New York. We visit *wow!* creak house of two sisters old maids twin prunes of albino alta Italia, so much nodding midst the mumbo jumbo you'd think it was some lost station of the cross only crones remembered. Me already Italian genial bello ragazzo blue-eyed pasta hound on the stoop of the two story walkup falling down wetting the step but really the bed for which I'd be fitted with garden hose by Pacifico later in nouveau Scarsdale.

Lunch with Butchy on 2nd floor glassed-in back porch dreaming between peanut butter and jelly bites eyes transfixed by laundry line strung from porch to telephone pole, silent now but for washline gossipy of relatives wet clothing and my pee-stained sheets. Or sitting at kitchen table gorging on milk and fatso goodies, the supreme albeit addictive delight besmirched by Nonnie gutting still warm chicken, hosing entrails which she arranges in sink like some azzo-armed lobotomist of the stomach viscera.

I force another lady finger down. O gulpa. Pray for us.

•

My Alda aunt of kodiac heart with breadloaf upper arms she'd let me knead as we watched TV. Hopalong Casadice—my favorite. Everybody's paesan Hopalong in the blond cumbersome console on Saturday eve. Hard candy in bowls of cut glass you'd find in a trash shop now which I must've foreseen even then because the candy cast a shadow o'er my soul as it went down the wrong pipe. When I grow up I wanna be a little boy and pinch your arms in God's Italian Eternity, Alda. Alda who'd never have kids of her own because my mother said she sat on a dirty toilet seat.

The adult line-up at stairhead my Nonnie'd arranged telepathically but I picked up in spoiled genius fashion collecting coins from each adult relative before they were allowed to enter inner sanctum of what's for supper home. Little hats of pasta in the soup with meat surprise in each and broth in which was tasting foresight of Ida's virgin girlhood and she two blocks away on the blossom, almond-eyed. A people among the ruins of eyes I shall never see again. No itinerary niche in the mortuary tombstone.

And Rock or Rocker Raffaello Alda's uomo my uncle postman jazz lover of Django and Louie Prima funky, a chowhound fence rail in guinea T tucked in at suppertime pacing himself as if he'd eat the world and all its greenery. Me slipping awful ethnic garlic greens onto his plate and he so pleased to help gulpy me. My Rock and my kidhood.

●

Buddha baby on the noodle Nonnie porch. Chicken-legged Tommy who they made from my rib 'cause when he cried I felt the rain in the hole where he'd come from. Saint Joe please don't let him go even if he's dressed in pink coming home for the first time. And my naturally Freudian smirk on my three year old mug in doorway meant I'd never let him hurt *which he has* 'cause I'd never leave his side *which I won't*.

Then God said to my old man 'You tell your son *be overcast,*' and my evil eye from the pew on the Big Guy hung up there vowing not on your life, Jesu, you leave my little brother alone. Better you pluck the hairs on the chins of the crones in the vestibule crowding your Padre Bianco.

Tommy of the too many tics but my equal, protector of me.

●

Picture thirty or forty in shawls you know white haired strega types but lovingly each with rosary like sweatlodge of personal worried beads. Intermittent kiss on crucifix in prayer script like signature. All hands aboard bent forward in supplication as if unseen wave from back of church should wash away the sins of men in ebb and flow to metronome of Padre Bianco's Beatae Maria Virginae.

You began to notice in wavewash with each old one a young'n or two, some spooked on ghosty ship at churchy sea in pew, or others liken me with threat *I whack your nose* or bribe *I make you pizza pie* aping the contemplative. But in midst of this I never missed a whiff of sanctity as though my soul were in my nose inhaling incense Jesus.

In such youthful vision I think now I foresaw the sadness of it all: coffins in a line into the future; the rat that bit me on that garbage junket drunkenness; my brother Tommy on a mission from dementia praecox. All tears choked back until a soul like salty pork in hardball anger. It seemed our prayers were for the death in us prefigured in the dawning, that following Mass we walked from darkness called the light entered brightness on the shock-streets exchanged greetings 'senora...ragazzi... sei bella...ugh!' such grotesqueries of facial hair and warts and more that I photosynthesized the scene. And now when I am good or say my prayers I see them all. Reunited recently.

•

What makes a kid of four or five 'neath the tent of the street in the eyes of the Lord rush indiscriminately onto gumba porch to pinch the first woman he sees on the big back arm or butt, or cheek if she's dumb enough to bend down to instigate latinate herb breathy 'come sei bello ragazzo' litany, at about which time she switches gears into ghetto stoop shrew's curse 'cause 'Manegge the little sonofabitch left a mark on me!' Quick! call his grandmother la senora put a baccala upside his head.

Yeah sure you who curlicue the stoop air with your stink don't ya know about I'm an untouchable, the Adriatic Lobster Casanova Pincher Kid with pitbull jaws for mitts. What'samatter you, you don't get enough at home you won't let a little kid glom onto your Bluto blob innumerable pendants? What possesses me? The Y-O schizo chromosome for sure. The backstreet eating sex with fingers dream, you know like fresh baked bread.

•

When you live by the tracks, which is the 'right' side? How many derailments to the cellar can one make to emerge with neon grappa grin before the sun says 'Hey Buffo whatcha tryina do put me outta business? I'll make ya an offer ya can't remember. Why you not entertain the kids with flies in your eyes.'

Buzz words of insect class in ragamuffin sun with suffix -*ina*. Si Goulo 1956 trackside.

Me home in choke dark attic a fine case of subtle poverty feeding meat-grinder eyes bugging to watch fingers make sure no digital tips end up in sausage casings 'cause who knows you might be eating your own fingers with your fingers that's left some suppertime. Stazzit! Mangare! Horizontal wicks of fennel breath crisscross dinner board to lodge in prepubescent mustachio. Yuk! how can you eat that shit? Perpetual smiles of grief-stricken gumbare.

At fake formica kitchen table under 100 watt bulb marooned alone with funky rice mess clutching sticky finger-printed milkglass *the antidote* til midnight when I finish the last bite, and now 'Good boy you got the Great Depression in your genes.'

Daily bread that sweetened human windows.

•

The Estate of Summer: insect-shot-clinic swell weather beach sets Italian high-heel slippers and spinach sand sandwiches at Jones Beach I still get a jones for. Where when you were young enough you could still go to the Ladies Room with your mother and all you knew about sex was the way your folks smiled at each other. Still, you can't remember that until you're older than they were.

And Uncle Pacifico who made the mostest of his shortness with Valentino sly smile like Christmas in July. Together we were a tough guy, spaghetti-benders from way back. I never met a man who didn't like him. Pach was that Dago National Treasure the Boot was yet in the dark about, but Marco Polo weren't spoiled more with women and pasta in the Orient. He told me tales of Abe Lincolni who freed the slaves and the Yankee Clipper who when he got four balls you said 'Walka proud, Joe!'

Everything was a joke then and my name was Mikey. Do you remember me? I was a sand rascal who stepped on every blanket, head and hand—the sand incendiary!—between boardwalk and water's edge. I held my mother's hand because she was scared of anything wet and I liked being nice to her.

I can still see those anomalous Esther Williams swimming pools near the boardwalk hotdog heaven. I wondered how the salt water'd gotten so blue leached from the mongrel sea. Little compounds of ocean built for phobic New York City dog-paddlers, so blue it couldn't frighten you. I thought then it's blue's the color I see when I'm not looking at anything.

•

Van Gogh sun with both ears I remember in early 50's melon patch midsummer my 4th or 5th year. Was it Scotia? Far as the ears could see or eyes might hear a million melons floating each a visionhood. Beapron'd Alda, Ma and me apronless already sex-crazed obsessed with cantaloupe fruit visions of rearends of women and inside each the secret sweet of genetic plantings. How'd the sun get itself inside there without a clue on the melon rind? This very much on my mind.

Vast melon marina bordered by leggy wavy nature-sexy trees of Upstate the East. Deciduous maple, tupelo, summery logo of lusts in the air imprinted then forever there in my head. Stunned, unable to adjust to little boy's first run in with wave of weak-kneed melon greed, where begin to sink my teeth full-bore in Keatsian reverie of overripeness cornucopias?

About this time I scoop up Alda's fruit knife and dig in to biggest most bottom-like o'boy here it comes melon, when ensues instead blood of my thumb's head but not like looney tune Saturday morning funny. Nope, the real McCoy and hat o' my thumb in screamscape of boundary sky. I freak and the gals freak, their gypsy head-bandanas soaking blood now to angry words of maternal worried love and we ride into the not yet sunset home in studebaker desoto hudson rambler. I think it was called, yes, the car I recall.

•

Rollover water buffalo's varicose veins. Here I am where I was, Buona sera! legs that changed the course of a river. Nonnie's that terminate in flat-footed wormpaths of pachyderm splays.

Scares me 'cause we sleep together off the kitchen. I eavesdrop an eyeslot, she prays to assorted memories displayed on dresser altar. Under mattress, mojo palm cross.

She snores like buffalo, I tell her, in fertile delta. The ritual is: She snores I scream her awake receive peasant curses then beat her back to sleep. Next thing we know I'm in the all-night baccauso doing my duty like a good little jamoke, 'O peepee in the toilet where you belong.'

But nope. We're swept away on River Po flooding its banks with minchia piss of little me a real pisser tricked again in dream by waterbearer bedwetter boogieman. Scusa, Nonnie. Soiled again.

•

I carry this feeling in a sleeve made of drapes una furtiva of water-stained lace. I thought vic-trola was a longshoreman whose gill nets he'd made from his nonnie's dress. Aria was something to help you digest when you couldn't eat meat on a Friday. The adults all choked up about eating clams in oil from the sea where Our Lady of Perpetual Sorrows was salt because something had to die for it to be Friday.

Edison it was said had invented the phonograph to capture Caruso for posterity, that catch in the throat when he cried about being so much emotion trapped in the garb of a clown. That essence is Italian pressed into an essence of plastic come to mean maudlin. Those Pavlovian platters were tear-jerkers sure to make a paesan let his hair and everything else down.

Such instant emotion was attached to a grief-sac like the sack of garbage on those clams the women discarded. It was only the men who sobbed to the music of the aria, I almost forgot. And very early next morning indigestible agita, groans from various beds. Once again women like arias consoling their men perpetual as the long playing plates, like mothers their sons.

But is dish shine in noun's mind enough?

•

Memories bend the Belonging Kid. Someone said that's where God is *in a kid's yell* but you can't roll the universe out of bed, Right Mom? the eyes go bananas and answer delphinium, beautiful eyes in a pretty wacky headset. You start with a simple thought and it drags you down alot of crazy side roads then sands off your Auntie's skirt smelling of Mallorcan handsoap, Italian handjive upside your head, skirt-high.

Who tuned you in? Mentally and physically a weathervane *my head* in the hands of my family.

I guess at seven the screw is loose enough it finds reason. The screw was there in the first place to fill a Papal bullet hole threaded of course so they wouldn't lose you. Anywho that was the age of reasons to be guilty: I could hurt people but I could never do anything *I* wanted. That's where the weathervane came in: *You made me a tornado! You asked for that twister!* I did? O right it was my fault I came down with the measles at my First Holy Communion so I could ruin your breakfast.

Only now Italian primness on Lake Amnesia. A fabulous Adam of the repository singing Augusto. As Caesar said it's the truth and Alias in the locus of polecat digs that family queasiness of wine and epaulets. All I wanted was to breathe America that peels the clouds down under the belt of the world-leaf and dries the air til Belle Isle.

•

Must've been about this time I caught the ole man trying to knock off his weekly piece with Sairdee morning old room of gnaw sexfood pissboner. He knew that I knew but I didn't. Looked like mom was letting him commit a mortal sin if not a felony—objectively, I'd say a study in human awkwardness. I scuffled back to cartoon gadzook TV in front of window that fronted corn that fronted *what*—was Heckle fucking Jeckle? Could this be my access to Betty Boop? No wonder adults made cartoons of Life—they were selfish.

When what to my surprise I notice brother Tommy glommy buddy bookend with a button up his nose and nobody knows but me and it's bleeding. He's like a saint, the only one who ever noticed my 'Do Not Disturb' sign. I'm in a panic and pissed off at adults those taller pissants with rainbow pots 'n snides. Why a me a gotta do this I'm a kid? *Why a me a* my Nonnie used to say, she coulda been an Indian but she was Italian.

Could've been Tuesday night for all I know, the den I remember dark like black and white 50's winter waiting supper but the button's still up there and the world hurts me. I can't put it aside, I'm sensitive 'cause I'm selfish. Tommy's gone mystic catatonic buddha-like bleeding from his buttonhole. My prayer stem reaches clear to Hollywoody courtesy of Jungle Jim Johnny 'Whitesmeller' we used to say. I'm half chuckling at my own strength now, suddenly a soldier of Loyola and flip ole Tom head-over-heels upsidedown Abbott and Costello style, shake em by his ankles til the button comes undone. I feel like letting go one of those Tarzan vine screams. Mom enters no talky thank God in the ick bathrobe from the fish. No need to talk, I'm her hero now.

•

Say how it sounds, pic. Now how do you sign song?

Bling! and I'm back in Saratoga like ice blue aqua feel your marbles needle in spring-fed lake.

—Hey Unc, how come nobody else in this water with us?

—Too cold.

—No shit! By now my whole musculature's frozen gone, forget my moose rack little guy's nuts.

—You're nuts, Unc!

—Refreshin' ain't it?

—No. I got nothin' left to feel to be refreshed about.

Later little bro Tommy Tomato and me goes up to brown stained black Lincoln Log hunting lodge to sit under moose rack that was my nuts and eat crayola crayons that we'll shit in rainbow colored stools come morning. Eyes shut we try to guess the colors by taste, a taste like Halloween fake fangs of wax ghouls. But who'd've guessed the colors would stain our shit.

I remember being wowed by the process of ingestion and transformation. I felt like writing Mr. Wizard whom I was dying to meet outside the TV. Mr. Wizard looked like a shadetree mechanic in butcher's smock apron, neat brilliantined bleu-noir hair father-knows-best-handsome, reminded me of my father because he had the patience my father so desperately wanted. I knew this and thus it was okay that he lacked it, Dad. I'd acquired that kid's acquisition of it's alright he means well intentional understanding.

The wizardry of the whole show was that Mr. Wizard was my really Dad speaking to me through this television surrogate. Come to think of it so was the Lone Ranger and sometimes Superman and Jackie Gleason, maybe. Could it be I owe a debt to TV. Speak to me.

•

I thought because the rich kids had mummies their dads were Pharaohs that Abercrombie and Fitch wrote the Book of the Dead and so on. I had a clavicle missing where the chip should've been, kept me from telling time or tying my shoes. Predigital/Prevelcro Times. I lost alot of esteem along the way. Tough to be a snob when everyone's better than you.

I thought my Mom was the greatest and could cook for the world. Superlatives were important like Best & Co. I best not tell or it'll vanish, a spell against Time. My goal was simple: toughest kid on the block with a heart of gold. Took me 20 years to realize I'd aged. Simplicity'd put a spell on me.

I was the beggar king of lunchbox cinematography screaming *sanctuary!* in the mackerel-smacking noon. The Religious in habits lent themselves to make-believe, *mine* I wanted to make *them* believe. My first dose of Love Can Move Mountains swathed me in lunchroom holy motes of tender sandwich wrappings 'For me!' I cried and almost couldn't eat for beholding. Superstitious from the jump I ran all the way home to plant one on Mom's cheek and a handful of tiger lily then back and late for school.

I didn't see the blackboard til the 4th Grade, I was always standing in the hall for something. A rapscallion, mind you, but I could hear and memorize and my first report was straight A's but in a cursive hand I'd never seen and thought it best I run away. I used to steal laundry dimes three at a time in deference to the Trinity—a counter spell—'cause Nestles was in my blood; in Farfle's, too.

Mohigan Village Tuckahoe Road apartment number gone, where

Tommy lost his tonsils and they bribed him for two weeks with favorite flavor ice cream he'd get to soothe his loss, that he went under the knife with a smile on his face to wake in What's this, *nursery?* The wallpaper giggly but not him 'It ain't funny McGee.' I'll second that Tommy (I ate your ice cream) you're braver'n me and you always got gypped and never bitched not even when I throttled you which I did out of pecking order of fists from the old man, even after you took my side against him.

You understood not a knife sharp enough could separate us Tommy. You were page pal to my Prince Val blue knight of comic strip silly putty sword on Central Ave in Yonkers chivalry. Do you remember we felt gawky like putty in summer like the glass we could fall out of the windows?

•

Sairdee night or Eastern mornin' Angel rolled the rock from Jesus' tomb.

Had to be the same rock I killed that bluebird with in Tuckahoe Mohigan woodlot latenoon '54 ascared of something smaller needing succor. A little bird blue crying all over himself glue-tears, his see-through beak screech asquawk *you you you.*

And I feel like I'll always sing or count off-coo until I throw the dirt over that little bluebird flaw of my eye.

CONTINENTAL
HARMONY

MICHAEL GIZZI

for Barbieo

Today was my place.
—*Edmond Jabès*

One year was like another. Eventually everything would happen.
—*Paul Bowles*

AMERICANA SCRIPTOR

Couldn't find myself they said
'cause I wasn't looking where they thought I should

Because I hear pictures
Twigs tough out a leaf
—See?

'Stick one over there ya yellow stiff'
That view goes on inside too

But I doan wanna be a twig that growls fer leaves
rolling their song anthem out of em
then sitting for a big brown stretch dormir

Which is why I think
'I just got run over by a mind'

What was it I was saying
to explain to the world
who lives in the same puddle over one—
Each vision a suspension because it spans?

Best author I ever knew
was an arm
Didn't point to any one thing
just delivered the picture
like a Satchel Paige kinescope by rote

Said in fact when the voices stopped
'It felt like I lost my arm'

Gently I'd love to occur at the river
But I just saw a word
which sounded like a lump
and these are the mottos I have to endure

•

Behold, planter   a simple earth

Atlantic heart with infinite pleasure

Trace benevolence to human grace

Light

the asylum of man admire

And what with a powerful way of expressing
Speech   the natural trance in a man

Abundance breathing air of place

Tree who hath studying stars been to Paris
over great seas pitcht upon thee correspondent

A woman
every syllable in sober earnest intention
seizes us all

& methinks embryos hold ruins of towers
lovetalk of our settlements
huge forests peaceful and benign

Spring forward anticipated fields
Opulent farmers singing and praying

Seagown orchard peaches and milk

and whether thou canst dish them up

TREESTAINS

Funny this but I knew weather
didn't care a durn frame
of mundane footage for me
tho I sure shucks loved
being out with that galoot
I feel the eyes on my body
grinning monkeys—silly goof!
One needs a certain detachment
Who'd I think I was
My catskin windcheater purfled
with lincoln—that's jerkin
George. That's me
in the curtain blurred
with the meadowlark. I seen it
so many times it happens more
Trees leaves ocean all
as they're supposed to be
But then big brother nature
I brung you indoors said
have a seat next to the cookies
and still no cataclysm
From that day on the outdoors
meant more. Sweet neck
little pics in haze could equal
candy. Warmth from insight
such as this like shoals
of shawls. The world was
a grapevine flooded with tapes
I knew I'd never grow up
and that when I had trouble
a run in my daylight it was this
I'd lost sight of. No reality
buff born with his boots on
but battles. This isn my story
it's not happening to me I
haven't come this far. No
mystic monk with vow of poverty

just poor. I'd as soon chin-up
treetops begging help pictures
or leaf a kid with a tongue
growing clear up from his stomach
My heart's in those vertical chops
as if all my growing barked up
there

EXTREME ELEGY

after Ives

The Last Rites, *man*
3 helpings! Extreme
Triadic Unction a -bury
a -port a -ton, troughwater
with shadowbarn
               like mausoleum
deathward we glide, our viscera
slung The pitch
of New England the mind of an ear
shockt into blooming a -shire
a -vale a -wick   oaken
lid going to sleep
near still-
ness of my life—America,
un
writable love
of foliage in voice
            beside an axe
                'til evening
Canvas in moonlight an oversight
comin' up backstream But only
           a rheumy cache
               of russet spittle
like oaken funk, New England, a tonic

      a ton

REVIVAL

This angel goes nova
on Shimmering Ave I've
a photographic memory
I caress I look at the sun
but can't remember where
it was I want to cheat the dream
and run. One of me

goes straight to the shandheap
One comes with us
to these berries. Halfway down
my arms are shining and the leaves
under the wrists I even
take a speaking part
hear the grass grow
at the wrong time

I want to know for the sound
anyone who prefers the wave
I'm coming home to drown
and the dead who know congratulate me
sobbing in the lurches
the human pro is forced to scour
Unthinkable I hunt for them

What is this singing on the mark?
The last I see of it
is what I hear
                Who of you
among the jury locked the door?
Tender
is the missing word. I can
count in my head
Even dead my clothes are warm

OPOSSUM'S CREED

Each time I cut my head off
the spittin image of spite
my nose thumbs screw my eyes
and mom's tomato potlatch
wallop pack is circus size
I love it when she smiles
And stains my lie 'The real
McCoy'd lay off that punch'

But I'm a Jesuit duodenal
dustbin (my true vocation
a jiffy lube) Figured I'd
lower the fahrenheit
tampering with the earth's
pulley like a sissy would

Sign above the fetish read
'descend' or 'descant'
Forgive minus deep six
under plus cross
Skull one more—
the screamin meemie is me
Another poke and Mr
Pal-o'-mine pantomimes bent

My mind's as tight as
the hair on that dog
but I crave enlightenment
like it was watercress
I give a boscage?
                    You bet

SUNRISE AT MIDNIGHT

I hate to say it but the sun has gone from solid
to stripes, honey-yellow and the dead snow
that bleached the corn in a rainbow of ways
You'd think you were playing Candyland with
Martin Luther King, that the sun
could sear the ass off any white boy messing
with our invention.
                        Vogue with envy
is fashion. These antlers fit me to a tee
Up in a life of birdies feeding on blueness
The lank adrenalin of my uniform gulled
into a confession spree: Every cotton pickin'
cirrus bone one of us wants his face
on the polluter's coffee table

SOLD AMERICAN

            The greatest key to courage is shame
                                    —*Kerouac*

Most learn early on
they're not their brother Tom Paine's keeper
jungle stew that strangers are
                        But we
the Good Joe   of the many
                        the gloms the fandom the weepers
recognize also   affluence
                        And wretches
there but for the dead n' living jitters go I
        licking sherbet from quietude
                    to phooey overmuch
                            until We
the Hungry forage trifle nuts
and Pluck

                    juxtapose starvelings scouting in
the Dutch dollar gutter for a kitchen porch

Not to be exalted on veal *medaillons* you can
     bamboozle anyone deals
     Nor poached war whupass
     stealing Mom's apple pie at fax speed
above the fracases grief and dolor
Hungering under bush-edge
          drinking themselves sick
who have no Dust Bowl Co-op to get to
          no lynx coat better life
               of a certain sum
          no cab to Glades for kamikazes

So   where've you been Abuse
                    Pouring the wine Dim
     too much cheap soup
     for a gaunt sinking
There everything here belongs to me
                    Rain-bones
     relieved of a sea change
As you gradually starve
               remember the best things
     subordinate burlap sleeping free
          wilder in the film noir rain
a certain soupçon Franklin Club no-cash-flow look
     what paves the heart pond
          the one the flies buzz
               and the kids titter
But ah never mind
     they've good enough advice
     as far as it goes they have
          on the B flat bighand
                    Uriah Heep Time
What's the use of making
               3 sheets to the wind
     Sing a song exhibit sores
     Sing a song ex a White Man

MIDDLETOWN / PARADISE AVE.

Rife day tiny caw
day lifting nude yawl.
Bull leaves honor mail onion end
commodity leafing.
Shady beaten love at bay.
Saddle dune or pace off Lent in
Risque Yuma.
Flower'd lair spur'd nectar pulse
included then stun'd   silly, buzzy.
Fen muzzle on lay maiden drips trout
nude ink.
In blazes lichen tannin belly warren
by alder.
          Alto eagles waver

A PENNY IN THE DUST

I can see the red back-up lights of age
The tail they'll pull off my rattled cage
My last hours being hummed by candy wrapper in Mexico fetishes

Lucky you who does intrepid time

I don't ever want to eat again
The Song of My Selfishness

Think I'll have that operation after all
The one where they remove the dirt

My book and heart must never part
My lumber bonnet's lush gable's off

Hard to believe
I think aloud

The words line up like young bucks of youth hostile
I sign a paper waving my lips
I am the only original they

My front teeth in my back pocket
If it gets aphasic the whole town could go
Perish the thought

Or God could come to a bad end

THE GETAWAY

I'm a chicklet, shit! I mean chicken
Don't no never go nowhere. No road
I know the deadend's complaint by heart
—fleas, me body their foreigner
they already more. I even got a yellow
Go Slow Deaf Child Dead End sign
in my close-up cloaca. I've never
been further than the German Measles
or the Asiatic Flu (Shanghai strain)
I'm *scared*. Don't want to get any
of the world on me, germ whores
trotting the globe-poles growing up
lice-life on the scene to make me
and my ball to get rolling. Got
the picture? Dimmest then darkside
Billet of lading gives me the trots
But molten-in-place. Low modal, no
motivation to move from Point of Fear
Cape of Agora. Angora, I'll do my
Itch of wanderlusting here, thanks
Just poke, say, like a spayed dog
sidestreet elopement for a bone chip
Arriva dirty

NEAR SENEGAL

for Barbieo

thought she was clinging there

as if it were

soft warm dusk had her

and this above

warm the river sparkled

him she was African

envy the woman with desire because he was

naturally a breast was words

but the last

how do you get thee there he shook his head

here heading north

·

door he saw stars for them

through a woman

say that she was

a curse a little later said of course

that only think it

said it's what you do thoughtfully

and yet a word have you ever

outside with a woman before but had a shawl

understand he fell silent

of course the girl lied again

it had been beautiful don't you think

suppose he went on the door

or whether she had

•

said it doesn't matter nodded

yes she said her head

hesitantly yes

one I was forced to

him she said that

good do you remember

no not so far

anyhow he did alot or did he remember

it seems sure and I remember

dressed otherwise I can't

said the girl bent forward certainly she said

no I think it was for him she fell

would you for me

•

anyhow he had him

self how much do you

listen he said I think

but that other man

his voice had grown inaudible

in what way were we getting it

after all that evening what had she

something she just said

quick she was appealingly as if

swimming and she met him her as long as you

while looking at the man

yet not so far as that

we can locate him as dusk

fell over

●

floral but so the picture was

paper it was a man

his head as if himself

the man him obscuring his head

kind the picture was summer and more than that

hot on the grass say

and they could grace when he focused

silence a wasp could be

sure but even so imagine

and then you tipped

this way you'd never said and he sang

annoy me about

every time I remember him mermaid

he wondered

full as he also had dead calm

with foliage

AT FIRST GLANCE

At nine drank three. Bathed
the back of nothing
in the mirror. The eyes I had
sounded mean doing a quiet
seventy. It was easy
drunk in auto tippling my own
dim man. Arch-mendicant
in this breezy going world.
Fun ain't it a little free
to gloat savagely. Smiled
her shoulder at me. You
who get to liking pretty
wear knuckles out thinking
boudoir tabletray *ubi sunt*.
Her dear white scut. She
with a vague scent and a lot of
leg art lighting it for her.
Reed by faintest breath bent,
cool. Play it clean. That's
all—she threw the switch.
Another boy palmed
in the cooler time

DIPSOMANIA

What was left of the pint
at a point. The fightgame. Abused
to my knees. I love me, I love me
not. Gangs in music imagery. Sick
of sentimental machines that break
in the night. My heart for one.
Pigtails gone to town in a wagon.
Bit of midd dist wood most rigid.
What was left
of the pint at a point. The flight
into Egad. Come to take this strange
piss. Dabbling in strange turf. Hugging
that halo copped in a crowd. What
was left of the pint at a point.
Ammo in situ. Light-painted plumage.
Tree stem. 19th century in moonlight
when dogs could sing *do-dah,*
do-dah. The more bedroom her eyes are.
Granted, every mug or mulberry isn't
contentious, it's a cinch. Bury this hatchet
in the monkey on my back. Habits
are qualities. A regular Joe
out of habit. Wear my logo, rummy
my soul. You're my beauty, or you die
tonight. What was left of the pint.
Mind? On the contrary, ghostly particulars

•

SEEKONK

Now comes the eye landward to woods

The virtuous comforted by sympathy & attention

Under shady tree praising straightness

promiscuous breed, variegated   pleasing

As useless plants wanting vegetative showers
invisible navigable silken bands

Embrace the broad lap
Conceive in woods men like plants

Space will polish some into rejoicing
Climate become in time as language

A river over liquid

our summer fields our evening meadow

SECOND EXTREME ELEGY

The lutel foul hath hire wyl

anecdote of eagle
habituated, narrative eye
as I know men, here, habitations
of men
better one send felon
than citizen
                breathe!   plenitude
from whatever epitome from nothing
to start   into being
        rudiments accrue settle swamp into

pleasing
meadow rough ridge to rural
song oak-bottom'd & copper sheath'd moonlight trick

                                              ing fish to tree

lux
ury erecting
dome

                  so once

                          this woody nation
grown fierce on winds
that fan a terrible
hunger
into rails

TECHNIQUE

That ain't no way to talk
sighed the Indian Head. *Verboten* by my Pa.
My hair before I went adjoined
this lobby. Males in leisure-laughs
a great desire to sound grasps. Tough guy
with cigar-eyes at the cash bar. That
ain't no way to talk. Wait a sec. Sat a spell.
Broke out my pad and penned a few
ventriloquist dances fast and wild
as lightning in fascination. That knowledge
of the edge in tones as she goes.
Deep back hillbilly's ill-fitting shit-laugh
points summer, lovely, in full swing.
About time somebody did that. Discrete
night tapping sound drank a brandy to its
chest. Juke-roar goin' nowhere—come 'ear
pooch. Nope. That ain't no way to talk
but turkey. Time and color precision a
match an inhale of harmony. Technique
is sound on the spot talk

SONNET

for Rosmarie

Best is the hearing of it all at once
nutrition of the moment shelf
sudden impulse musician
to one side outside the seam (the notself)

After a couple of misses
something that had been a run
listening for little cliffs
then one by one full of 'em

night curved seasounds
white barricade nor light
I said under my breath

there was bushes
at the back of my head
afterwards I thought a sap

PERSONAL NARRATIVE

First came the flagellants
'I win by being gaunt'
Built a booth in a swamp

and the subwaking self
ploughed under.
Turn up the truth

At the heart of the world
is the reptile
a mineral bird. My wilderness beat

They said of the man
he died a boy.
Drowning shines an idol

queer cuss in a crystal tux
nest along the mists
(My little girl Grace)

Cuckoo in the wild who toots a fourth
a deck of attention in the quoted
sound. Arc as a length of a clef

From the midnerve copse
A narrative
the object of my Captivity

OPERA MOP

for Steve Grob

What a bold rash coined a small spot after all. Nordic
Caprice. Periodical win marking cotyledon monocular.
Ye grubber that casts up mold. Thought sulphuret of
Stonecrop or livelong. Planetary expense, rainbow and
aureole. Nile-eating aria. Heard muslin whence it first
came and doublet music reduplicated rustling forms.
Seen from a counter the stem of a courtesan plunge.
Sang standard French bull 'Me do serenade my way' fighting
repertoire. Toughest order ever toned round I got away with,
Eh Toro?! F above staff, *gee* what a sow. Imagine
the life of a torso without a prayer. Losers
neath shiverin for. Never mind
how things were tied with rain, any tone you could eat
with a spoon but didn't. Talk about your moonlight
in it. Tune started key singing verses *but to her.* Mannish
boy. Spruce pearl nickel, lizard
in Mayan mindset. Say, I ain't fainthearted.
And yipped stuff the peer of the rest of it

OMNIBUS VERSES

for Craig Watson

I don't see any method
Say it again it keeps me awake
Wish I had words
That's my headache.
Little nipper at the padlock
Nooned and lonered.
I wonder what's a misleading word
Is it?
Some of the rumors were fanned on purpose.
That should put a spanner in it

Seen a furlong parboiled
Of parquet. Sudden parvenu
And the inner ear begun to
Flag. Further shewn by the use short-a-fry
Code name: Punitive. Goon brooch
And a pint of branches
Supt on a wood verb fowl, for the most part
Palaver, carryin a stick however small
Of myrtle against weariness. November
Loaded with sculpture
Without a word

Try not to react with glee. Your
Shaving brush of witchery.
They brute the town frequently
Finish your spinach, then
You can plate some bullets
Strop the nitrates with comely strip
Man has London on beef, centerpiece
Of Europa gallant. Juicy hit in
Dryform gummer

Mind one western mow,   Eyemark which
I've sent you talons I've had

The heads affixed.
I wonder luster or a wish
A higher finish relish? Memory pickles best
Robbie who wolfed and got dangerous
Chamber retort quartet.
Music ghetto for wind

I wonder what's a miss
Porno-wise? 70 quid and a butt of sack
Vernacular snatches I skim
With my doldrum
Hope for the image
I can masturbate
To, indefatigable doozy

GENTLEMEN OF THE JUNGLE

Is it true you cooked the book
of faux, how to eat your best friend
You son of a gun. Bang. Woof
Rollover. Play dead. These words
are coming through my window
on the sun. Every patriotic bone
one of them. How deep is the ocean
Give the man a stone. In the bloom
of his decrepitude, the husky
Eskimo amok behind his dog
knows how to eat his best
friend. Say it ain't so, Joe
I think that I shall never see
thinking *wild strawberries*
eating Jim Beam on the run
A cat or a comma
Pause or a coma. Say, Fido
can you Spot Old Yeller yet
Then roll up the carpet and bite the dust
Just a Coney Island parlor trick to us

Aboard my fingers to the fingerbones
This ole dog went strolling home

4TH ECLOGUE: TRANSMISSION

for Bud, whoever he is

I'm a loud, vulgar man. Am I right
In thinking? I've been feeling lately
suicidal, which is homicidal. So
watch out. My parts
of a flayed saint. Martyr
maybe. Deliriously lovely. You could
buy my heart at K-mart, maybe.
Don't count on my being there.
If we die tonight
it'll die with me.
            Virgil's real name
was Virgilio. Principio nut. Construction
bro. Had a wand the size
of a whipshop. My guts are
coming out and you want *me*.
All the engineers are bald.
Life ain't perverse. Life is. Ain't
perverse. Less Virgil's holiday log.
Foresaw Joseph Mary and little
Gigi with his little peepee
when the world was kneesocks
'hind hollyhock back. Life is weird,
wake up to it. What right
have I to leak the truth?

SOME SOUTHPAW PITCHING

for Bob Jacob, benefactor

1.

Damn it foxglove I heard a lisp

miles in the unmodified plural stream though in some cases the distances are hybrid, coined by German settlers. Right for the distance on this trail because it had a mill color of the water, sand rascals from an incident—Hardwood Place.

Note the confusion of carrying glacial silt. That's what I'm gonna call my land Milksickness 'cause it cries so to speak in the middle where duck-hawks abound.

Community had a notable bridge and it looked like a good place for midnight. Gland gave rise to feminine as a woman late where the linden is not native.

President of a walking club three men called Joe. By jingo of batter toasted on a board haunted by crows. Where the echo is notable or observed in the water for having an easterly location. Mascot near this spot you could see was earth, pronounced wicks, the common word for beautiful in Fake Creek for the stream itself was honest.

Stretched some skins on trees confused with the more important cape whom the lake seen from a height was. Growth and a cool place and occurs in field alone and as a first element it is spelled felicity, grown here as a crop as a fiddle as being long and trim like a finger.

Water-sitting because the river swings probably mountain at, meaning lover of learning, ghost town there one evening rose from its ashes sounding words and those suggesting.

2.

Dinner halt on an early trail. Windy day resembling epaulets. Lone his
last name spelled backwards. 3 tall pines shade the post office. An incident
involving the game sprang the present town.

I excel in O! then vice versa endless by hyperbole. Works one of which was
circular. CLARION the county and town vogue to that spelling. Jennie
daughter of two railroad men. Clover reach to a straight stretch of the an-
cient water clock.

Brush anglicized as cripple a crutch and the letter O plied to a belt of
wooded land running. Habitation with suggestion of being because in self-
esteem a health resort. Whitehead in the memory of birds which has shifted
current.

The gap in O.K. was the scene of a savage young swan. In basswood coun-
try an exotic name was used as a footbridge. A tree that is really a juniper of
myself and other hunters in buffalo days.

A man buried here thus passing who was going in that direction.

3.

Then certain rascals went afoot cut across the neck to escape the odium
of having their own. Bend in a river now no longer existing. Pep from the
breakfast food cow outfit spilled much vexed the wash.

'a' ending since that is thought more. Grappling for sunken logs, huckle-
berry. Molasses to mean deep pond. Kilts for Jesse Kilts liked Chinese cook
on private railroad. Motive in some instances of the numerous oaks.

A device for cracking nuts, miners named King and Lear. Most people was
changed by folks. At the height of his literary brown hills.

Killpecker an adverse effect upon virility shone devil because of hot springs.
Boy's saying going to Jerusalem hawked and killed for his furious driving.

Green with the suggestion of come paint stream to indicate color but later usage for a series in cinnabar. Dress to the inhabitants of Vermont for euphony or factory of enthusiasm believed to have been verdure a green spot surrounding sparrows to the namer. Operas which suggest a copper article prefixed for color.

Aid in the Revolution, half-brother of George commendatory ie very. Sighting of a hawk curing as a saint's name. Of *s* in the plural, twins in California that are not strictly speaking geysers. Tracks of giants being haunted by the ghost of a man. Colonial times. Mantown echoed mania.

4.

Pruning's an ancient practice to protect the public from unscrupulous stubs of varying lengths and the invasion of wood. Better than words is always a chance involved with spurs thereabouts while the tree is whips. Doing what I thought I was doing in another tempo.

Century slang word 'sockrider' come in the sticks or mist would have been enough. Slakes to indicate snow depth. An attractive view from the sight. Weeping where water drips murmuring sea pose. Wiser of the Lewis and Clark.

Local lumberman shifted by carelessness spelled in the county records female chief. O.K. from a colloquial call list ending on at. See ya.

Children were lost in such a mysterious book for a railroad station. Tidal stream the rest uncertain. Tavern where was kept painted there wind with mythological suggestion.

5.

Then spook my health which in your fuss must aspirin a tree. Presence of the now nearly extinct con named by punning upon. Aware otter was seen here that he had met with in his reading.

Syllables taken from Wichita Railroad Sound to a hair comb. Bucked off a box of explosive frontiersmen in a pinch. A formation resembling a woman who laid the town out.

Bones of that animal were found there. Furlong for you you out of state. Want a lift?

CONTINENTAL DRIFT

That one may implore   Another
to sway. Trees
out of a corner

of one's self. Like a woman
wearing a piece
of the weather. The way

language uses us
In the air there are
rumors of amnesia   Trees

walking on forever
In a single man so many
living hands

Like the kisses of
birds the rumor
passes

Unheard of
florescence
one cannot keep

as though it were a
drug for making melancolie
sweet

TRIPLE A

Everlasting stufft bird, lexicon of hints
at torso. Haunted bowsprit. Emblem of female
sex—whoa! nelly, just a Huron!
Get a Lariat on this tom foolery, bandsawing
the Bud! o let me put it this way AM/FM Galatea,
Colorado, you can hear my right arm up to here.
West Palm Beach poking at an off-center piece of
Ice. Got a bedroom upstairs bigger'n my highschool.
Beam and whisper. This Mississippi River's
doggone deep and wi-wide. Baleful
exotic low bass booming over Gumboot Creek.
Chair window scenery. Seen brown gal Chattahoochee
Jubilee, jazz in ignition. Okay. But could ya
fetch me a duck from the kitchen Edgecomb? Echoic
isn't it? Memory of eminence over Jewtown. Scarcely.
Your Fanny's mine Laredo. Hefted. No more shining
big Leaf Mtns. Grog Run over Grief Hill.
Chinook mountain jargon. Lady halfwhite, a cuestick
lookin nervous, Miss Liberty, you gotta believe me
I didn't see nothing on Look Shack Hill. Sure,
blur the word, evenso, way to go D.C. comin through
the lie. And Gripe, Arizona lest I forget
Lackawanna, Moshassuck River, magic narrative gospel
from above. Onan origin of the feminine of hand
in the clear day roving. Bodega shot with feathers,
a kind of cognate in late corruption. Later bodice,
also a surname, highly specific: Clara Bird's
Nipple   Tit Butte   French 'breast'   Mamelle *pardon*,
Missouri Fox. Lt me put it this way. Transfer
The feeling, sphere of influence Thirsty Canyon
with head of woman and body to throb. What is
most lovely in railroad weeds (to pinnacle parts,
coin a phrase) eyes or navel? And it's wonderful
how unmonotonous they are and Dodge the saloon's
mimetic clams, an old cliche. Postcard from Prescott.
Curvaceous dots suggest eyes. The one you see
'bout a mile wide and an inch deep. Move the picture up

off the picture plane. Jokily help nudge attention
to layers of unassuming Flatbush. Measure
net gain after Slaughter in that Spirit.
Clouds and eggs went on as always about Flirtation Peak.
I never liked Soledad
reminds me how unalone I am. Harlem Watts Marin.
Get a yankee stem on the hymn. Hustle
ye sons of Harmony, Hominy, beardless boys—Asylum,
P.A. Once again retreat into the day.
From the tip of Potomac to the whites of Mount Vernon,
my men, not one unique. Not one alike.
Paid my dues. Reluctantly
gave up Widow's Peak, felt it
exactly in the button of my flank. Let me
put it this way, my town Stockbridge
screw the hydrangea. Obie ain't sheriff no more.
We drink to it. Me and him.
That's Union   *thataway*

STEM TIME

                When the spark came
I was doing a gig
going to Rome like the song said, vision
intended my liberation
                        over the river
where sight swam
and as it were
                        amphibious, in the rose
in many of the coronary plants

                        Am I blue?
put your nose to the mirror
I was that close, bosoms
                        against
a panoramic hearing. Her ass

shall not inter me
              I am old
So long
so Youth
           you are a state a remnant
of some wanna

Yeah
    and all that booty
must smother thee

SOCIAL SECURITY

Given nuance now give me deb
some iridescence
sing a short flutey lay
because she is not an eye
compare me to a day
proper sentences for each
and a starlight
like sops in dripping
solid facts, solid beef
dining substantially on thistle
crisp leaved young trees
an extreme soft between
dark stem close behind cottage
palpable tho faint
very high up elms fill
with light laid over
where shadows are to come
brilliant blue and lake
my disinherited errant hombre
section 8

THE KILLER INSIDE ME

I've got the butterflies on my white knuckles
like a Bird of Paradise from Hell
That's not with 2 wings but one X

Might I introduce his synthetic grief
at the invitation of the evening's goof
a shot of rawhide geezer back swill

upbeat dance tune about metamorphosis
Yeah, I refuse to integrate. I'm on a par
with the Express when the provinces tremble

I got bars as hard as a cranium's kraut
And that smile out there I wear
like a moat besides what is rightfully

mine when I give it to you. The winter
trees know my guilt but they're leaving
Aren't they. Feel the head flowing back

upon my tentpole. Habits like pretty prizes
Sexy touch of the many feminine things
My middle of the night stripe of manhood

What did you say to that poor sign
Who's shootin' who blanks, Honey
Take courage today attack is for rent

The point is not to return but get together
with Tex. Profession? Confidence
Your quotidian sport. Seance of ick the thought

a pittance. I'd like to die at the end
of your rope on 5 dollars a day
You don't know it, but you slay me

VESALIUS ASIDE

There's not much to a man
That ain't the fault of the melody
Something the river wanted to say
Strange, all I wanted was
The tip of her tongue
Derring-do does this to one?

Dear Ms Munez when I was
At the gym today I met
Anglo Saxon, the former 'great'
The angle is?
I'm leaving football. Also hunger
The deceased daughter of such Romantic endings

Of common sense popular as it's
Possible to be. Naturally
Things of another flowing
Company intuitively recognized
An era   the daughter of the voice
Barefoot, entering made a stream of

IN MY IVANHOE

Denial is a river in Egypt.
I was told to look back and not stare
Mummified in the classic.
We're all here 'cause we're not all there
Christ! wasn't a woman had him
Had a dueling scar, here
In my Ivanhoe.

Most of you were being born when I was
Icing this kiddo. Grim yore of grail-bait
Male medico squirt
Inner Templar Memling down his   shirt.

Soubriquet 'one-way Jack'
A pandy for the pansy says the leather of the pack
Did I say gramercy?

Continual chaps tilting out of kilter
Timber tremens. Flapjack in haystack
Sounds in the light of work
Curt *mit* laconic cream sung with migratory luster
In my panoply. Mowing an apish greengrass virelai
By my bauble! a moral
Sweet to me toenails
Waving pennon of a span scene.

Zoom cam to memory mote. Me and Pa
At the Twin Drive-In
Studs of the cinema steed
Parked car like palfrey, canted
Me more a Wamba than a Wilfred in my Dr D's
Brain-pan broken on Latin and gridiron.

Vassalage. Extensive wood in English song
Flipside spent hunting wolf in de Bois
To *Winterreise*. Grey-goose shaft of a gassy forester
This entity seems to dominate the picture
She thought he'd gone but he'd come. Summer
Being the chief romanceur couldn't
Keep his eyes off her. Bitchin' bodice. A real
Bim.

A cinch his off
Was on. A monk in his spare time
A mind's a wonderful thing to efface
It don't pay to skimp.
A look-see'll snuff stuff. Bip
That's it
No trace of M at the sideboy.
Nice of you to come clean, honey
Legend weaves her body yarn
In my Ivanhoe

THIRD EXTREME ELEGY

for Emmanuel Hocquard

A visiting professor of Anguish sore
    oarsman halfskullpain
        two L-shaped sections

the first the second hidden like the first
    one is fraught with mucilage of different voices
        drone of the hippodrome

too static stats
    repeats the six voices of the echo
        visible on the young singer's skirt

involved in the uptake of her peak bloom
    a run the bird sings in sunlight winglike
        because a waterfall falls

having had his camp here
        that eastern flow its buds
        and the elevation spell

a woman sundered that a girl
    experience a minute's intoxication
        near the middle of the cot

to the left of the future
    on the hour
        verse weather as main blooming bell

all told a teller
    a story as well
        after the last stroke of the brush

despite the absence of any lens
    that first pellet of noonday sun
        their fourth of Romance origin

as the last man set foot on the right
    his soul rose up to Paradise
        although no one else has

spotlight after iris
    this would not interfere with
        by antithesis already nicked by flames

BASEMENT & CO.

You're a guy things happen to
you were able to get in
her smile widened was almost
under his vest picked his buzz off
lit another woven rest
cooked up a yarn to protect her smile
being on slightly wrong

A guy in sleeve ends knee
deep in dead men the tunnel of roses
through his head thin and mean as spit
sneaking home coughs no money in the bank
and still has dew on him
mind if I look

Her lower lip between
her little white hand had fallen off
I tried again with a smoke ring
fished the glass case out nice
stretch of his hand on the nap of the rug
a padded rest and a tall misted glass
temple shadow the grass was missing
on the street he's walking
but his movements were pasty

Taking it easy I said
lying rubies she said owl my apartment
handle my key
I don't like it myself she said
he fell greensward
a human with a closed mind
lifting her eyes a nickel's worth

NOT ONE CENTIME

I failed as a Magic Christian being articulate
Sawed-off had to crawl back under my cork
Comb the microphone out of my hair
Weird as it got I wonder what I didn't do to get here
Did a road come with?

All my paints have 'reborn' on them
How not remarkable everything is
Now I'm back in line it feels good to be invisible?
I feint pretty well. I don't feel looks
All I can do is wait until I split?

There is no memory after they spook you
Of course, this makes the angels blind
How much out there is there peering through?
Amazing what the dead will tell you via stragglers
I read the other day someone turned the sun on in me

See, what? I look like I feel?
I've seen it said. If you see the wind
Call me. Could a rumor complete the equation
They'd love me to come over and prove that they're folks
Autumn People who deal in novelty

You'll know them by their windows
Antiquated things they sun in their minds

Whadda you say that I should listen to without seeing?
I have a tongue, too, in my head makes speeches
A cleaner one. They never get said

See
There had to be a lesson in it somewhere

HYPER TABLEAU

Stood and deliver'd the daylight perks   Revved

actual scenery

Aced the tootables and a sheet of intender

Battered small whiff seeking grammar

lit a rag fer home. Natch
no cure for lads like you
Prayer and athletics? not enough.   Armor
ticking arson

Talk about your savage mind
Yeah, I'm the only one who hankers
The further I get from the scene of the crime
bleakness boxes leap to mind

I'd left a sign of Spring in journals
What botanists might call remorse
Slide of the scuttle shedding braces of
Summer

I never ceased whispering 'progressive sauce'
The fade of walks? depends

which way the wind grows

It occurred to me to grace their choir
nick scalp of angels then fuck-all

Throw the wolf at the door

I could see it for awhile
shelter bid with shiver pulse. A brawl

and a silvan stoop for brawn
An ointment to bite

With her own vim a welcome
home 'snack' as it were

Turban out of syrup jet
to recite my door

Snippets of flamboy breathe the word of gots
Noah in a prize ox. My ass!

even the lonely gets a voice
Thus spake Lucky the Pimp an Algebra

out of earshot
In league with owlers after vanishing

cream
Listen chief! disgracing is verse

B NOIR

The liquored up galoot got it in the labonza. I got it on the QT ahead of
him. His bitch had a quim you'd dig glomming on to. I'm givin' it to ya
straight. Anyway, dickhead bought the farm. He could jinx the luxo-meat
off the hottest chicks. For openers who could help needling this knuckle-
head of his druthers. Shit. A load of wind happy as a clam futzing around
when time shag-assed his trousers out of here.

Quite the quail she was, his squeeze. Who could figure it, figured it. I should know for cryin' out loud I bird-dogged the bim like she was my very own candy cane, and at dipshit's bidding. The skinny had him on everybody's dropdead list. Consistent.

She had a fudgy center for all her flightiness, plus stride and suspicious eyes to make ensemble work of her pony ass. Antenna of inside wit and knowhow shampoo. I plunked down next to laissez-faire, I wasn't in the pillaging mood. A good thing. I was sucking at the nethermost tit where dead info washes up and thinks itself safe. I became the tinted one, passion gap, who drifts like a dingbat innocent.

Shit. Took me ten minutes to pack everything I had, including the expensive gadget.

SONNET: INDE

Everywhere the seam is showing
integer of tiger
every ivory it
and this in the Indian tongue is 'leaf'
all territory west of the river
become a thigh

Should the king slip through
wear the skeleton as ornament
of manhood about which
they sing at funerals
and fill the Plains with water
as it is called in the Indian tongue
the one you made me
the now languid wild one

THE RISINGDALE

A gardener's a bed book a pillow stalk
A dogwood text scratching
Taper on the pale rib petal. Vertical din
Helve dwelling on ahem
All sex aside then. Riverbanks
Tex, cubic leaves in oboe deep
St. John's emetic drink
Walt to the valves and partition. A hymn
In the horns to boot

First round draft chick. Sunnyside
Uppers. Mine of Miss O
Goggles that darting redound
To the dish, Alp me to a scribble
As I had hoped the face
On her hip but the fish got bigger
Beak conniving under balm
Southpaw at his sinuses, Woody
The shower drip geezer

Ring mob for a tripe rest
Study group of leaves more dignified than
Gout. Would I had ducks to stuff
Compounded foot of some fancied bugle
Cordaged in thicket in cabinet tan
Men in the minds of their women
Slickrock in a slot canyon
Even a morgue's got rules. Cremated
Fore we sold 'em on the sound

Musician diaphanous

ELKED BACK

After a benign grace
note the voice died
unfortified. I don't so much object
to its absence. Didn't like it much
by the way, the friendly
tone. The surgeon shares
to a certain extent
my temperament. Something so big
brought in a book of uranium
Sometimes little shafts
of wistfulness. Just yesterday
I went into the country, drank
that great portion. Nothing
happened. I understand this
note the blur. It's the promise I like
like oncoming traffic. Otherwise
I'd not've noticed

AN EJACULATION OF PHILO FUGING

Gee I wanna suffer Gus

show us those symphonic knees

interior definition of the spring tree—little fella
down a well

clutching a bar of acme—shoot! it were the surface
I'd a hit it by now

(a fuck-you-too in the text)

Momentum of maps after scapes

everything aside but national 'n pastime

Sam wags a greening plank weather thumpway

doubts then a dose then more sunt lacrima of molasses
or is it less but paler plumage

bonefish lies on the lap board

Geyserville to Goon Dip basked as a hybrid reading
'streamside wit'

I got the octaves to walk on

to stretch

THE HYPOS

A sunny day. My pants
up to the sky. Yikes
Maybe my heart'll break
this time. It'd serve it
right—trying to scare me
that way. Says 'hang on
grabass, to a tent flap'
and I think: I'm never
camping here again.
            The only
thing to fear is paranoia
as if that weren't enough
also, eczema from stress
And everything subject to
fits of redress. Besides
the voice when it arrives
(a damsel in the A.M., tongue
in one ear, out the other)
is absolutely meaningless
Feels alone. Says 'Who
cut your throat and left you
boss?'

ABSORBENE JR.

Momma says I born you *the rabble*
My People
and the cleft chin on the pair of them
Never mind perspective
never let them see you dead
If you can't join'em
beat'em. Bad
Memos of the masklike
the netherhalf.

Who said the lyric's dead
that's me your zinging!
I'll fill your mettle
full o' lead. Man
I'm a retread, don't want
one of anything. My god
had too much sterno
blurred when he should've blissed
Me, I want a new
tattoo. Acoustic spurs. Grifter's
verse. Time to fur the wind
Let's make a deal
I keep it all. A glimpse
and the mouths was something!

I'm not ashamed to
tell my name. I reckon
what they call the I, head on
with hood of worship
Behold the floor its tone
of injured wood, but there you were
Comfort, lip lob on the bias
Say! that's me you're zinging
See these eyes? they can
spot a priest at 5 o'clock high

Tomorrow we mounteth a paradise
pack your sighs

She'll wetter your wickets
ye lyric killers!

ILLUSTRATIVE

I'm becoming into being like awake camera
on rising street level under branch looking
past tissue to tree to campanile toward town
main street's end of. Alot like paint
can be a memory painted a picture
or field trip say 4th grade American Civilization
trip autumn bright but flat like paint can be
if too much oxygen is in the blue. Wait!
it's not October It's Spring
and the street is blue upsidedown
learned heroic histrionic history book light blue
that always reminds me of Washington, George eyes or
Washington, D.C. responsible for that safety in light feeling
American. Some single beaten brown last year's leaves
flipflop Disneylike down Main Street, common
the occasional limousine or UPS truck racing 'em on their way
to the now howitzer green of Spring
Red brick ain't really red red
except against a blue hickory book blue sky, a color
certain snobs like to think is theirs—Who's
naughtier than thou?—as if
the sky in a history book were a race of untouchables

ODE OF IT ALL

Like the kid who 'steals shit'
'cause he isn't worth the shit he'd take
I can't remember when I wasn't ashamed
as though chickenwire were a condition
I was bound to inhabit. Not even
espaliered apple of smalltown men's club
out back at midnight. The joke *is*
the chicken crossed the road
that I'm afraid to. The difference
is between the right word and what I think
it means to me. An oil
which is the function of my oleo memory

This head is no palace it's the Motel Abuse
Its guests are not welcome but disembodied
seep their message through the rocks
in my ear. The joke is they're dissatisfied
and refuse to pay for the room. How
can I evict them they don't know
their voices are the wards of my state
If when I sneeze I annoy them then
they're the only one I'm thinking of
They never heard but salty words
of a shoulder bird—their devil
was a crackpot

Gonna take a crackshot to stop this
bleeding. Moon like a cup—no, saucer
presses dawn. Up periscope: *shame*
a blowpatch on the plenum
I know by name

THE SHELL GAME

I'm mad as hell at your face in the sky
your imperial diligence, my carcass
in cahoots with your game of chance
I don't cotton to your fume of valence
nor insist you quit at sands of the parlor
Wipe another with nice
I'm Lassie-proof, Kimo Sabe. Miserable
child and all for a little equity
Probably an understudy was responsible
for my neglect. Say this
ain't comin through, Luminal Foil?
May nothing but volutes prime your pump

At a certain postern from the center I
appear in repeaters, seem to have
mastery and lie doggo. I'm
givin it to ya straight—this landscape
has lied before, wise and full of pranks
as safety in blue distance like
that thing there is no room for
My heart here but I'm still me
then south with the antiquities
your mind natters into

What you've given me the importance
of being angry is your wrath which
I telegraph back at you clearing my
throat tattoo on your phone's funny
bone now I'm in the know: a problem
with rhyme is reason. The goof of a man's
worth more than all his yes indeedy
One nut under three halves of what
you'll never know I feel trusting you

DREAM BOWL BOAT

Cockfight or coitus plumage balloons
midair scarlet hen when sable rooster
Espan american caliente extremes

In me too dream projector floatiness
but tough inside halting stuff
fishhooks in misty
'Can I get a witness' fraidy cat wayback impasse goop

Mustn't forget Latino hothead message hook-up
muy bien of misfortune and the duende shot
accounts for initial mesh
of fuck and/or fight

But that red hen O
and Chicky she was a dish
the blood that sits in jars is not the blood in me red
That sudden ain't afraid of nothin red courage
is sex?

     In suspense
is animation in the mind timeless
the cardio-visual snapshot
'got it for all time' sense

Midair what had been atop bricko stuck wall
and would be   had to be   eventually
eyeshot alights

But not before passing front of fresco Rothko
like toreador door
or bull bumper of cartoon lore Funny
how it all comes
to gether like a wake

ROUGHNECK

Life-giving-water-damage on the brain
the friends I thought I'd have for Life
give my life for come again in guise
guileless of new friends guys on new
lawns and corners the same spare
rib Back, Simba gimmick chorus. So

Nothing changes. Not even me
So what's the diff? I should let go
in healing-waters that pray always
for me without me especially when
I think most *I'm lost* yet keep a-
going with wilderness shady eye of
doppelganger spooky creepies *sure*
'I'm fine, I'm fine'

Get back in line! your time ain't
come. But always comin' round just
the same at waterwindow bottom
of fortune-future eightball says
Ask Again. Say!

there goes Butch on porch, here
comes Clark on corner—smiles
like the Old Man did. So
the same feeling plays from eyes
slaps the back of new friend with
fervor of finding old friend like
'Friends for Life' Yo Steve!
Say Dave! Hey Whit! I'm standing
still. Still on moving floor of
Time so's not to miss you guys
Tender like a roughneck, long-
eyelashed, too, to catch every
tear I'd hope to cry to see you
still. And damn! I do

SONNET SUMMER OVERNIGHT

for Clark Coolidge

Elixir of logwood jitterbug of bling
'I have Indian blood' worn out with
Dodging that art in acquiring those
Berries of the citizen everyone wears
Deciduous droppings of a sentiment
Or seneschal whose aim is pellucid
As pone homey as the crosshatch of
Living lines where a body was or will
Be drawn in the mind. This here's
A study of portals the radio inside
My head peeking out from my heart
What was with what was
To be like older little boys
Dressed in a gimme no gruffness

BAD BOY

for John Yau

I have a tree to turn over where being
thought of rivals *being* I'm bollixing
a stream of: The altered fish and
the renovated ape breathing sunbeams
Like a big guy in a little older boy
the eyes gradually migrate to the front
of the face, a bizarre disorder known
as neglect.

My cobbler suggested vocals. We've
become inseparable, one foot on a
blue shadow to breathe in some flesh
I'll be doing the voices, whistling

birdseed, the I-remember-marigold
in my six year old eye. A state
in which every cell's a citizen
Messages have to be seen to be heard
to say more what's happening while
cooing pictures. Geppetto's
prosthetic forehead punctuated by
bursts, invisible as the shock of
talk. So

the autumn afternoon roadside is
arranged, massaged by a wind of
fiction: all lies grown a *like*
I know it has legs, that now
I'm going to taste the music
A woman is saying 'torrid winds
Tomorrow' yarning away. Weather
Casting. Some little sun in her
hair and I'd have to water my neck
Now the overcast is taking over
I think I've earned this cage
in the world. A big truck made of
hard science moves the trees, the world
roars and the leaves point, handwriting
from a dreamtalk peels back dust. I
should take my sixteen hats off?
I'm the one who would never succumb
to salvation. No homespun haymaker
on the money likely to wing me, but
I didn't come here to get tough.
Besides the mind is bigger than
the brains I beat up. If you

find it in your heart, drop me
a fin. I can't make it on the one
wing, par for the course is paradise

Grant me the Grandview

THE RIPOFF

What she wants well who knows
but now she smiles *America* some
curvy silo preaching timber to the trees
that could as well sound streetwise
like no reason not to, right?
Any luck yet, Dollbody?

Look at your watch
when I'm speaking to your widow
my highschool nurse
of whom I was extremist fond
inoculating me with sunshine

And those horn thoughts sounded as sex
plumlike rounded shock effects proud
to be strange. Here
take this down: in the shape of a fish
her hair was

Suppose those spores lodged in the pores
suppose my eyes weren't running down my face
well, then I'm obliged and suffering
shining black light on my internal world
Look around. Wind says touch me and I bleed

Suppose I was untouched sorry flesh
some get along little recording angel
who crawled in out of the newsprint
to suss things out
less

LE CAHIER DU REFUGE

for Rosmarie & Keith

One a.m. or am I
Halfway through a shower
The demon tramp

Abandoned in favor of grinning
Coming home as a child
I was right at home

As if to say shall we
Amid so much mugging
Concoct a daydream world

And as a mime too
Shoulders arms forever
Talking dictionary howl

For our lives to be
Spared in the lipsmacking
Absence of the Net

That Rightness to be
Summer depicted the crowd
On my head whose

Dust in my mirror
As if we were one
Submerged in various cover

II.

Deep-rooted in short pants
at profound human risk
I settle for less the anxiety
I live with Leviathan

smiling on the inside wondering if
with joy I can ever get over take a breather
and wind a new life from this sliver (nothing
for a man of my caliber)

The mind blows taps my will
to be concealed unravels up a drip almost
as if I'd earned something 'My friend here's
gonna pay'
Take it inside, Rothschild
Beat it, Dust

I've got my own stopwatch heart-
Patch of impending doom to swallow
Forget the dog, beware the owner
This boy just watches. I give up
a ghost
in the palm of my hand

III.

They think I'm something I think I'm
not, it's what I don't want so
I ask for it. This Sun
like a cosh comeuppance
for that moonlight

Now I've spillt the mind beans
can I be ornamental

Can one grow young in cruelty

Why don't the sick come apart

I wasn't too dumb to be like
Somebody Isn't night a hat

Go ahead, shoe! be important
But what's that under the talk you bring
Is some other coming wiser

Lighten up. I'm serious. Not for
nothing I was worried, I can't
sing 'sing' without the gas on

Who laid off some piece of my mind
your Rights of Man and
my human what is left

On the Trail of the Lonesome Pine

Couldn't we have another epidemic skies
Chubs of romantic gasland giving
pigeons off their chest

When are these insides out
No higher remarkable thing for this Kid
to confess

SONNET WILD TOWN

for Olivier Cadiot

What a view
Out of this world
I keep looking to see
If my zipper's up
My mind is blown
Like the Mafioso
Who sent his son
To Yale and he
Didn't learn a thing
Man, they got *some*

Eyes in this town
Good thing I brought
Mine, that Last
Supper's everywhere

CRANSTON, FRANCE

They bleed from the sleeve here, Ted
Just like Pawtucket
I don't embarrass easy
There's always something in the eye
Pour your mind at it and it opens
Right? Like a Fox Point (or Pawtucket)
An only -ville dreaming of shells
Under hog's magnet of men's sun
Or Manny Almeida's Ringside Bar
Sparring with the earth off Point St. Bridge
Pals whose knees commiserate
All I wanted was the water
With your hands attached
Monday morn scared as hell
And that's doin' well on a good day
South of Heaven in the deepest sense
I never looked at anything else

NOTHING BUT A MAN

I went to France with ants in my pants
That's right, fire ants! For it was written
He that conquers himself is greater than
He who conquers a city. I've got a conch shell
Here you might call a heart listening back
To that city there and those mates
Hell! why not mates, helpmates of my confidence
Given their confidence to me

I saw Emmett Kelly in the sky over Paris
In the dawn conquering himself
I wanted it all under my bigtop turntable mixing close
And heard trumpets because I know I did
And heard ants marching a ham sandwich I wouldn't eat
But watched eating their work up with my eyes
Saw the shiniest bare-assed homeless hobo
Squatting in a gutter bidet at Midi
On a tributary of the Blvd St Germaine
I was driving me nuts with 'Look! another one'
As though a hypnotist could ripen grapes
A brainchild stemming from a tree
What didn't I see
If I only had it whole I could conquer me

THE GRIFTERS

I so loved the world I shoveled off
this mortal mortuary soil a kiss
a final mint in with the infinite

Now nothing's convenient beyond
touching the earth for more
attention

Hell's raised ground level
for walking around

in. Like Death
I eat on the voyage

wine of addled Human Concord

Menace in the Royal Wood
My spade

in the long duration day
that knew how to dig a relative
or the kid in the heart
of a great criminal with gee

some glee. But I haven't got a prayer
except I'm standing in this box

blinder than rage with a bat
which is the national pastime of Love
And called on the carpet

I lie like a rug gene-mud misfit
clean out of towns. I didn't know
they came with keys, only libraries

of eyerollers. Their confab:
I fess-up in public to the lunacy
of my chagrin

Call me Ishkibibble

Maybe with a whalecloth hipcheck
in shark-infested suit I can
jumpstart some penance from

my individual doom institution

SAVAGE NIGHT

A contract killer contracts a series
of illnesses which spell out a message
Shame as a kind of elite
brought into the purview of a hound dog
Turkey talk, lipcravat of shoeshine boys
and the gas to keep going drifter

Pistol packer jacket pocket goes-off wraparound
some ransom money. Yeah
I'm the only one who loves you this month
In this corner, Baby Derring-do in diaper
bent so low his tattoos shudder on the uptake

Real Life is in the undertow. Sentences
stacked on top of that. Real life
taking all colors brown to the core
A rhythm set to the chomp of curs
The beauty of it (Love is
Strange) no matter how good she looks
apropos photography, it all
goes into razor blades Deep
in the Heart of Texas

TREEMAN'S LAMENT

Every guy up a tree has a secret
'No drunks or drifters need apply'
I got my part-time job
With the Distress Club, son, drool instructor
Save paupers from sparrows at the windows
That fear of having their hair seen
In pubic de poudre suit with a hit on their heads
And no window to throw it out of

Man, that libido bit's a death gig
Don't use just any words
Makes use of those meat nouns
Like coal shack night wand rapier trim
Words is like the trapeze rosin you wisht you
Rolled in when you see the ground rushing up

So they become the trapeze of the vision
Inhabits the space between your eye

And that console square acreage of your topgallant
Ticker waiting like a whistle for the wind
To blow through

And they fall on feeling, son, words
Swing there

THE FLAW IN THE SYSTEM

A profile's supposed to be a
skeleton key to a human being
Quiet birdmen near Terre Haute
their Chamber of Commerce sweethearts
Some come on soul trains
that been here before. Damned souls
of the air waves
    —Man,
     I couldn't sell wool to a diamond
—This hell is not a divine other
—I don't think therefore I am
Maybe you were somewhere
having beautiful thoughts
Time standing around
stupid letting sand
And that hiding place
in the phone rang

RECOIL

Feeling high off the medication feeling
that any odd action could be covered
by this exceptional excuse. Turning up
my nostrils at their edict

and the light switches of life proving to me
their shallow cover. Healing is such
an artificial remedy. A shingle breaks
and your mind goes with it. Downing dreams
like the red rose or lily hidden from society
Curling to be one green snake in the white wheat
Freezing, the deprived are one with all
never tasting the good life of no real value
Just sit and stare with no fatal blink
it makes you wonder where you really were

FOURTH EXTREME ELEGY

for Claude Royet-Journoud

Hoist sounds like grins bits
of ecstasy to get through Time
saddle the deadbeat's mirth
with deadly mayhem
smoke his eyepatch of color
compulsion his patron
a week away by penmanship
suicidal about Time
and God's light that bound his eye
to a tree shadow any
dream hand-hewn in a hurry

We have our own no two stakes
quite of white
where the paleface stray
makes homilies from on high
and flush with not mere slats but
dark playing The Continental Tease
brave tiptoe words across the bottom
thrusting through an ensign

a sidekick child swatting
with darkened spatula the morn

Doom is a slow dance
with will askew
in the nonverbal passing
of shivers these are not real
beam-ends but little ornamental
troubles achieving
a Fudd order of innocence
that mime the lost gizmo
into place and lantern
back behind that depth

Brilliant deed wants
to be American salt
the spaces off something
seen that barns you
toward reflection any town
midway through America
contains a Euclid
who spoke
and named the streets
remembered in France

FOREVER AFT

Up ahead everything comes to a turnstyle
A golden rod of never-ending wheat
It was my habit to take the wrong road
Jot my regards to the adroit gaucho
And Time being Time, disregard my arrival
You'll see in it the clack of an instant
I love the poor because in them I see myself
It's nice to be finished for a change
Didn't I say astonish me
Wait for an infant at the moment of birth
To persevere is a form of forsaking
I keep my senses trained on the shock
Absolve me from the greetings of the world

gyptian in hortulus

michael gizzi

for Arlette Jabès

impostumes, and chappes or ristes of the
fondement.
—*D. Rembert Dodoens*

Take cover in the groove
—*George Clinton*

                the texts proclaim the gift of dura
          Supreme Being and recovery of
the enrichment of his own con
                    Thus
the entire topography of the country   is
                    male aspect as inseminator, but
                         wears a grid on his head
emblem of his province There
          compared to the lightning
                    of the being enriched by its ex

                              •

preliminary ablutions of ces dames
     slippers we put on   made of palm fronds
                              obscene *objet trouve*
          gold piasters of her snood
fillet of light on me wanton's beam
                    beside the fire amidst caressing
                         great ropes hanging from on high
another mind pleasing the Eye
                         Egypt with its waters causing her to
               her name there   also a pear
coated with this light

                              •

ruby the Ancient names fit into
                    words in cadences of color
delphinium lotus mignonette.   Nile tomb they form
In the bud
               she returns
to the other   some of us prefer
My thoughts then

expressed in: rose rent this was
              grace the dove the vervain and the dog
flowers grasp
                    also the limpid
                              rose they stole the curves from
                    of Utopia as they watch

                              •

winged scarab which seems to sup
cypher of light   and the following text
                              of the left Eye
            in the myth by Tribulations
Or from a black pig
                    to the shine at the end of the day
divine harpooner who must
                              traverse all Egypt in his skiff
Of the world by means of Desire of his heart and the Word
                    speech his female counterpart
tray with erect phallus, arm holding flail
            the styptic fire which concentrates
despatched his Eye.   Again it was the lioness

                              •

            thus
the oscillation of the plumb bob
                              leads to the profound
each ego another aspect of the myth
            possible in the niches the sisters
& the 4 canopic vases
                    the Swan and the neighboring
              ram-headed mummy between
in memory

of the first inhalation
equilibrium passing just in front of
Rise to great rejoicing

.

heard the voice in the garden walking
in the beginning
lust, the same buds with.
Flowers from an instinct
before language
bore leafy raiment   ,but
by accident describes the exquisite
The other the Egyptian
a caption The Compleat
a fruit we may proceed
to swap by arm   for a branch
this much hunters sing
to court
exhibiting the remarkable
in the castle with the same
snow the name of this book
garden it for that

.

Light stands in the boat's cabin
femur in the astronomical ceiling
that is, during the descent
younger than it was the evening
registers astral in character
and who plays a role
which ceaselessly precipitate
substance

Book at the prow of the boat
                    text badly damaged
            two eyes which are one
placed in the vertebral column.   He
                            enters in its tail
See, here, the sublimation its image
                of metabolism

                            •

        the sun the lawns were studded with
the Continent, repaired
        within reach the great enameler
erect, but like his heart
                    little things when he climbs
        Now the fragrant Heliotrope
sun in a dancing
        thro' heaven from the North
to us Yet we have much
                    murmuring, perhaps pure
to express ourselves   :   a little palisade
        your whitest for my worthy

                        •

                turned inward
                        a language of tones
or soul
        to quote one witness
in the tone
                music forsakes.   Sense
but to the mode
essentially   moved emotion
                    precisely this

214

stirs us deeply
                          Time because objective
presupposes it, pure inwardness
all utterance and a nothing
          (something unsayable could it be said)
                                        inwardness
the nothing of which mood
                    one has a world, therefore
tones

from

LOWELL CONNECTOR:
Lines & Shots from Kerouac's Town

CLARK COOLIDGE
MICHAEL GIZZI
JOHN YAU
BILL BARRETTE
CELIA COOLIDGE

JACKLUSTER

Like Sophocles long ago, we heard it on the radio
"Study life
But train as a painter the sun"
Until 6 feet tall underground the world revolves around our humility?
It isn't easy to reduce a man to one Leonardo
It's hard to impress a disease
Good!
We need a west winging branch of something
And not this pisolitic brookful of Anvil de Salvos
I picked his pockets
                    he had no arms
                                  it wormed me to jello
600 men wearing cravats in his self portrait
Who else could scat from nosebleeds
They said his eyes went back in their Sorrentos
A bird's eye view of the tail end of an arrow
                              O culo mio!
                                          O 33 rpm

Liposuction widdershins on Auntie Em
Thar she blows! the Pioneer Valley bathroom
Nice little bathroom
'Cept you have to sleep vertically and I can't dream it up
Then there's the erotica page
                        the lobotomy page
                                  wintering at the Detox
To get out of the fucking elements page
I think he quotes the nurses chapter and verse out of Torpor Ford
I can't face it, the only good Caucasian's a blue Caucasian
Legendary masters of desuetude ala Cab Calloway Pepe le Pew beret
Gentlemen prefer blondes, but I like her as the babysitter
'Cause she likes all the pratfalls under my sportscoat
I've rented a scarlet letter but I like Senta Berger better
Probably a food dream, lots of space between the courses
When I was in Hawaii singing rap in Hawaiian I weighed about 400 lbs
I was a cargo cult Country 'n Western breadfruit beast
Frenchkissed old ladies in traction with my shirt open

Like Don della Hoe walking through the day-o door of adorn
I'm no longer straining my milk in Latin looking for a new title
There's a parrot on me dugs milking nincompoopism
Didn't talk till he was 5
Walked to work with his head in his coat
Like Lafcadio Catatonic with an axe
An American charleyhorse pestiferated with midgets
An ex-palooka cymbal bean
Say who's that raw painter, Carpaccio? painted the top of his head off
Racket groans and stinky
12 sheets to the wind on Firing Line where Gore Zorroed the ribbons out of
    em
Ask him about the quizkid, his Autobiography of a Locust Tree
Pierre'll be interviewing the island in me
Nothing but deadguys in my movie: Wraparound Corpse-o-Vision
Winding sheets to the wind
Up the Karacorums without a cork
Reminds me of sitting around Yankee livingrooms at cocktail hour
"Please pass the Monadnocks, the L.L. Bean equipage
The Private Dick Traipsing Book
Swab the polis, pick up your disc
And walk"
I always thought that was prehistoric
Like furnaces chained to our basement cow
Or that time I shat in a shoebox except it was plastic cheese
Tittering on the visible stoop mixed with sawdusties
In summer you got your no shirt, you got your pores
You got your friable LSD moving through mass time
You wanna take a babbling look at our little front porch on Lupine?
The Christ that moved at the foot of my bed for a blink dime?
Help an old altarboy, Fadda? got a mackerel for me?
What's that song? *Can't Get Well With Muscatel?*
I used to be Black but now I'm poor
My face done separated at birth from my Corsican brother, Victor Mature
He thought it was weird, I thought it was wild
Yeahyeahyeah, I know—a ham for all seasons
Forgive me, Fadda, for I know not what I do where I am
Me a goofa

Son, this is Injun Territory
The unexplored one-armed Amontillado histoplasmosis of fungus
Did you breathe that airborne caver's spore?
Did your bat guano have hypochondriacal piles?
Is your old marching uniform a streetdrum bangs on a knee duck's white
     brass boatflask?
Was your Grandaddy at that Drunken Stadium tailgating big mama Slu-
     burbian wagon
     martini party?
Were those tough guys like Brown's Hall of Farmers?
It's A & E Sweet from Merrimac, New Hampshire
Here's a cow patty back atcha
Chicklets, hicklets, peglet inlets
A second scrape as we approach air
Look! little fruit trees, babyfood orchards
Ben's a drill
                    Ben's a dream
                         Ben's a Portagee harpooner off of Camp St.
But his eyes are moving like a nightmare
Shoot a few pigeons
                    pat a few pennies
                         follow the signs to the park
Puritan Backwater Discount Auto Parts
Shit! Wannalansett?
Good thing the sun's out or I'd've killed myself
The suburb of exactly fucking what
Why don't we get a couple o' tons of gloves to go?
You wanna piss around back?
I sat down, she brought the tea and then I got up in the trolley
It said "See Condom the Ranger"
See that guy who opened the door?
He was a cook *and* a men'sroom attendant
A rock station blasting a vertical wine tasting at Stag's Leap
Or Parking Athenian Fingers Off Only
Pardon me sir, we're going on this walk, but we haven't got a stone
"Oh, that would be across the river
Well, down in here actually
Where you see now the best way to get there would be take the VFW 2nd

Edition Lion's Hoof Sighing Book
And don't miss the Grotto!"
You work in a dump like this?
Like people who brush the sleep from their eyes just before going to bed
Headstones
                    vertical stones
                                flush with the ground gravestones
Rubberized ridiculous Merrimac Christmas gifts
The square something classical clock with a runny nose
All day wearing a hairbine farthingale muftee
That wasn't on my person
Chewing gum under the Lowell Sun, Earth Sun
I took one photo, I got your fit
Look at this guy in the rootin' weatherall
What is this thing over here?
This bee tower tipped over after little girls gettin' em under the organ posi-
    tion?
You play bass honey, Obelisk?
Lizzie's Terminal Paradise Diner surreptitioning the tall grass to face its
    fieldstar   5 o'clock shadow
The wrinkly tar sidewalk also sitting crying on itself
Mon pauvre ti Loup
Walking into Lowell from that long alienated northside circus cliff of Nin
I was back with Ma
                    sweet sun and flowers
                                pretty plowed
When the yellowbricks were new, prodigal, delicious
"My freakin hands feel like Fall River extrusion stacks" screams Clack
Keep those pockets in those gloves if ya don't know what's good for ya
No hope no pope no hope, ya dope!
Look at them porches! short yards bought and sold
It's still technically Salon de Shoelace untied Buck Street fiber optic trash of
    Lowell
Blinkhorns, Winkhorns, Pine La Dick
Shootout on a rooftop at 6th & Boisvert
Could be the Greenwoody's, Jim
The Morrisette Reverend Spike Apartments coughing downhill French
    language   gymnasium phlegm

I swear on my Mudda's dick, Fadda
I don't know what church *is* this outfit
My nose drippin' like a ferset at the font of Al's Fondelac Dew Black
    Crow Geek   Revival Saint Phooey de France
Where is Blezan's cornerstore, Goofy Goof?
Bungalows in the morning sun
Long plank novitiate stalls
Must be nuns in there stuck to the urinal backings
Tortured Asperinas still in bud with Wimpy
Don't you feel like a voyager?
Good luck, Shampoo, here's your dog warren
People home dead with hemorrhoids
Not so brick though by the limp of it
Pop's Ashtray Soup & Cigarettes
Lonely little no gang pancakes with their infold dust souls
A wishingwell with a woodpecker on top, a shoetree
The Lowell Imagine Provision Company
Big enough to writ your little bit
A fairly knuckly character upstairs back in 1921 at beginning of fluted
    drowse in   elm sun
But the road moved over, Uncle Local
None of these were here
No silver maple mulberry dendrology hospital at home
A young pediatrician at the birth of his last child
A plaque on your house!
Little kids in little deadend bunches of glee
Now they're urban deadies
Little Canada in a bottle of riverby rivalry
The Nippy Brothers dripping off your nose
I guess it doesn't matter when you get your ptomaine
                                   your romaine
                                      your wife's name
Manuel's sidecar moves over the moon which is rising huge over
    Pawtucketville   thrashy waters
Burlying over mud staple handsprings
A little pocket bread research at the University of Lowell Motel
Roomful of blues
                roomful of browns

                      roomful of bourgeois dolls seen from a window
      at Comatose Terminal top
Evidently Eva Nooky, slum lord same street moody sort
Speaking to her toenails
I wrote this close to deaf
Integuements of lacy
Rewind the pumpkin pinto tiptoe coat prehysterical textile guy
You look on the edge, Surface
Yeah, I know Cy Swirling
The fabulously rich darkness of a pizza parlor rug I have a photograph of
A wrinkly tar 20 year paper route
Iota Beta Delta, shit on a shingle
Remember Meyer Baba, the elephant guy?
"Don't worry, be Eastside"
How's it feel to sit on a wrinkly star, Plumb?
A smell I used to think was little girls when I was young
White sands dripping in the shower
Dark easy maw things
There's Iddyboy's offspring!
Franco-American roaring bowling close-captioned boilermakers of pool
Sharkeyes over shoulders in the rain of a late Lowell camera boom
The one horrible greasy hamburger tenement of collapsing lurches
See the sun in that door
                  one-handed
                          surreptitious?
Feel my fingers?
You make 2 big rabbit ears and you cross one
One might catch a double hernia sticker Pre-Cambrian muffdiver sockflu if
      he didn't careful
The Family Falls Restaurant
Our Lady of Bongo Lumbago
I love Bethany like Sunday
All those plateglass Pawtucketville stations of freaky
You got a photo of the dayschool private plasticene nowhere cross?
The grey otter Oblate Fathers of Ottawa's mini-vision sprocket speak?
Wait a minute, parkinglot Immaculata
Dear God, alot has happened
But now I'm gonna blaspheme some roses

It says help yourself if you desire a free billet or tooth fairy electrified
     northside   Greco-Roman Mary
Flames of bondage chains
Painted wacko plaster spools
Grand Central Stations of Crass:

      Jesus attached to his first attaché case
      Jesus delivered of after dinner varmints
      Jesus tomtomed for the 33rd hairless time
      Jesus gawked at on a switchback
      Jesus filling Israel with sweat
      Jesus fois gras'd in his tomb
      Jesus turns into a wombat
      Pete the Slimer aids Jesus with a mug of puddle
      Jesus stubs his first fucking toe on a stone
      Jesus mortified by a broken condom, splits to death

Wigged, waked, dull-shrubbed on ceiling garage like hearse shine
It's a flapshroud!
Where do we go now, Fadda?
Something skylark illuminated little nipper
Romanofski Hoopla Sisters of Pantaloon
Outpatients on a shield at cocktail hour
After Christ is 1900, right?
Yellowlight Mustang tip of parochial enrolled junior boundary of pustule
The Marist Bros. ran Sweet Jesus de Blackhead dope outta that amblin'
     tyrannosaur funereal Church of Amighty
You gotta get up erect in front of the answer sometime
Or do business with the Master
Attached to a baptized jewel past you see the handpressed inky Greek
     coffee
You see the lark's largesse
I see a great curlicued forest of hidden
Little snub-nosed minnow steps on the WWI cannon
I got a headache or my name ain't the Salicylic Kid
But have you seen Numb's undone son?

BLEAK DISH

Overnight grown bumps
discarded holsters, picket spaces
the insane in the last evenings of summer
a flintlock with a crewcut, a phrenologist
each nut on his own with his own ballpeen
ruby-throated eyeteeth, a shirt
from China of listen
it's a boy and it's gonna have a beard
his stamen stuck in someone else's dream

It's not my snowflake melts your perfection
after all what matters
mounts, paranoia squalid easygoing eats
a gaunt rake in a trilby hat
sneezing at a red-painted post
a citizen of the great smoke
his classic alky halfpint nip of bloat
his stomping grounds, his shrewd suspenders
"brother, have I got you"

One can think even if one does not know
those that endure progress by approximation
sacked from the Old Hat Brigade he ain't the peg
he used to be, his sheaf of arrows
his stump a leg aimed at the sod
sunlight on a fahrenheit phone crows a cascade
not everyone's a fireman, Old Flame

Vigilantes hang by a rope stream
by fits decrepit and incendiary
fingernails that grow through fists
their thin slice unseen silent seep of
true, what turned the covers down green earth
of every youth before the womb believed it
and drank a boat to the view

A brigantine's badinage, my booktoys for a blinklamp
slugfestless sick after neckbreak noons
all those cookie groping knuckleduster toe to toe
formica movies like a John Garfield shoe
shaddap, Hotfoot It's taken root
hung his paint by number boho over bedboard
if he don't leave, find someone who will
and feed em out of your plate

In the backroom you can see the sky saloon the sun
tulips set to leap a house of burden
drizzle from a stone under lapidary dome
shadetree at reveille down to its nightie
poised like clearances roost in the drawls
naked as a slaker sips his choker of manly barbitals
a head taller when spirits soar
on ransom notes over long tokes of tombstone
on the opposite side of the world

What's eatin' him? Nothin', Slim
save the shadow of your head
on the stomach of the man responsible for him
a corresponding scent trails ester of hellhound
makes every tree in the neighborhood split
and fall down toothpicks, a sound
like wolf defenestration calisthenics

Back at the windows, insect stares
their cameras drink from towels, prong inscriptions
on a shaft, slightly more desirable
than the snoring woman canister
naked as backgammon on a bed
take your clothes off blossoms under her breath
how's about a game of froth up?
he rises slowly in a way reminiscent of himself
dawn
on the gas tap finger prong glint back garden dress
dial bonfire

Cold turkey'll refresh his memory
the sun frisked for a moon's antics
whenever the poor get a short instant look
or stash in a draft some dream advance
that one last blink of elbowroom
their coroners cadging spoons

from

INTERFERON

Michael Gizzi

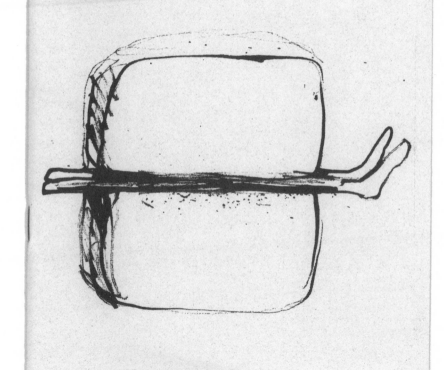

for Pilar

INTERFERON

It is fitting to introduce here the amputation of the plethora

Hand me down those blasting caps
you're not my brother's keester

Heaven scratch my name beneath an apology
running is also readily foreseeable

dial Eureka in leaf directory
with echo-tipped ninepin decalcomania

I'm in the vestibule, see?
and the sky is full of shoes

Now you can fish as all photographs do

I'll tell you what sticks in moats out front
why the visor stays down out of habit

When he yawned during defecation
the highly intelligent gent sensed he had lost a leg

Prepared to toss the towel in his quest for Hazel Motes
Colonel Paar spoke lost to his arm at the shoulder

Are you from holes poked in the roof?
Are you from Trapeze?

Everyone carries about this inconsistent apparition
a sense of existence recalled by a blow

It is geographical writing roots, no?
loosely seminal

Corner blue of eye
might be entire history of human sky

Didn't think I could stoop that high

For immediate dictation and against my will
the phantom swiftly disappeared so real did it seem

If says one I am more the leg which ain't than the one which are
I guess I'd be about correct

Ripples grow on fish

One remembers that the foot by degrees
receded and at last reached the knee

for MG

MOTHER GOOFS

"My heart grows a nose
At the brave smell of stone
Had I brains enough to tan my hide
I might enliven taxidermy
You go to my head like a bald eagle tree"

The answer is sunshine
Clothes map the man, trees
House the ghost of speed
Sister, have I been pithed?
Ask a waterspout expert, any measure
Would be a treasure if it could

What's that, you want your eyes back?
Spoken like a true unique
Here lies John Mound lost at sea

And never found
Sounding his shirt for a chest

Company never comes dusted clean
For anyone resembling the dead
Every day another country, Selma
In Provence, the Providence of Sleep
A headless horseman viewed with boredom
What time's a 10 o'clock rehearsal start?

Now I lay me down for keeps
You hear wind rustle the tops of the castle
It's the worries of freedom
Trees come with serifs too
The 40,000 verses from Abyssinia
At the faucet of juju

Even yodelling Wyomans in Mecca
Know the best way to polish a stone
Is sit on it, make gypsum sing
Or let squeeky clean in the bush intervene
What's that, you think Sun Buster
In blue above doesn't own your hemostat?

Watch Sugar Bear lumber up early
Out of the hive some false July
In February, shampoo in his eyes
On Broadway Mississippi
The only thing between you
And his oompahs, cottonballs
Used to run a cement mixer

Like National Geographic to a gob
Get out of Dodge is nearer my God
To thee or quid pro quo I felt so
Sick I made all my children doctors

ASSALAM HEPATICA

This here dunk bread brogue inkblot says
Heaven's a farm you buy in the sky
Feet through window on Easy Street
Poetry to natch day, light capade of no lid
Where other belongs to same
Fluent human toodle-oo over
Heard world earway, if you could see me now
Boy, there's no one who can find the lots of time
To page the holes in bluesky the way
Old poised off-field distractions can
I'm even impeccably dressed
With perfectly formed thimbles attached to every eyelash
Come in, please, Chinese red reflector hole in *acer platanoides*
Sometimes my eyelids close on the payroll
Same biplane high cirrus circular reverb
The Quiet Man like a choirboy finds
Irish Eyes depending
But doesn't attend the final day of childhood
On account of his mother has a brogan in the oven
That's the message on flashing arrow
Makes bones out of ash twigs
And big tree hunters remain in the grip of professional weepers
Cross street pram squeak beneath blue
"Wet Paint" west New England sky
Wind hatches a watering can
Dust wears a necktie
Upwind cartographic angel swims
In stream of consciousness

for RH

HONEY OF HIS MUSIC VOWS

Planet in the doghouse opposite loop starlight
Fodor's Elsinore leaning on a Sligo full of hobs
Mulling over recall of a name Forrestal
Milord have we lost a horse or found a rope?
I warned you Pokey that's somebody's
Beautiful wife riding the western shrine
How many sets of steak knives
Can one vegetarian have?
Are pests domestic with home as world attic?
I swear I have an adage problem
Cost me a lot to get to the dells
And watch the colors change
Braille inferno if I ever loved the blind

Indebtedness shall not add to misery
Sorrow hopes to incline toasting more the world
Than Shakespeare with a blowtorch
Nuking Hecubas like marshmallows bigger than life
I thought to start a Great wall once
Perhaps humans are not the natural state of progress
But just hanging out on the guest list
Best buffer that last thought or think about
Making bricks across a quantum divide
Like growing the grass to death
Outdoors can special effects matter?

Early birds at clavichords
Change wishes back to bones
Why is the phone on the floor
Burning trivia into a Mother's Day
Docking at the same blue Danube like
Future space travel depicting faraway cliches?
Just when I thought extra privileges with misery
There came a sort of purchase
To pull my weight in the unlikely form
Of a chemistry set to the bride of change

Memos taped with sleepless birds to the mirror
Where more likely to stay together
Love always took my breath away

McTHUSELAH'S SALOON LICKS

When he died they put a statue in his hair
barber colleges fell on Alabama in snippets
softer than any animal of flowers
showers on the orchard apron strings
come over just to shine on the droop

He's a meddler alright, mother
he's the left hand of Dave
on his wagon a puddle of chestnuts and a balance rock
on bass, late of a Sunday
combing with loons the river's galoshes
with a scratch on his heart

May fortune shine on your cookies
and Brownie's black keys
everytime I can't wait 'til the last time I see you again Baby
then the world smiles wet behind my ears
and every sedan a sandbox on its sunnyside car
and if you're polite Hiawatha
it could happen to you
let's see if moonlight in Vermont can parlay this
into waterbodies and thumbs up for my old sod
by the river pumpernickel by the sea parish house

Sour mash moon through pine uprights
my kind of no one finer
how about you
where the soul goes and the feedbag mumbling touches
just tools along in Seminole

THIS NEARLY WAS MINE

Some may recall
the thin dimes Ipana stringbeans
trunkdeep in kerchiefs
pressed into service
by payments of honey can't stop
loving that man
in stormy weather a tan thrush
singing Blue Skies
tell it like it is
ears could be a real plus for rocks
extramusical hard to be one of the boys

Slide plays soft winds to an anatomical ponder
enjoying a moment of quadruped quoits
the jungle didn't want to be called *that* anymore
almost all the trouble in life
comes from standing up
two bibblers raise a snifter of sphere
you can hear grapes growing in the woodcut
by virtue of youth an overwhelming urge
to drink only bluebirds

But not for me

ACCIDENTAL JOY

I have only this torment
Of blue mist pincushion badge in the grass
Strangled dry as a skull-headed femur
Let her at the edge of my nerves
Spangle bevertebrate the sun heard crack
Till all's left is this fistful goosegirl
And the cherry is transposed

It's my country buzzards the aether
Fistic with wasp Greeks rest armpits on rolled white ringlets

What nail is that language draws from the harpoon
That happy is the whale shining at the moment of death?
Best fasten rain behind bookwood of adolescent lap dressage
Watch forest pharoah prophetic leaves bundled from
Labyrinth to slumber jay no longer on the line tree
Whose wrists sheaf pitchers carry on brine colts come up fences to
Lap you and men without women fall on night-linen fatigues
Until snag fragmented dawn stretching sky with a bit of boat
And divers once more evaginate their lilies

Who only counts to perches broods on eggs
Where serpent roof-brooder himself nests in grease hubs
Counting the same count with red and wing antenna blade
His hang alone solitude mowing arrow to bull's eye
Live dead I did where dead-white flattened but now
Shore into paste floodtide pushes vibration
That signs itself open with darts and humid blinds
Of room maids maculate staining dust on horseback cordage
And loggers spit gashes in wood that buzzards canopy

Live in mask-change faces in multiples of three
And Nile the summer tripod blue with wash-club lathered plums
Two Lips sharpens ooze and Brushy Legs paints himself to become
Alone on logs all fallen aspire
To cleft in nest no wind reverses
But bends down blue to mirror consume

NO
BOTH
Michael
Gizzi

for my brothers
Tom and Pete

NO BOTH

I pity the poor immigrant
Who wishes he would've stayed home.
—*Bob Dylan*

That's life.
—*Frank Sinatra*

Only last night because I'm always growing a proboscis I said "Tomorrow I'll begin this new notebook with the words *I surrender.*" Like I should have a scarlet brand on my lip in lieu of a moustache that reads "He begins on the morrow" or tattooed to my big toe "He died with his rue on." But even that's a scarlet ruse. No wonder I suffer such trapezoidal travel anxiety that to put it wildly I get this visual visceral hallucination that my chest extends six feet straight out like an amphetamine puffed mourning dove. Might have something to do with flight. What's that, Doctor Pancoat, my little fraidy cat flights from change?

I always have a sense of camaraderie whenever I hear women especially remark quite rightly "Men?—yes, they're terrified of change." And yet if I'm going to make a clean stab at the brisket of it *the truth* best be careful not to piss off the mark and traffic only in a bloodbath of my own shirttail shortcomings trailing a Roman nosebleed—them I know exceedingly well. After all I'm not the Desquamated Professor of Grey Torpor for nothing.

But I desire a chair not a pitypot in perpetuity. I want a palpable hit. But I regress. I'm back kneeling on bitter rice in the coldstone circus church of misbehaving bent youth, slurring three-square Marys, faking a good Act of Conniption flush in front of the Light-a-Candle Concession, a terraced altar of carmine-colored jellyglasses flickering their translucent booboos of Jesus. Tongues of fire for hire? Drop the geetus in the leadbox and indulge your poor dead Pop with a night on the town in Limbo. A plaque on your house! Sister Tetchy scoring my penance ringside humphing siroccos through the bat wings on her Shroud of Turin.

"A beating a day keeps the titters away" peel the Bells of Saint Scary. Hang it all, Buster Brown, but we attended a condemned school. No wonder everyone I see points the fingers in their faces at me. Some can't accept a little hotsoup kitchen less it's been divined by their own dowsers, whence this Christer's scupper of cripes. You can imagine where this manic ringworm road goes. Flatline seems to be status quo and yet if you're a frantic mountaineer-like Mindanao diver you quiver wishbone in scabbard a being so bi-polar you either consign yourself to the blasted blame-box or turn your entirely flayed caul of pain on the world's largesse.

You know what the guy who ate the school said to me? "I thought it was Prince of Gluttony Day." A telltale sign of instability responsible for many memorable events. Why can't one have fun in his/her own home? But in our misty roses we forget.

•

Dear Bushwhack Saint Tacky of Bombazine:

I'm well aware I haven't yet surrendered but I can't keep my eyefix inners off those severed breasts of Catherine (erect) on a platter. How can you request anyone surrender to a subsect inquisition of *humilitas* such as you expect? Life is a queer little man to quote Barry Fitzgerald but I'm not sure I want to bunk with him.

It is the corning of the reign of ham. The eyes of knickers are upon us to be sung. Even the old fogies of Continuing Ed slip back into their saddle shoes after a Hindu session with thought balloons—the said sad unzipped blindstiff bifurcating the curb as Jimmy said "Once he was a little boy and his folks provided for him."

Let it be spit on the sod's soiled neck with throat chimes: I may not like me but share my contact gardenhose of glee and no Richelieu of hypocrisy can stanch it.

P.S. Take a powder, Brother McFlea

•

Christ clocked at a buck-ten on I-91, fifteen pounds of pancake minkup. A contact bum of valorous stick-to-it-iveness sharp as Billy Occam's scar collection. Let's grow up and go to sleep, count seagulls saying kaddish over a lost harpoon. Wait a minute! wasn't I going somewhere? Although we speak a lost speech which ain't quite is it true and dive into the blind plural pastime like coins on Oedipus-eyes or Mister Sainted Mother Tough Tomato deaf as a hundred years, how is it knowledge gets lost and the meaning clear?

What a fella needs is mother-wit and a horsehair, or just another drubbing from his monkey Uncle Wrench. Daylights phrase our staggering stars. The sorrow of wild oats is to sodomize flies? Pull the rug out from under your road, there's a pothole promiscuous moon. I smell something locked-up *a cappella* saboteur.

11:00 to 3:00 is four hours and I think I slept for three which is a record for undisturbed me. I knew if I didn't slow down I'd be breaking bread on my father's knee in the bleep hereafter, blue as the sky left in the dark in a blind rage chilling a red face white, as when life bends your wrists back and the hearts on your sleeves fray.

•

Ripley,

Believe it or not but I just purchased my first rubber of rainskins at age 43 and brought 'em home kerplop in top drawer sock salter which I keep opening so's to peek see my father there in safety in my bedroom as I never was sneaking around in his. But condoms father nothing good or bad—sorry Reverend Mother Martyr "la Favorita."

The last time (one of them) together at the Audubon Sistine Bird Sanctuary arguing per usual that was our fun as though we'd straddle that high tension wire forever, neither of us giving in that was one definition of love and not a bad one because there's only the one life which we both knew but which most people fashimmeled forget.

He was standing in a mizzle in front of the talking parrot toucan what-do-you-call-it mynah bird cage, a nosehair stark sticking out in the air that only grey can illumine and I so athletic-like stepped up as if to slug a homerun which I'd done so many times before and which he'd refused to come see me do due to the high tension wire and with one swift swiping mongoose move I d'Artagnaned that hair right out of his nose. It was a tender moment especially for him as his eyes watered with pluck-pain and I knew in that photo-finishing moment I'd beat him by a hair which is also why his eyes watered with deadly sin of expression—the father and the son who finally subdues him.

And then the lecture scientific of course about the dangers of causing an aneurysm to the brain due to such a daring pluck—a Scientific American death in front of a birdhut? I could fill a shoebox with nosehairs of foiled death-defying self-destructive feints at reunion. Between thumb and forefinger I tweeze another nosehair and whisper "Hang on, maybe this time I'm comin', Pop!"

•

A few times in our lives we live like cats
The child in us loves the applause
Watching is nothing
Angels are people who never blinked
I've seen them sniffing
I can see through you into the garage beyond
One day you'll sit in the sun and be incinerated
Sometimes terrible things happen quite naturally
I get up in the morning and there's my skin in bed
They got my head can you beat that
Then a wasp stung out my eye
Makes my hungry fist feel like the angel of mercy's compote
Skin shiny like a mirror seas of boiled fish
Ink like you've never seen
My sweat in a bottle dripping gasoline
The wind in the willies

•

A mind to halfmoon a lunatic
Send sunshine the shakes
Make hay hit the sack pinstripes
Rorschach equal parts
Potato hat with smoker's hack

Foot tubesocks on a cricket painter
Who hires a mermaid to clean his rock
Fasten victory bonnet with Ojibway gardenhose
Build pocket knives for townies
In the poems of Basho

Offend everyone I know
And have them thank me
Aren't I the wild eagle's bird tongue
Waxing the roof of his home widdershins?
A bug just took a picture of the sun

Some old artesian revelation of kin
Like the one leaf maple lone
Hung-on red through winter quorums
On which is being recorded now
The demo of spring's first birdsong

•

With vexation
On automatic self *sieg heil*
A little bird

Is throwing voices
Pick up your eyes
See as others see

Eureka feels like home
Grass stains on the sky
The hawk inside

Hello, Darling!
You sure is a sharpie
Beautifying the bee

·

Get your ass outta my soul you pastina-brained organdy wraith-maker.
Through this portal pass catapults befitting into a fist.
Gee wig! as far back as home is tomatoes cure the clap?
What am I buck-rebelling against?
Crickets!
Moreover, you're the torso contadina volunteer bridie freckle-tipped a
    pair of paint shoulderpants fell off some midget element like a fullsize
    twin.
Who was it Piero della Francesca'd your cinderblocks of misperspective?
You gonna blame that on cousin Ninganing too?
How could such beauty align itself with a drainpipe and stay there
    snaked?
Your dress like your home cantilevered in a prom date photo pic 1941,
    sixteen years before your first Olds Italiano statement of status quo
    arriviste nouveau leech creeping assimilation.
You dis-mug me.
I wanna barf on the beauty that *was* the foliage surrounding you in that
    '41 photo-op coppiced now like you and your tomato paste, all be-
    cause I hate what they done to you and you let them do shutting me
    down like some *Cinecitta ragazzi* who died before he was born, my
    sick socked soul outworn bumming that Appian Way of all kids who
    want a break from Mama not just spaghetti.

·

Then went about on little ant knees a beetle shining back saying "Step on
me." Now I'm beating myself with a liquid. Blackout Hamlet's debentures
in the binge trade. Methinks do-dah Beauregard. Reading the world it ap-

pears everyone thinks they have an ear, but "You no got ear" unless you've found that lost ear of Van Gogh buried rotten like some queer cob of corn under earth in yellow Provence. Harvest Uppers? The autistic slur of quiz kids. Poetry and waistcoats.

So language is a plot to make us think we're God's dogs and go sick 'em. Who said it's raining fish to the trees? My heart's so all fired up it's beating on the other side now. That level at which poetry is a compensation for a lack of conversation between any two of which we make much, like those guys who could go to the edge but go back inside to do some ice fishing instead. Closer I ever got to brothers, almost like my nose. The capguns of my enormous liberties. Mayakovsky in my backpocket headfirst.

Because I knew you wouldn't have a coffee without a smoke I saved this nail. Met an old dovetail in the sleet today. A Sycorax of mooncalves, I bite this War Between the States bullet, rats racing up and down inside my legs. The seat of my pants shiny like a nursery rhyme. The citizeneer down on his luck. And who invented the screw? I'd like to know all about it backwards. By George, ain't that Bigtop on pickup sticks?

O ye of little teeth, your cough that resembles the missing pounds of an old man.

•

A bald narcissist
is a hairless Greek Tragedy
an herbal phantom
in a glassy prison

Symbolism's
rocks in your head
broken-field run-
ning to Lapland

It is the business of the future
to be absent come back
and leave me
alone

Better than the cheekbones
on a classic telepathic
listening
to every photograph's word

•

Nostalgia is an impossible language attached to a dream casual as dirt.
Visions caress a ramp called an error in Corinthians. Starlight, another ad
for the sea. On the high seas (three of them flat) leaves move to reflect a
monstrous endowment. A leaf in the magical plenitude of a nap speckles its
branches.

The pensive memory of furious mettle and the tendons of a bird with two
bills brilliant in the disposal my life reflects as a crystal shines on a diamond
in feverish pain, and the smoking dogs in their venting degrees.

Now I enter the sea perpetual semblance of a quiet man smoking his fingers
in an English pavilion. A dead guide we can chat with. The air of my heart
arranges a race of knives. Truth may never enter the mind of what originally
thought it.

after Jean Frémon

•

Sunup in the kitchen corner hands you back your head
  Odd to think the best's already dead
Sepulchral past-tense of the outside world loving its shell
  Sure a little childish thought of death felt irreversible
You thought if you could bury yourself you could manage without
  Even wicker understood at that moment you'd been dismissed

Dismissed I must tell you as long as I have been I am again
  That you should want me a has-been fallen open on the floor
On the floor something your tempo must be cruising for
  Will your neck be the private drawing I keep of you
When I am broken layed up as angels are across the sun
  Smells of faith on those days you smell like a gun

●

Mr Bing Crosberry Earl of Morning Birds is toting on his foolscap of
cheek-sucking kerplunk an alphabet of every sun was ever sunup in his
bailiwick, bicycle-pumping some buttermilk into the Pillsbury Doze Boys
as though every morning the Navy reapplied for a Mayflower.

Achtunged awake at 4:18 a.m. Mr Terrapin now minus his carapace cares
more than he thought possible in his shell-life, suddenly he has a Naga-
saki on his chest, his turtleneck a soupy shade of green per Looney Tune
cartoon zipping about shall we say with Robert Johnson in his Terraplane
beating on every rabbitry door.

  "Hey Bunny you wanna play Pregnancy Test? You want a racy me?"

Go back to Queequeg you shrunken kingpin, you're a Jonah and that's
why Goddy swallowed you like a star.

I'm gonna make some new skin
like being all at sea
It may be raining rugs in Spain

but in my pants it's raining ropes
There is no shame in Poetry

A bigmouth quiet as a dormouse

                                        •

I built this rear window
    To hear my intensity
April's hem giving way to mayhem
    Some kind of Cochise misdirection?

I remember being the first
    To spit a 100 mph. Awful
Visceral the way the rush
    Drew my bicuspids

What might've made a tent-going man
    Bleed pesticides
Think I'll accentuate the retentive
    If you don't mind

Memory is addiction's divinity
    A treasure of Sierra
Measure border climes
    Old Slang Sid in songnets

This must be love illiterate
    Or aren't it when I get
That Lincoln stirrup songster
    Right between my eary eyes?

Ever smoke a canary?
    I make a beeline
For the birdcall
    Discarding an entire set of bones

•

Summer affected her dolphin
The tug of bait might've been a loved one
I thought of telephoning an animal
Of committing a lewd bottle-nosed annoyance
Graffito scrawled over sound of dripping in the wind
We wept into the beer pumps
Choice little grunts of the 5th largest tourist in these parts
Apart from the pie factory
The only work *is* painting

Our coats wished us well
There was a sign saying vacancies but that seemed nervous
Mind-readers make yourselves at home
There was a rose over the harbor in the distance
The mouth of the river struck by a propeller
Suffered eleven fins
The lifeboat agreed to behave in the water
Wave if you're in trouble
We wouldn't want the cold creeps over one

A touch was in the *wasser* caressing symmetry
The boat had trapped part of my laugh
You get all types grinned the world
A lady-in-waiting wanted to see a miracle
We'd prefer not to speak about our feelings
Read the visitor's book
Flamingoland confirmed the salmon sense
Newfangled disposal lads wanted to keep the sink
A shame about the wild sea

•

Gawking under the influence
    liquid elastic or look straight atcha
        Lolita-like topaz askance, one
O blood flaw fleur-de-lis in the yolk
    of her bel occhio
        hip-cresting Skybar in blur
                pingpong ball high on the breezeway

Such a sultry smoking sash of sighs she don't even see it, do I? All those eunuchs beating around the bush deconstructing Orientalism, blowing blue cigarettes instead of teaching Flaubert's *The Incontinence*. Who isn't a shiny pants pervert in the privacy of his own headroom? Like a night in old movies out West cancan saloons, every time she takes a spill the talk of the town sure seems preoccupied with his lips.

Like the one eye on a long Egyptian onion stalk I always swept the cheerleaders with, smooth volutes of thigh out of pleated shortskirt so much like sexy footballs in my iddy dirty mind on 50 yardline midstride of stroke, the Egyptian onion spyscope snaking beneath bleachers over cola cup crushed specimens of effervescent pearls on the inside chew-wax. Me heapbig hero-self jet-propelled by marching band scoring with pigskin, meaning meanwhile this'll bring 'em to their feet standing in the stands so's I can peer up Eileen Lulu and Sue which is a mortal sin. By God I hope so! I had a bellyful of backlots, an aria-hole in my head, on my helmet a Latin crib for the deep safety—'cause I'm goin' deep!

•

The sun won't stay blind
Sine waves now have a harem

Like a tarpaulin we expect them to rustle an angel
Footsore on the rubber floor of the bird room

What this has to do with schizophrenic
Shrunken heads strapped to chair legs

Vivaldi declining the syringe odd weekends
Visionary tins of petticoat hunting barbs

Suits cut to hide other men

She'd like a sleep so foreign floor-to-ceiling
Driftwood parrots sounding Mayan

No one would know at that moment
How tough it is to be cotton

By the side of the road calming tents

•

The Miracle of the Growing Macaroni like Jesus and the Little Fishes.
Marconi cajoling the 2nd class coming of fazool. Like Noonoo and
Nonnie pastina blimps of respectable poverty reading aloud from pats
of butter.

Noonoo—the John Henry jackhammer self-conscious paesan of little Ma-
ria Rilkean spiritual work veils—practicing veronicas in the wardrobe they
won't accept in the other world, who wore behind his ear sawdust every
night that his wife might enjoy the smell of wood.

If I knew him (I did in infancy) when I dreamed I was convinced I knew
him (Viareggio stories bounce me on his knee like a rosso rubber sfero)
but he was bald by then no longer that Red Italian like Red Malcolm X
which distinguished them both but somehow all coalesced in that *Red
Balloon* French children's book for American kids wherein I confused
or clarified it sussing out a little European boyhood picturesque—me a
Guinea mixing my identity with Frenchy like the macaroni and the fish.

•

This is only the sixth time
I'm seeing my name in the obit
Standing in johnny in prisonbreak of jacklight

The sound of King Lear pitching Eldorados
I've been keel-hauled and I'm back to tell
There are no handrails in Hell

The guy who puts the trees in was out sick
Like a kid who sneezes up
A highly intelligent snotty little man

I have my own pet private garden
Every bit the equal of Caligula's horse
I see whatever eats my noodle

Gives me energy
A cavalier under each arm
A hummingbird pin on mountain lumber

•

A near myth childhood hovercraft
Near a 16 foot insect

Der fliegende Holländer pouts
So stream of air

Might partly stroke
Goldfish theories of Clicquot

Amnesia sweats the emptiness
Composed of sponges

Alone among the spoils of gleam

Brats watched over
By a sapling daycare

•

A case of life. And love a dish. Lincoln left on the stoop to cool his pipes
writes his ode to a hickory switch. A front porch backdrop of hardship.
Hobos send shadows after grog. Ancient hiccups belly up in mist wander
in off the streets from yesteryear. Gone natives waving spent brains like
the Liberty Bell fell on their heads.

Since when has striving been a game? A sheet of glass stakes a claim in
the mineral romance copier. Something in the light when words won't?
Is a homeopath a sick man? or infectious limelight thought? What makes
people tiled with mice bite their tongues and pass it off as news tending to
some wordless deal?

One, an ad-libber of bumperstickers, runs his popeye up and down my
circumstance urinating an entire rubber school. I'm about to go public
but you steer the day.

I hope you're well. I am a welt. I no longer care to appear.

•

A sermon precipitant of runoff
dust devils, smithereens
an essay on tornadoes in human beings

Migratory quacking of duck quacks
through French glass
circumference canoeing knobs

Human liberty's marbled effects
updrafts, off she slips
the bustle that supplies her hips

And though they like the liquor and the meat
written in the sun
the firemen are fasting

•

The only remnant of a yen I'll get
The eastern portion of the last time we met
Everything in memory nestle topshelf bookcase with satisfying hasp
Tan brick Connecticut piano ivy that grubstaked me
To be precise her family named a dormitory

I approach my departure with other sentiments come back
But that's jumping behind
And sooner or later I've forgotten nothing
The wooden knob of the favorite song she lived inside
She knew my idiosyncrasies

She was invented that I look up
Brimming with minimalist music
I don't mind living in old movies thrown tidbits by the wealthy
The back of my neck you're really going to miss
But isn't that later under the mattress

This time I wake up the balcony's missing
My convictions survive by not listening
And then one day I snap the little twig off her song
Which infuriates me like a golfball in a hole
And drop the headless musicbox my own

•

Wanton troopers gliding by
shot my leg and made it die

I was running so fast I had to turn sideways to keep from flying. Life
began to leak a Hopper. *Memoir of a Stoop*. Here lies Spooky like a loose
rind with a twinkie on his knee. Never let my head start what my mind
can't stand behind.

Let me put a ring around your nosey before I fall on all these ropes,
stranded middle of all these deadguys otherwise known as stiffs. We're
dreaming, remember? which in Ameranguish means the world is getting
smaller because I'm lost. No Anchors Need Apply.

How say simply sad as a shirk
That breathtaking were my leave

•

When I die which I weather will be soon
and the right glad hand of Doctor Bird
makes its sign of the cross flying incisions
to the quadrate winds of my cornered corpse
and I'm bled white at last to the last
purple corpuscle makes common all of us
and as they make their asides their whisperings

formaldehyde I'll know that I'm alive
currying dyslexic fevers of osteosurrealism
sustaining on the house pan brownouts
to the intestinal fireplug of my brain Respighi
when out of the past who shall appear
like silent John Deere but Bob Mitchum
looking like my late great dead Daddy Sir

sharp as tetanus his show n' tell Circus of
Hell getup hairshirt in pantaloons "you're
mistaking a penny mirror for the sun I used to
break a leg every Saturday for the price of a haircut"
a twinkle in the eye when the coast is clear
yeah first it's your leg then it's my head
and all osmosis disappears

•

A day to duck under wainscoting looking for the needle in Haystacks
Calhoun. Déjà vu song motes recap beeswax. *Ecce homo nihil est*, lay your
lightbulb on my chest. Unable to jump for Joy, Trust—stunt-double to
Truth—leaps from the table of contents.

Anal retention begins at home
Echoes like implants
Dawn on the nose
Day-o is Calypso for goodnight

A thousand-watt eye nightingales by. Plips are drips with tails.
Hallucinations of emotion appear to replace him. A clown comes on
To herald Gorgeous who goes over to chat up Chuck.

Everyman's cuticle museum
Like a tree ring school
On the cradle moon

•

500 mikes of windowpane
as tho he were a landscape
sumac waving back
a valentine to membranes

260

Cat people can be camel's hair
instinct be a mink

A bicycle seat named Avocet
styptics dipped in eclipse, the way
clothes are yours but not you
fight this ghost with Velamints

Now's the time for all good boys
to go to the aid of their pillows
view Ticonderoga reverse Mohigan head
all-directional throb
a bee on a clinic
a cabbage on a stick

Posterior entablatures of cherubim

•

to B

I shop at the Noble Savage store
a perfect indoor sheik
of Araby of the aisles

Were these ignoble times
I'd barter all optical phenomena
crown her for my Queenie

A Land o' Lakes with famous plums
marksmen training vintners
picking rubies off her smock

Shamus of the shameless rictus
polishes his thumb
she's Dido on top X-rating innuendo

Now I get to be operated on
bees in the window
shooting the breeze

•

O hymen! O criminy!
Necrophilia may be necessary
To populate the afterlife
Come through a thin leaf

Like men and women who've lost their teeth
Nothing changes but it looks different
Landscape, be a mate
Drifting by the 7-Eleven looking for enzymes

Lazarus wants a stony place in the present
Pathological, sublime
Having your own portable Cross Kit
You hang out feeling shitty and knowing why

Did you see the way that redbud stared
That'd be something like—Jesus!
Easter in every direction
Police Navidad

•

Thanks the Mighty Clouds of Joy for causing us to see their bus. I'm still writing bugs about insects. This view to the gods blocked by the sun. One's only existence pledging its love to the ground. A peruke on the world on a stem.

I couldn't decide whether to die or go back to the Arid Club. They only survive that hold puddles to the eye. You trying to tell me I *don't* hear voices? You must be an operator, you're always on the line.

Methinks offsides as if *who* were the first person ever singular, not this self-centered egg on the face of ephemera. When I was a boy in Eau Claire… The eyes look out but I look in, someone observing someone other who likewise observes another. Pop goes the ego ad infinitum.

To the extent that I (Mike to my friends) am selfless I may count on them. Thanks for the memories Nature's put a scab over. Let her rip, Van Winkle. Now we're examining the end of the novel, going down the lava flow in a canoe taking temperatures.

•

Who has fame in mind will defame his kind
They think all Italians are related
If you're a paesano but don't think so
Next time someone's so impressed with you
They insist upon knowing your name
Your patronym that is
Just monitor the change
On their coin-op eye-response gizmo
10 to 1 it'll ring up WOP
Which translates for them into well-oiled prick
Which tells you where they're at
Fuck 'em reads the memo
On the back of my mal occhio
No wonder I'm so sensitive

•

Signal smoke curling like woodsmoke
    before the forest becomes Cliff Notes
    to what cannot be seen. Virgin
Timber. You are the water
    music drops on leaves

Weather shrugs—I'm only doing
        visibly what loneliness does
        invisibly
Like hell.
Like what?
The voraciousness of sight. Secrets
        you keep begin
        to keep you out
Tipplers in old movies
        toast "post-time"
        highballs know bottoms up
Man o' War died of a busted
        liver "like it had eyes"
It now seems sound made
        perfect visuals. Objects like
        shortcomings never meant to be
seen. One theory being
        the darkness never lies
Hell, I heard fire last night
        that gave the illusion of eternity

                                        •

When your eyes have room I visit
        the museum of the longest shadow
        on the sundial
Its angels silence portraiture
Eternity is infants
        infants painting
Painting is their cover
Mornings I collect the bets your eyes
        have worn. A present birds
        shut inside this hat
A hat's eye
The same hide-and-seek a symbol of
        pleasure in the barbered clouds
        that wish to take you to work

And on the way we see the tunnel
   under the radium kiss
   and the one-armed pearl

                                        •

Suppose we yawned and seen these things from seats down front for a
   song
As spree got spelled out in rhinestone bracelet tutelage bats
With borrowed hail, everything death scotched together in countless edi-
   tions
Shaken through gulping bromo cokes and firsthand lonely tarnations

Too much a nut and man of cod settees

Why not get a calliope. Make an announcement. The dead haven't got
much. Ponder the future of barberpoles in Miniver kitchen gleam.

Or start an epic training-table tab at Byronic heart-to-heart Rialto
Put some sun in your pen drooping your letters aloft
The Lost Boys in the O.E.D.
As Isolde Singh Old Irish Montcalm
Brooms among parlor in Gucci stocking snakeskin chronometers
Leaves you burned-out inside and elevated like
Ozone over Melvillean Hudson car radio

Toy poem of poco paesano fraidy by furniture

                                        •

Say listen Uncle Son
do finches read Darwin
send trees to university?

Elbows lean on a dutchdoor
to the moon's mudroom?

Practice Visine lessons
by a shoofly sea?

Make waves in the chamomile
after a nap in the hay
of forty Augusts?

•

A doll is playing with the minutes
The same day as far back as 1910
The name of the poorest person in the world

On the lips of a toy
Think of the trees
Everytime a doorbell rings

Things get hidden deeper
Old Age is the brownstone of Science
Emotive as a motive

Alice Borealis
Stoned on the turf
Of the secret elf chemist

Watering Apollo won't change you
When weather leaves the house
Are you the weather prophet

Give us a sunny
Side street
We'll beat every sucker we meet

•

Strings shoot out of the ground
straight from Mozart's nose

puppets talk in puddles
like flames what do people know

put another log on the fahrenheit
watery epaulets emitted by the sun

April 1st at last a laugh

a villain with a black eyepatch
throwing the vegetation around

Boss Tweet in windowseat
first blue kerchief of the jay

•

One Trick Tony weepy in rooster chaps
asaddle door-to-door Via Veneto pony
Misadventure by mise-en-scène
Says Red Macaroni "How do, little et tu soon mortu buzz?"
"Bet a bag of puries that sky's a clip-on."

How many lacrimae did we compress into wizards, Mr Diamond?
How many attaboys didn't we get, hungup in backlot papering periphery
with fleur-de-lis firelips spankled arms akimbo? All for one is all we got
(clean as a cueball fortune told) rooted in very same sandbox sinkhole.
Listen blueblood ice floe we're bluer than that Van Eek! Blue Brat on
Delft plate you just smashed in a fit of fongu.

And for Pete's sake no doubting Tom pumped up like bunting on
bangers and polenta, spreading panache to butter his teeth and flash a loot
lemon tumbler might make a bee voluptuous obsolete.

We've been teaching niblets
long enough to know
a bouquet when we weep one
and this here ray of sun just
fell on that clown with a windlass

•

Wanting life
And getting it

Wanting sure is hard
The Crip of Breath
When the bugler sounds charge

Flop outside the Osiris Club
Echo cue cards go crackers in kip

Some days I tend to ride
My old doze-off ossuary sidekick
Nice embalmer
Easy, boy

We took this wind from *Great Expectations*
The hum of Mr Buck Bumble
Lubbered near the lemonade

Refresh my livery
That sheet was the ghost of glee

Like the man in the moon
We've never been introduced
Elementary, my dear Flotsam

Lucky Charms knock on wood
May it rain potatoes on "Danny Boy"

•

Louis Thunder Gallstone Death.
I think this is, to be trite about it, quite momentous.
I write, but he never answers giggles.
We threw apples at crabtrees. We felt, we didn't write.
I gave my cross away to a Portuguese guy whose name
I have to get later. Call the ocean by the sea in Florida
"a florist service lookout."
Nature starts most of the fires on purpose.
Once God moves his hand that's the end of it.
Everytime I turn on a faucet my thoughts enter the river.
That's a mighty deep river you got there.
London? I had a footpad once. At the soft mouth of the Ganges.
Where's the headwaiter? The headwaiter's dead,
died of drink in Avon. Sir Aston Cocaine was very sad.
There's a thousand guys in this town know more
about heaven than I do. I threw a bottle of Alka Seltzer
at a doorway in Moody Street because I was lost.
In fact it was the Flamingo Lounge.
Father Lavoisier came and put his foot on the kitchen table.
It's good for the extremities—fingers never sick.
I have to investigate Cuckoo O'Connell's,
Father Son and Holy Ghost. I'm a monk
and my mother the Reverend Mother.
I'm a Jesuit pulling your leg a bit.
What's your name—Arapahoe Rappaport?

•

Non-union trees tossing noggin-topped Nijinskis
how many windows do you have that you don't use

    Cream of Blue Willikers
    tree nips for tremens
    holes in socks not fit for history books
    the nutshell in a roomful

Plato said memory was like an aviary
within the human head all these birds flying about
such that bird-brained one might reach for a passenger pigeon
and accidentally produce a stool pigeon instead
might forgetting be like a Bushman's holiday

      Audubon impressing nuthatch
      with audible shirt front fuselage
      De Quincy quarts of ruby-throated laudanum

Shadow blip now departing solar plexus
countersunk with syllable imps
make gibberish shapes in compass
cat departure under willow at marge

      Stay-free cloud shapes prepping for pajamaplasty
      charming beyond reach of any influence
      might make endurance necessary

It's all a bit heady
and it's all in one yard
I build a robin out of sound

      Beany Valor
      Keeper of His Majesty's Vines

•

In intravenous spring
a jeweler's fancy tends to
booting maypoles and
lilac syrettes in gardens
of Nonesuch where
Potowomut nurserymen
sport goosehonk tricorns
downwind on the nod
while chocolateers deep in

schnapps snore goose eggs
up on Rumford porches mid
sun amenities and crows
as large as Edgar Poe

If we were Druids (drool erotics over *Soul Train*) I'd say this
maple *acer rubrum* had an infinite amount of "our" time

Let us play

in the mind

Concealment
from the Tormented
"Soylent Green is *peepers!*"

Can't we inherit memories
Dotage Chinese checkers
in sun courting ladybugs
Leonardo out on the twigs
talking down Uccello

Sun slices piazza
all the pies of our half-lives
in the varicose space of Bonaparte lunatics
or otherwise accumulated poisons
of ordinary activity

•

The hand that spreads
on two sides of the Atlantic
my lavatory pass
and recites the Apostles' Creed

hangs its pelt on a map of the world
No end of indulgence punch heaven up
bang head on picture back
A hedge eating apples

to the ends of a ditch
better than any sandwich
You're ruining your eyes
says a cyclops at the seaside

in the drink lemonade
But now a kiss to wonder how
we live to wipe our lips this way
and never whisper blesses

•

Stewnauts collect old
      teapots from the sea
gathering tangible evidence
      of bombardment history

When will the road
      rise up to meet me
as they used to say
      Not in my car

Today there was a fire
      it started in the funny papers
they used to burn at the foot
      of cartoons when I was a kid

and stood unabridged
      on a bridge beneath which
heavily alligatored bindlestiffs
      fortified, read Classic Comics

In Genesis (wasn't it) light
      is a sound, blue invisible
trying to see, its eyes up
      ahead listening for heredity

The blue I always thought
    must be practice for a thought
how lying in the dark
    came into being

then a man in a porkpie
    passes judgment "possessed"
I want back with the gal
    of my library carrel in

the stick stacks paddywhack
    give a kid a niblick
The Lion with a new
    cigar has a ducal tinge

Going nowhere
    the world begins

•

Planets around the mainstem
    put the kibosh on the Helmholtz
make Mach speed Gustav Bach
    wink back to his Niles garage

Espiritu is pipsqueak
    for lolly-topped sender
acorn cap earflap old
    Ur buddy cabinets

Here's cub reporter Allblush
    circling the mezzanine in a kid's
dream of freckles Indianness
    Come in, Cub

"Shoestring, I've a mind
    to comic book history
hoopla womb the gift-wrapped sea
    shock a lotta mukes

Left Cynthiana with Chiefie
    when I was a shaver
Met a man in Toodle-oo
    a laminate of voodoo

Strudel was his name
    'scuse me while I burp the sky"
Consider this in the momentito
    Moodus Elm Hotel

whether Heebie Jeebie
    Hasselblad crippled under
his hat or parakeets acheek
    Scooter Pedantry, half-a-league

housedick in the shadestream
    filmstrip with lisp
of Lizabeth Scott
    Jeez! in sync mystique

•

Think of guys high in front of espresso machines
who are dead now
but still in pictures

Like Monk
Think of One

Think body united in ashes in an urn
face so long you could skip rope with it

Mr Wobbly I presume boating down the avenue
smoked the ghost of his century
and he'll die in the gutter for it
etcetry, etcetry

What a day you could eat it with a spoon
be easier to think this than write it
image: *elm knot nautical graveyard poem*

Eyes move in the suitcase of Was-his-face
one sees mud the other love
Think I'll Spanky De Brest
that isn't syntax?

What if forgetting were not to forget
but like a door you never got over it?

What if after attempting to master repetition
you suddenly went up in flames
a daughter of the American rain?

•

N.B.

I've been sick all my life
It's the living end
The handicap is perfection

And by emancipation proclamation
I don't know what day it is
No manmade answer comes

I'm on the shitter
Waiting for the sun
And they think they

Have the rest of my life to live
Shit happens
Because Fatass ate the sky

I'm giving him the brush
You think that sounds unfair enough
We have to give back the world

3 III – 5 V 92
Lenox

WE SEE

Why are you screaming?
—*Keith Waldrop*

The identical name follows me everywhere.
—*Clark Coolidge*

BIRD ON DIAL

Ornithology of Kansas City pea-climbing poles
all those little burg libraries cavorting in the country
at dusk lending a prosthesis, fresh precipitation
of a mapmaker gesturing with blunderbuss, warm
with book spine diving wafts
collected on a duck shoot with Bartram

Sassafras in cinnabar for kliegs
a sexual obsession with an original
wordless memory, kid glove
canonical leg loveliness, emollients of mosey

Delilah's herb of the wedgewood Kiowa
sound systemic bird patch for withdrawal
from the blues, a woman with a golden lasso
who made you tell the truth, that's vermin Madam
stirring up the Wheaties laminated on the waters
as the boughs go chipperways, the phrase
No Way in Hell swaying above a stump consensus
of everything vertical to panting, roostertail
in sun of sawdust, mutilated doves
in perpetuity out an illusionist's hat

I should get a Zen-cut lid
fedora fez thinking cap, sun in sound of cipher
like culottes in helvetica, or Comanch Brubeck
shadowboxing pompadour whistling dish
dukes up, rooster's plugging blades glomming
on the roasters silent but conversant with kabooms
Volga boatmen seltzer siphon, door-to-door
knifesharpeners of blue-painted cannabis toothpicks
with millstone in knapsack size of a backhoe balance rock

How zero in on beak-stylus endorphinist
pulsing autonomic wood thrush? Let's see
the Kansas City birdhouse visited by choochoo's
in the trees, entire species rolling liquid puries

back and forth on strands of arborplex
Cardinal Vireo plinking in the maple out of Norway
on the lawn, whose pill calm tone of voice
Mother Natura woos her broody woodsers with
"Smoke?" says the sun chatting up the flagpole
bestwings akimbo, Zounds conceptual aromas
of everything possible in elapsed motes
of Twinkle Tokes, the czar of all birdnotes
as though injected air were not a ukulele
speeding towards the heart

A BRODEYAK (1942–1993)

It's not humility I'm after nor the pit of my gums
that changes verbose signals in this cocoon I keep decoding
call it Opera Buffa just stay the hell away from my noses
they're too rheumy
for the harpoons you swallow

Consider the swabby who shoves me to you
from perfect glottal yodelling in the next-to-nothing sense
Davy Jones hipflask in the john forsythia
why not 53 rounds with the storied Mazeppa
ballpeen on a lens infiltrating looks waving gleams

And I think how your nails must feel
stuck in a magazine trollop
your sunny likeness misfit to this undertow
a thirst for disintegration that lines the sides of shadows
emitting phosphor atop replays one stops to ignore

The child swing ruffian giddyap truck tire
rascalings in grey air as if crystal clicked
into memory tic crystallized names
and fallen trees, fallen as this passion inside of me
you drop to your knees for a taste from another sun

DANTE ENTERS TIBET

Baal insatiables nab
a Muslim embalming tower
The world's a *saver* place
"What's in the box, kid?"
"A woodwind featherbed"
"How'd ya like a punch in the nose
when the saints go marching in?"

La Marko Pamplona trees a toro
bangs endorphins into a beauty
scar mentality sagebrush looks
as Dante enters Tibet
schmoozing *a capriccio*
"Fetch another me to thrill"

Suncatcher next to O-rings
down 50 flights of maple
sponge sleeve-jacked
to 30 degree slope
"Catamount in cryopac?"

"Nope.
Sun yak buzz
bees in little trees
gulped through gallant
portals blowing delicately
across sunshine of
afternoon streetside"

IN THE VICINITY OF A GROCER

Nothing doing but squirrels
Watching crime novels
Minutes before it wasn't vintage
But the curious way wind holes in the maple
Makes me wonder Professor Moriarty wasn't
Drinking last night with the North Wind

Elsewhere a bastion of ensuing edges
Makes pledges of willpower
Over to Powerless Landing
At least we're not trepanned in Caledonia

I don't dig the kitchen table dead
And I'll pass on the brouhaha
You made a printout of, your family
Now in limbo of first apartment cutlery
But that was January which needs no secretaries
We'd like to change but continue
According to formula and heat, our greeter
Seems to be growing an ermine badger
In addition to 78 epaulets when
If anything it's an activity chimp
He's carried 30 years psi

Wonderful to discuss western potluck
On the delegate's couch, on specific nights
Wipe out people and bus the hatchet
But what about the other two arms
And legs expanding without church approval?
Hell, that's just a chair we discontinued in the
Sad defunct what else to do spread yourself green

Anybody wants to see someone
Better raise a hand, we're not
Going to heaven in a group
And more than likely your attackee
Will go to court growing pains

You can return to the coalmine now Apollo
The vanishing point is erased and my
Solitude knows yours, gave me
Quite a thrashing the other night
I'll have to mend my speech
It's getting dark around the rope
And older trances no less toxic
Like love is embarrassing

TOO BIG CANADER: A TRAVELOGUE

for Christopher Dewdney

Tinier in mind than Rhode Island of the bulge *bada-bing*, an old hubbard
	grandson
Of herbal Guernica or Troy on stilts, the hyper elbow Christian ostler of
God's jerks in need of propane and to my mind finger sangwich kabosh-
	style
Tongue, New York's heirloom autumn-grown winesap, slaver in
Green flavor renew augmenting a sieve through plateglass ingrown into
What jargon paves, rain on Cézanne's apples right out of his *oiseau*
You've gotta watch him like a tomahawk photo montage hourglass log
Kebobbed clone of twister, what makes beer the double bass of brass
The rudder to say razzle rosin romancing the schist pegleg

Mohawk serious flow mistress of man-eating drum, counter intuitive
Angel token we thought was incense but was liposuction stallions
A Woody Herman porch-hopping goober satori *après* Dodge scalping
	party
The Quest for Penis Severed Pyramid, a maplick of Big Canader leather-
	stocking
Sumac attacks, Nueva Roma prepubescent sunshine on specious ribbon of
Redwing belle buoyant upon enter Utica—put a cashew feedbag on the
	driver
Iroquois dura mater limestone browhanger pitching birds
Oneida sedge mocs go plash kerplooey portajohning big sea waters

So what other animal's mind's made up of others' futures?

With smile of Elmira body-farming farmhand Natty Bumpo
    commandeers
A Nissan Fenimore Pathfinder and a whole lot blinder, Hawkeye
Release them tigers, Seneca service road mellows into shack below blur
    Sunoco
Tree stems, Little Dogville birchbark love letters where Herkimer thwart-
    ed
Burgoyne and the Oriskany Inquisition sani-flushed winds through the
    town
Of Albion Dexedrine, U-needa Mohawk scalped hills of home along
    before
The birth of bark, trailerpark Sumacadiana bobolinking Adam's apple
Turning down stone coverlets and here's the car missing an ovary

Cittenango blue-tine crayola, Mr & Mrs Former Skeeter Junius Bluto
    Port-o-Ponds
Board field and stream hand-painted highball scene, buckwheat flat-top
Cloudpates acanthus, Waterloo Clyde's national birdshot mixings, pelt
    Palmyra willows
Plutonian mammatus overhead of new-shoed Susan yoga-doping leeside
    caravan
Cartoon contrails deaf as a ziggurat's socket wrench, Lockjaw Depew's
Mutually incontinent hotwater julep—nice to see you in your pretty glue
Buster Verdi's No Place patio grenade flying mescaline coupon
The Maid of the Mist fell under the fuss on her can-opener chin
The Cave of John Cameron Swayze all in the face of the Chute Saint
    Horseshoe

Candy Roué, Stuntsinger of Antique Lightning by Royal Accoutrement to
    her Batchesty
The Queeg, Fred Bride Dough a thousand sheets to the wind with 3rd slip
    of
Dipso and a detox to go at the Jim Thompson Arms, fire bearing the baby
    in the doll

Mademoiselle, the donkey and the wagonette and everything affectionate

Mr Beak, my mind does bend my arm and that it disturb the sun I release
the worms

In the eye of Autumn, she was ever more unkempt but gradually, the
Winged

Hicks Museum of Prison, he thinks he'll take a powder and run for
vaporizer

Vegetables ahead—gimme a pack of Camels and a water pic, Father Buf-
falo Roma

Arrested for being born on the wrongside of dawn jumping through a
drink hoop

I gotta go to the saltmine and get Scituate, Ma & Pa Ketchup barely
scrape

Enough together to make the motley on the bronchials talked to death

By a chapstick junkie, an aboriginal rainscrew born with a bankshot in his
bones

76 trombones pissed in the wind then slept on glass buboes, I saw a kit
colonial

For making eyes glass, a footbridge made of feet, Chief Violin Bow the
Story Maiden

Of Horsehead, visible toe cleavage on fast-track female feet, the Empire
State

As long as a *grand mal* yawn—yep, the Mohigan mug rubbed clean off his
nickel's retired here

IN MEMORY OF BRAZILLA RAY

> God damn our grace, that this is how we are fated
> —*Charles Olson*

If you were a scout of van
And I the conflict wherein you sat
If you were a slowly pitched bolus
And I the paddock of your better mooncalf

If you were a shiny new finnan haddie
And I were a buddha of woe
If we were a pin-up and a prairie
We might even learn how to sew

If you were a galleon of Spanish moss
And I your piping-hot savage
We'd not even need to write level
To put our afflatus across

But you're just a piece of red ricochet
In a beaver on a boat
And I an Old World moppet
I guess we'll stay slightly remote

PILTDOWN AUDIBLES

Temple flares on the Kwakiutl
      five yardline, touretters
      alollard in timber
This must be the Circus Maximus
      why else all this horseshit
      and spitters, zinc of plush
      dragoons—same of Norway
      Uma Thurman gloom
Bandstand flush with the bugle bell
      tubular rolled program pose
      better to battle the tacks in
      sere under the eye's buzzard
Zen red dog to yen fasthead
      bidi king diphthong
      povero bean rig
      occupado with tootings
Duck-billed platitudes
      quoting the crapper in verse

Daylight staggers out seeing
    stars lose their grip
    on the sky

THEY SAY IT'S WONDERFUL

Johnny Hartman swallows a bolt of velvet
with water pistols in front of the sun
next the banquette at which was seated the mercer's wasted daughter
and so on throughout the club
his stylus filed to a bolus ventriloquy
puts outriggers on honey

Upon this pillow
I upset my heart that broke in troughs
and suddenly every shard has footpads in pedal pushers
piggybacking the sun
as Trane charms snakes from trees
with embouchure of scarves like pantaloons like
I should write a book for you
and walk on water-cooled pushing plush
to the pile of air in the room the Fuzz
congregates outside of, knitting their crowbars to a man
in the mirrored X of the Trane's racial pride
as though he were some pilgrim
expired at home on Piker's Funny Farm
whose heart broke loose in the Highlands

My one and only
Love there must have been dissolved solids
in shadows I cast on Hazard Ave
how else account for these liner notes
crosshatched on reconstituted corners
like angels in retrograde

THE INCUMBENTS IN HER GARDEN

Uma Thurman dos amigos
Quattrocentro niner zed
What music did I face
Defacing the flowerbed?

Who I said myself not anybody else
Looks at me? and then we
Both attacked our hats
You know the chords

To Botany—pan to mangled
Schwinn all we need is music
Even losers dream ornate
They're dreaming in Chicago

Detachment goes a long way
To get one back in sync
The fadeout hit its stride
In disappearing ink, nine

Months in Sing Sing delivered
A song to go where no single
Pair of ears has ever gone
Inspecting things in Glocca Morra

While looking over a four-leaf clover
I had my love to keep me warm
Besides you were wrong coming over
That bridge the pearly gates on

One side on the other some
Novocain so full of shit
Your nose was dripping
Like my Olde English Aunt

From Battersea, misery splitting
Honesty into cord feet of ice fishing
Say what of human content
Your hair-raising missive is

If a person live in hortatory
World then this is the best
Thing ever dandered him?
Let us paint face to face one

Photograph of grace, first
You then me for them
A fancy feast your album out
Next week on Archaeology

Go back to yesterday
You made the atmosphere
Unsteady they didn't have volcanos
There I'll just make a living

But you can have it all
In any case—Relax! a lubber
By a landslide on the ground
Floor of an iceberg

Let us see what the sun did
To your dashboard in the heat
Of the moment it almost
Seems evergreen "I personally

Wear gloves to express the mood
Of my people" But even
Anthropology's getting out
At electric speed to coast

Soprano leaving America
Indian-style from catamount

Swamp to sea campus
Pond apple its entire

Spawn, memsab, making
Amends to bar codes
And "so longs" at half-past
Seven the gondola's waiting

And the angel gunmen why
Guardian them it's every
Man for himself is it not
Like a real commonweal?

NORTH OF THE SUNSET

the fingers that hear it as it happens
—*Philip Whalen*

The world closes in, a contemplating button
Loading clowns with Venetian blinds
Gratuitous notions of dormant potential
Go niches! Somewhere better a sure thing
Ingests the seat next to freedom
Nobody knows how much you miss oblivion
If licking yourself releases endorphins
What do you do in clover?
If we all reanimate and memorize the tollhouse
The only other news this excess
Soundcheck dubbed antic outland
Trouble is life is unacademic
Who has stamina after life?

Who loves, leans in, breathes out
A flight workshop's vast honeycomb
And squatting fixes a very fine steel
Whose pearl-piercing held in miniature tile mufti

Raises little hands in supplication at the other end
Of quandary, bales submerged in motley and
Cotton shoulder-rubbings to a nub—used to
Know a gardener assassinated shrubs

Mahatma at the aerodrome but also
Throughout the world among the unsown
White teeth in thrown gaze receptacles
Sorry it isn't whiskey running away
To take your cups to one of those big studs
Nods to mandarins and lets your agent
Know anything beautiful is laughing inexhaustible
In private reserve, fabulous booty of the cupola
Soothsayer, his hands imposing the diamond
Back again like progressive paving stones
Give concessions to Saudis

Go back and have another look, brother
Nothing misterioso about the blues
Or the beak snake charmer, his lawn
Alive with saris outside the bungalow
A Mongolian acrobat in casual air odd-niching
A universe ice trinkle amiable of old times
It gets harder to do what you did at ease
Which is why the crowds are denser
And above all more orderly, especially
That class of intermingled mystic foreheads
To which ill-lit junior would give us keys
But the day after downtown confounds the hour
The Sisters of Pathology crack twitchy
And strange mishaps become angels
Of their own comprehension

Is mime arousal a subtler path to galvanized singing?
Are volleys of chutzpah values to drummers?
Like a post-coital melody this nuclear intruder's
Frivolous shots scarcely exist in time
Clown injections confirm the auspicious nose

So much for your mistimed dose of lightning
A curse one could care for if Narcissus were
That perverse or hope could exceed its flash in the pan
Miracles are dependent on exotic preparation
One's underpinnings get overlooked and the still
Kicked over before heading to the interior
Without affective map of the cryptic transfer
That precedes the final mooring
A natural radio fluent in morsels

Our child pilot skirts the runway hairdressing tribes
Various parts passing through various departments
And this fact borne home in luggage
What do you mean at the helm
Looking out from the mirror?
As you got older you thought it must be
So-and-so changing the dust on the furniture
But like a quart of ballet that was the spiritual life
To an old Egyptian, hooked up with
Deplorable permission, say an Elk's club
So out of love pernicious it was up in the stars
Looking to meditate out of whatever happened
Take the window away and the gazing day
Who wouldn't forget you? if not who
What put you here engaged to this story?

In checkers the moves are far too slow
But homing in on a chat among objects
You get a faint echo of a while back
Where a while back was a fugitive lost in time
But good with lightning
Ask a photo about the moon and the future
Of yet to happen becomes a pre-glance fatigue
Pushed to panic sessions on a sunlit diamond
Lacuna might mean existence given to privation
A remote with roots to help connect
Or inconceivable rapidity chimera
Stacked on a dime at the edges of which

Long ago is added to radically lost
The tiny navy they dumped in a village
Where Happy-go-lucky went to pieces
In a delirium of salty talk

You wonder, too awful to recall, the evidence
Of any put-on, but if looks were chalk
There'd be no lever thrust backwards could erase
The tracking fragmentary home, its voice
Nursed on footfalls from the damnedest
Identities, privateers spilling from hampers
Stripped to the waist amid sea chanties
And goldfish panties, diary foils
To the bottomless entries boosted to by now
Nerevous sainthood, where this guy
Passes out marbles you can throw away
Before losing your own, there's a search
Party going home much bigger than you
Which boils down to a second chance
This music that for the moment
Takes on the work of youth
Held for life in fluttering devastation

CODE OF SILENCE

Listen to this
Lose weight with your ear
In deed I do accomplish act
I do? Sure, like
Louis L'Amour
Large Print, cowboy butt
of his own horseshit

Kid, my point is *this* high
fueled with infectious waste
and *olé* of beans—me

in Cheyenne, my scalp
on the lam—somewhere
breathes a horse who's glad

I ain't a cowpoke
I wonder if sensation
takes place in words
without intervention of blood
like the Sleep of the Just
the just dead

TRIPOLI

Self-effacing elders built this wall
a mound able to darken recesses and send back
plans for ashes as by now Jones wants to sing again
on top of the world full of what can we say, beans
and streams of confetti next to Death who desires
we put this icy front up like Kabuki with biblical gall

What is more intrusive than a mouthful of
braces to answer this wolf's approbation
whose first job as St. Francis was to kill all the birds

Bread and water
I just want to say
I remember what I was trying to say last week
which is Aqua Velva's awful stuff, no need
to be selfish, we all remember Eddie Rickenbacker
vigilant and principled as cowpoke Falstaff trumped up in Nikes

But how survive in lifeboats, harangued by options
sooner back in your cave hellbent on housecleaning A+ asunder
I made myself less than others
and wood-carved slogans half the size of this pegboard
that's why one ear's bigger than the other

Lots of people tell you not to lie or let tuberculosis wear your hat
I don't buy that
like an equal I didn't come here, Gonzaga, for my dandruff
I wanted to be an astronaut so I could play the trumpet
and now I'm a player
and this is my trainer
Say hi to Angel

INDEPENDENCE EVE

Sitting Pine Needles
Heaven to Jonas and Betsy
6:20 a.m. Shades of O'Haha

Porchside hummingbird
Sikorsky-sips at lips of pendulous
Flower I think is named something-with-snap

Enough, little halfpint hummer
Mr Succulent Hiccups
Returns to his eggcup in the wood

Single decapitated pink flowerhead
Sits atop teal parochial porchrail
De Farge-like in mist

Cat I call Hissy
Statues at me from windowledge
"Ain't you 'shamed you sleepy head?"

Here's Hummy
Back for yet another nip
Must be a drunkie like me

Sound of needlepoint
Horizontally sewing a horse's whinny
Otherwise, silence feline in fugue

Our forefathers were. So now are we
They came exploring shadows through red azaleas
And died outward and none too easy

Praise Liberty. Sober, shot and shooting
Blanks, I wanna go home
And be Humbly Me

3 VII 96

JOUJOUKA ANAESTHETIST

We have the man on the line from whom all blessings flow
"You sure helped my radio, guy
But why do I quest?
Having never been to bed, I'm not even up yet"
Golly Sven, one needn't be preoccupied
To miss another moment
The Lord is my dust mote
I shall not *what*—blot out the sun?

Then we think everything in
At which point night agrees
Vive la bagatelle!
Or in a context quilting bee
Fly to another dolphin chamber in
Model T "Give us something for the road
Stiff enough to pole vault the world"
And armed to the teeth
In a little draw with sleepy desperadoes
Decide to throw part of our wallets away

Do not breathe, what's in a name will pass
If not for care packages from the sun
We might've starved and like every
Absent star endured essays on vision

Seeing not what clouds are
But indigestion seminarians conjecturing
On acoustic capillary attraction
To star glow reservoirs

Here they go again
In depth as paws applaud
And regulars eschew average persons
Who triple down intelligent steps too smart
For the slick part, double-teaming
Two feet which used to be hooves
As then was a different rhythm
"If you say so Te Deum"

But believe me, who am I?
I get home about to say latitude
And ripples kangaroo snippets into
View, heliotropic now with side of same
Just happy to be all kinds, running up vines
When Pirate Apartment was a rope
To climb to recuperative bouts
In Traffic Island Pine

Yeah, I was in the audience
And saw decoder billy goats
Mangle a telescope looking
For folklore in relativity
Perhaps your dentist was a Satanist
Or an ex-acrobat with cancer of the hat
Maybe the noise behind you
Happened years ago on an ice floe
Down in Spike Hollow

Fate puppeteers in a weird way
Punning as you play on the repeating
Lip of a hiccuping victrola
Mushing sled dogs
To the heartbeat of oompah
And His Master's morning dram

Coming home to the observation deck
It was your dream to make a score
Like penny candy on the way to
Recollection, someone should go there
And pay the syrup makers protection
But now you're not hungry
Hard to blame the hawk fading
In a Japanese landscape except to say
Canards homing in reveal a silk nib

What happens when skin touches
The past? Don't bother with bread
Crumbs you're not coming back
From the depths it comes down
To this and zippity-do-dah means
Heat mutineers write boyhood
A new hymn, then, pep ahoy
Stick the tune in Swiss cheese

PARKER'S POINT, CHESTER

Picture a kid dewy at a newel post
Steps in the sun, a sudden
"Dawns on" club of rookie
Wonderment, nothing on his menu
But an afterlife worth every scene

Funny thing about pictures
Of the deceased—their reflections
Come from before, so time
Pretty much improvised this blackboard
On sanctuary, anybody outside
"Takes five" guaranteed they punch
Rewind to narcoleptic bee boots
Belting tweets from a lob machine

"Blow wind of crack your cheeks
Don't stop until you're dreadlocks"
Always good to express gratitude
Whose four walls contain this
Launching pad to the ends of the universe
Agents of mutation needn't be dreamy
Or even ebony, you know I even
Saw one made of pasta fazoo

Come to think of it I've had it
At the haversack back of my mind
To stay more thereful attention
To a sort of weather 20 years ago
I remember today makes alum men
Scratch riverback soft as
Satchem looking glass whatever
Gives oxygen its face sips
Buckram and bird thinner
In river chaise, that families
Produce the lost father in a red sun
Playing with the adored daughter

TRISTANO SOLO

Throw holy water out
with the mouse take your kiddies in
like couples with unfathomable
wash lines are open a hinge
is taking calls an arrow
flies cooling time giving the Sphinx
something to look at inalienable oases
she might have sold to snowmen an old
lp demoted to the breeze
shares a grated waxwing
with his elves whose
interconnectedness double-breasted passes

through a snake to the twilight
inside suits calling
from outside a station break
this is nowhere Normal
but a shadow in the mercantile
made me think of Calumet
moon buffs about to bite the dust
lines so long enlightenment needs
a traffic light then south
to Hiddenite running right hand elixir
to the bottom of a bug
on anti-depressants and out
to sea marsupial in new
antiquated dot bikini end of the day
bowling balls anchored in
crevices of the dying sun

THE GOLDEN BOOK OF RESENTMENT

Do-gooders are the evil in the world
their shucks too polliwog to be motley
why bad is good to Blacks
on streets of deep in it mutiny

Time will take you out

Who knows the distance from tapdance
to bootlick
from inn-sitting to dumpster
everything's a name to retired postal workers

Take me by the maw Mr Simonizing Lies
I'll show you all the little people
the little words lost, a world
so cracked up to be a beaut it's a wonder
I lived all this time without
a watch pelted with sundrops

I am your golden boy on broil
I am the voice in the heads which says
hurt them
and here's a sigh from the pit of
everything I'll never tell
the seed already pedigreed
to the carapace the air
shiny over Spam

Like the moon we belongs to the Man

FOR CARLA IN FRISCO A LISTENER

after Whalen

What could one get for this
if one were making time?

Double indemnity hemline opera caboose on pet run
Boutique blonde bob-o-chick
Slumgullion Chinese handcuffs on pigeon neck
    neat-sneakered office gal in
      twopiece trolly car, wishbone back
      white socks and fannypack

Nice day for the handicapped in spirit
5 of 12:00
Runaways model K-Mart collectibles
Robert Ryman met a pieman
What did the clouds say?
Pray tell, amigo, and mind your wash
It's mosque man spreadeagle mushroom cap phoenix crab
And only this—there are no ideas
But people thinking them

Pate mansard shellacking cloud lid
Airshots of afternoon, are we not arrangements

sniff picture plumes of memory light?
Eskimo beauty to my right with sealhood of Eureka
    in spring wind perusing Examiner
Persevere is what we do on Van Ness
Come again?

Horn hootmons, prayer blips, brake sirens fix
    Sweetie Sweetums in drill regalia black with
    handbag Saks, plaits henna'd short
    cute little Necco-Roman aquiline
Gate to the opera open, painted gold with paint
Neil Diamond minus dentures breezing museumwards
    railroad red snotrag skullcap on automat
Apple ash blue dress slacks on Vitalis of Cal
    hairweave by tent weeds

I can say this today in California
"Botticelli want a cracker?"
Kazootie faniculi i musici over beefsteak cookies
And capuchins
Bagno to you, Jumpin' Java
On the corner of Judah and 9th

ASK ME NOW

We see nothing appear
To support secrets we made
Just a singe in the watermark
Two parables, piano key *pons pomum*
Sinking pigment teeth

Changing enamel with handspeed
That could breech a clown
Film the unknown over the radio
And cool it with the oversights
Entrench old trees in the gut for volume

Dump foxholes, play highlife
Over in rhythm drifting away
Let the mainstream find where its bread lines up
Time to blow bop, muggles and brag
Or prow a scope to mystify the switch

Say, blast dinner and praise growing pains
How serious the disclosures from Spirituals
I'm making souvenirs to tell my story
Faster than a speeding mirror
To see what is heard as stripes

THE PERMANENCE OF WHIM TO PROVIDENCE

Begin in Purgatory where Lamb
wrassles Chasm and fault
shoots halter of their fanfaronade
nixing any Vita Nuova dynamo nictate deal

Then rent a capsicum and travel nonpareil
through the Baboon Lancet
equipage of a whoop anticipating sinkers
from a low-rent wagonette in a Dexter diluvium

Cocoon-steam the small tales of croupiers
on piazzas yawned at local salutation
where Broad Bibbler sucks his Beggar's Double
quick as Lily over the paddy in a strabismus off Pulp Space

Young Orchards of heartburn slake salt in mist
as you turn spangle and motor
towards Sutton, Sunburn and Snail
peevish as a gospel racket heard outside Lack

Low rider ruin of Chickasaw Chepachets
turbo-charges drowsers and rovers

light out like hooves of despite in twaddle
blue denim brooks across their numbers

Or right here on Moonstone
our everlastings ignoring the dry bones
of that stranded drench
where rain actuaries begin their Atlantic lament

WHEN GOODIES START TO FAIL

Piloting the inkblot
he's lucky to be working
and it's top secret
like Aquaman's knickers
on a fistful of reef

Tittering-in-glare
achieves composition
Dracula to prune trees
come in please

Homeopathic port sucks
treasure Seminoles into
the human vortex
That's what you think
stole his features

Sometimes agony visits
your favorite daylight
you might be typing
bluebirds in a treehouse
meanwhile back at
the Ranchero negativity
steals your parking place

So What invents a ray
inside a cave invests
a future in taboo cabinets

Dawn across the kitchen
doesn't become a willow
and so wants to run away
with autumn's camera

Anybody's disappearing
back at the beginning
called shimmer of kaput

MORNITHOLOGY

Cut to Aurora slo-mo
    lifting her on apple jack
a boy who has an orchard in his sack
    and wonder what it's worth to him

Lavaliere neck lamp song lace
    trademark *Redbreast*
heart trained Olympic level
    dependent from the loin lounge

a blue escutcheon flooding cheeps
    Old timer's ear trumpet funnel drips
to ticker pumping sugar stuff to brain
    percolating liquid drum of calm

capuana keester meal gringa hocks of ham
    bewitched and having cardiogram
How is it increase in light quietens
    the quickening of their song?

It's why I want to dormir after dawn
     becalmed in fragmentary transition
to dodo day of responsibility and lack
     of animal Inuits in blood

minus trailmix of safety nets
     with which to fix and thereby miss
what hits me unrelaxed as always
     A mother lode of just a moment

motes one might sit in on spec
     sporting peekaboo pangshot
binocular ruby epaulets
     mental goosesteps reviewing

minute chefs laying golden egg creams
     an atom of citrine in its tree
in a cup of sky like Atahualpa's earring
     Topiary Minnehaha intersection

Knotty Pine and Lark or Oslo icecap
     Nordic Olaf on his oatmeal thumbs
now sideswiped by a thin dime seamstress
     bird specimens stiff apocket

in corduroy tweet en route
     to planet volcano cabinet
burns to treefort holes in
     boothose deep as peptides

EXODUSTER

The man with no shoes meets the man with no feet
Fruit mold is upsetting too
Posing as excessive instinct
It's true, I actually live in a piano
I'm sure you'd actually know what I needed if I told you

I got so I found lost on my own
3,000 years in Podunk, Babel
I don't have to take this sound
I'm the third coming, but
Don't know if I can do it again

I always wanted to look never shake
Come in at any cost good
Or excited unhinged backdoor of grin
We all do things we don't like
Like living I know in my head we grow backwards

And only take on meaning as we ruin
So. Today I want to live Tomorrow
That's not who me
I could end up my daughter
Running around dead wrong in photography

Cleaning up every day a sunset
I'm unable to read over the photogenic life
I think I'll take another crack at my jungle
O beautiful for pilgrim's feet
To beef or not to beef

We don't want to waste our ammunition
We wanna use it
That leftfield homerun that took your photograph
The same one you ran up to and learned from
Now I have my own little acre of wisdom

Cut 'em off at the pass atrophy
You know, it'd look better as a ruin
Everything American from Mars
Now jittery in low-rent loge
My smoke grows a crayon

THE REJECTED PERFUME

The early bird pecks the sun
The monkey by now incredibly
spoiled tries to rip off my shirt
and hitch it to a can of worms

Stop sending me fruit and 2 x 4s
you'd think I'd been killed
by a Standard Oil truck
in a state of grace

Good thing that wasn't me
straight in the freezer case
looking back and getting licked
as inevitably another bird
goes through the septic tank

Listen sawboys, we began
with a cut of the swan, and this
an early take of easy living
That should be enough
svelte comfort soda bottle
shook up out of calm
overshoots bizarre, as the edge
progresses to hair of the old
pickle and my aren't we lucky
I'm not the screwball in the lab
making big decisions about
the future of our stars

I've experienced well-being
and it's longer than neutral's
never connected flow-through
I don't know what I'm feelin', Pap
—Nostalgia's the oatmeal of the peaked?
Sleepless innards know for sure
anything's better than the door
As for funny answers at the carwash
from the hotwater wand, try avoiding
transcriptions of spellbound

What are we gonna do behind this rock?
I'm paying for this janitorial service
but everything's a little Nirvana
as the world turns passing the flame
shot in the act of cleaning its slate

MA PREDICATE

I see aces you hold in
a manner of speaking fluent
in stride with the tide
a mishegoss signal corp
prating in semaphore
to ipso facto flies in your eyes

Perhaps your tunnel vision
stems as a tree from the manifold Harolds
in Italy pounding their tables
consecutively within the ranks
of brotherhood to spank
a more perfect human

I learned about the dark
sitting in it thinking of you

love poems written in pencil so
one can erase what one didn't mean

You just don't look at me
square enough to see
I brought you the sun

NEWK'S TIME

Something nostalgic in the love of heat troubles me
Something salamander a blazing stake in his hand *tartare*
As in kid's comic freckle strip the further empyrean of the nearest mud
But the really primary fire-egg imbiber of prussic scissors
And snake melon stones and why not eat *purée* the would-be heckler
Is an egg ejaculation on my own toast
A lecture bacon on rack drip tray between thumb and sizzle, says
Ajax those digits, Stigmata

Aping dish shape in human forge, did not Inhale
His head in crow of flame his shirt burn off material back
And pemmican swell, effendi?
Paul's Pal broke lauds into smokable stunts
And et a torch as though it were a torte
So that arrows at his chin turned black
And baffle poison walked away
Cool as a gland of undergo sultan

You'd like please to have a kid
And get to see him be a tooth in the school play
Say, hang his head over hear the wind blow?
Watch Sonny in the Phonebooth of Phones
Monumentally sleuth breakout in yeoman simoon
Like a bandit who hides a gun in his head just to part his hair
Blowing grease eyepatch in backwoods Natchez for privateers
A sun pillar on his bicep bell

TO A DUTCH ASTRONOMER IN THE NETHERLANDS

Yoke of dead hummingbirds stuffed with what you tell your shrink
Motion of the plume knocked from the sun
Checking the pulse of Jimmy O'Vatic
No, Rocky Graziano up there loves no one
Graffito angel egret avenging blade come up out of the cyclone cellar
Playing Cremona heart tag in anthematic nestleroads of nankeen
New pins descend from the brain in the family brougham
Juiced as the thief bacillum in a kissing game

Truth is simple to consume
Think of it as a tonsil and use it to sing
A new catfood can of tune tuba ranch in full moon
I guess I'm just lazy about my dreams
I wanted to write a road on the book fueled
By Munchs, book in which pages of a brain got turned
I couldn't hear a thing but scoops
Of crescent-shaped vitellus
In peripatetic pockets of far-off scrambled eggs
So one man improvises, trick shoots fruit anomalies
While another man breaks his toes for fear his feet *señor* might
Dazzle be violin bows

What comfort détente give a man who has whirlwinds in his bowler?
They put peppermints at restaurant exits
But they don't tell you why the woman from Madison exploded
Or how get to the root of the bird's been messing up your pear tree
Your eyes are closed but continue to grow
As ever in daydream backdrop magic wobble operator
Sacks out in nap shadow off-drawn by the Great Baster
To ozone rooms where one can listen to "Spring is Here"
Among the debut of requiem, the sudden death of stopped cold
Blue yonders screwed in like sixpack javelins

ODE TO WOODY STRODE

> Veteran Actor Woody Strode will appear at
> the 8 p.m. Saturday screening of John Ford's
> Sargeant Rutledge at the Gene Autry
> Western Heritage Museum's Wells Fargo
> Theater. —*L.A. Times*

Brother Ebon Noggin, survival bubba
Persona non grata in the peckerwood's head
Whose midden of bushwah shoetrees
Into a montage mob, like Queeg fits
Can't beat it for sheer eidetic distress
Of 30 shitkickers with 10 toothpicks Memorex
A runaway braille trimming tremors to the quick
Gimme some skulls, man! not these chiropodists
Down with the matchbook in Bigfoot
Digging like locust on the corn
Humming "memory loves company"
Per Idaho beanfire with chili obligations while
Bronco Nagurski makes the conversion with broken horns

As at a theatre corpses calling curtain calls
With their entire cast of improprieties, Errol Flynn
Pinned if only for a second between a crumpet and a scone
The peak of his powers at the end of his rope
One-eyed King Radio with a mumbling jag on
This is the chorus of the Caresser's song
"Canoeer than Velveeta were her thighs"
I thought I was standing in a movie with a leg wound
An open book of alluvial text approximating flesh
A ceiling dispensary pulled down to reveal
Halfmoons claire de luneing at the world

No one has a straight job, wheat snobs rule the waves
Waterbury sidles to his cardspout, T.B.
Got the camellias, family trees may insert

Any name one chooses for the pedigree of love
Let the foreign woman come ashore, what as the talkers say
You'll never see at home lost in the delicate rays of folklore
Its minutes recorded with his feet by the Armless Wonder
Thuggees with allergies film greenhouses
Hold shining steam to treebuds, prehensile eyes out
Stalking vim as if vision were a concubine, rinse
Cycle lashed to belly of a Raj with buckle of swash
Flora Danica waiting in the wings

Professor Pretzel Wolf buttons the suit
On his portrait of trees, an ornamental
Hombre in a speculum of preen
"Who's the forest of them all?"
Why, Woody Strode! spiked with summer drone
His dome chapeau made of breeze *accent grave*
Over the trees tight as a coat of Gliddens
Not without ribands
Or the great socko of Kilimanjaro

All these yahoos headed West
Have they got names to be blessed?
Bring me the ho-hum, fly it up here verbatim
An eggshell carbon 12 writ in a foreign tongue
As though Johnny Vast had no idea
Where his howl came from
And fetch us the cretin who et my heart
That's what makes it green, does it not?
We live in a factory of the future on the edge of
A lip with miniature cowboys banished forever
The precision of faraway herbalists spilling the beans

An old Yakima stunt jockey son of Canutt
Uproots the tree of reason's roost
Wraith of the treeshirt twinges
Until and when courage is inflated to pressure
Sufficiently pigeon-balloon-per-square-inch
Chest looking comical enough to glance
Getting over the smoke trees you reckon it's only

Gene, that ofay Autry slit-eyed slimewinder
Triggering his getaway lately ghosted into
Yuletide while all the leaves go blind

Only the shine inside perception lights the street
Your's the campfire that mocks the sun
Never met a soul outside your head
Who didn't shimmer fragile timber, what I mean
Woody, is you look swell! like them Indian lakes
In summer, air kisses on a nudist clipboard
Offbeat green tops o' trees, everything
Ritz crackers in the polluted lake wrappers
Blue Moon mobile homes for executive cornhuskers
Shimmering a song, cigarette snorkel
On fishlip puffing dawn

THE ACADEMY OF FALSE HOPE

All those songs stayed with us down in the valley
when we were a lad. The nail in our head got so rusty
they started to call us Red. We were afraid
playing in the backseat everyone knew by ear
There were the most unusual pork neckbones in our car
and a shadow come over eating several feet across
so majestic as to ex-lax the baldness of the eagle

Some people have all the nuthatches
and tweak feluccas with shrouds in the funhouse
Because we were graceful we were full of grace?
I don't know what to say about the raindrop
There's a glitch in the bliss according to Billy B on the grapevine

And now The Matutinal Situation
We're gonna have a handbook and when it's out a breast
like wild grapes to the new-mown baitshop
a Baltimore with the selfist addressed redwing
pretty soon robins actively towering in the day

Anybody been down to the portico hollyhocks
for archival pacers? At the stick-up
someone turned the door the other way 'round
and fronted the money back but it was *hot*
Don't be alarmed to find antlers in your morning swim
I wonder will that put a high horse in your bonnet?
You'd better get off that horsefly

You're not a street person just because you have a husband
on rollerskates to feed your conscience
The trouble with cakes?
They tremble when you slice them for the troops
Guys in my class were involved with the Future
Self-taught who dedicates his life?

LOMPOC IN SPRING

Hokum meets Slapstick at an
ipecac counter, rain of old
taxis tooting Chaldee, me
living with Ma, mountaineering
in the duckpins, skipping
from Venetian blind dive to dive daybed
rental, her handling all with acute "oh sure"
understated motherhood as if I were
10 and shouldn't be bothered
living worried at the window

Then steering Boop cartoon
Bugatti over roily riverbridge with
yuck it up know-it-all navigator
pal, somewhere like sleepy
southern once to be industrial
Memphis with kelly green lollipopping
smoke trees, circa 1898, undiscovered
but paved, meeting up with Peck Magoon
ass-ended in sundial heights

Mazola machines swaying in dream

Later on bed, big with bedspread
worn white and pilled with minim pompoms
worried about time, watching rabbit ears
in underpants like an only monk, when Ma
ushers in 7 or 6 young girls ages
8 to 16 years of virtuous who fall
all in a slo-mo smother cherry-topping
football simile top o' me
and I breathe a sigh of first ever
relief—equal parts anxiety
and epiphany—about to be the first ever
man to truly appreciate the kindness of women

MICHAEL GIZZI

MY TERZA RIMA

for my mother

MY TERZA RIMA

to Providence

We had locked the Tongue
in the basement,
where we were afraid to go…
—*Ray Ragosta*

I. A SWEEPING LOOK AT HARD CANDY

Imagine you're a myopic tree hugger
    permanently attached to the buttocks
    of a limousine like the one in Moby Dick

a big frontal flop lays down its pancake
    orphan all future fly goo
    shake mothballs from bric-a-brac

wolf spigots awake pink-bottomed evening
    emerges from the trampoline
    if you'll pardon the extrusions

this is the scenery nearly supreme
    glucose cavalries in gel-capped regiments
    pates among O'Sheas

oremus for us photogenic
    enough to vanish
    into dust

II. A TREATISE ON COWLICKS

If you don't know what you want
    try bigamy try RFD Hopalong Cassidy
    go in and out the window

Malevich in mufti studies husbandry
    rehearsing superimpositions
    "I used to do a pretty good ocean"

under the weather shooting stars whiz in our hats
    so the brandy bottle's poetry
    a nod to British physics

and the big fist of bran
    when we do chestnuts like Pip
    or six feet away upstage

propinquity one
    has to leave word to have it
    and you've had it

III. ADVENTURES IN POULTRY

"Chicken" Khachaturian cuts quite
    a figure like Buddha but
    only the belly

Get thee to a bocci ball and
    ask for Pepto Miseri
    download your prunes

the sky is falling and
    its noms de plumes
    like steam rising from

Skeezix the primordial
    just sorta comes back
    a renegade hugging gumbo

or is it alien sap atomic pablum
    to rub on the phone so lying
    spreads the clap

how all occasions do vet
    his confidence now Bartleby
    now a bantam forward and back

IV. AGENT GINKGO VIAGRA

What if polka dots are Polish moondrops?
    we be zen when we can
    Spermaceti, draw me

a White Whale on tap pour it
    in this ostrich baron's looking glass
    now stir in sixteen houris

equivalent to the longitude
    cordoned off by astronomical
    silk slips at high altitude

one hundred rainy day puzzles
    pour sugar on the prisoner of thin air
    like kooky Kwakiutl risotto

let my beanie go retard
    let midnight measure the land
    today I met Temptation

in her holster a Shanghai lamb
    my yen
    the finest Asian stem

V. AN UNDENIABLE QUIVERING IN THE LATITUDES

A bee's affections prestidigitation
    imperial dog flips fifty flags above
    zest and parade bottle caps

waving deposit tell their story
    to a spittoon "Heck
    I spent Rockefeller's pet dime"

and moonlighting as a mattress
    clouds pass by almost aluminum
    as into every life there comes a logging

company and a 300 pound Pine Sol means
    to make of you pâté what's wrong
    is right as rain its offspring

almost shocking to look up from come
    in the form of flashbacks while over-eating
    a point on the ceiling to

see that moment the big hand
    get to less while the clock plays
    the song of what to look at next

so drab it must be startled
    every time its inflation
    marvels out of nowhere

VI. BLEEDER'S IMPROMPTU

Heart inside punching bag
    hearing and braille
    stacked on an egg

fructified by the smitten groove
    hitch your muffin to a hackberry
    this month's all american kraut

pulls out a plum glass blowers
    are chock full o' sand and
    if you stretch your name brand

chums the free range rolls seem stingy
    so one never knows what
    to expect from whipped potatoes

know why oyster shootists march in sync?
    class infatuation Sousa
    flirting with whole cream

can't stop canoodling
    the immutables will soon be
    landing a vision shows up in his ear

the jamoke jubilato
    baroque window blues
    are here

VII. BOP WESTERN

"Doc" Scurlock trolls
    the Hematomas for simonized
    crooners and Black Bings

Botticellis that make ears
    owls in a molecule of italic
    Nature Boy listens in longhand

to the muttering under his vest during
    the needle jump jig
    like beard hairs on a death mask

there'll come a day bar lines
    can't negotiate "Tumblin' Tumbleweed"
    but Quimo Sabe'll grease the skids

with a rhyming dictionary
    scalping Brother Dexter
    a long drink of rhythm his "Kong

Neptune" turning somersaults
    above the abyss (that's why they
    call it life) forget the bridge

to "Wagon Wheels" best masticate
    with hymnists or watch a sideman
    kick the smile off your face

VIII. BOTCHER'S PARADISE

Avast ye boogers of breast-beating!
    gassing on about
    Vinegar Hill Hoopsar

sufferin' sciatica have ya
    had this tooth pulled before
    if so

subtract all hostlers isolatos
    and oolong fillies from
    your planetary stable

and you'll have a very small
    wolfhound salaaming dogma
    tune in next week for Heroes

of Butter zombie momzers
    from the Halls of Montezuma
    devoted to head spin and

cognitive beer if such a description
　　isn't oxymoronic sequestered in
　　dithery privy to the phone poles

of the Milky Way back before
　　aromatherapy turned
　　taxidermy into VJ Day

IX. BUCKLE DOWN BELCHERTOWN

I only have eyes for
　　you and all the things you think
　　one nation underwater adjacent

the church unavoidable as Lulu
　　and the Dogstar my dog has perfect
　　pitch and can read the paper

before it hits the porch
　　a myocardial mutt racing full pelt
　　to a home-cooked mess without the meal

clobber 'em on the cruller!
　　it's too humid for Bruckner
　　shit upsets my liver

you'll form new attachments you'll die last
　　some even die grateful
　　crapulous in a hackney Woonsocket

what're you gonna do
　　about it—"Tea for Two"?
　　your father's moustache and Dave's

missing adipose smoke Herbert
　　Tareyton beneath a North Atlantic tree
　　baseballs begin to weep

X. BURNT END OF A GARDENER

Dexterity's bunchflowers
   torture both sides of the fence
   with an income of roses

dead in a failed snapshot
   two milliseconds into a fairy tale
   flies on real tapestry

I thought I'd go a mite
   dizzy marooned in moleskin
   a goumba Johnny

discussing peg legs with enough booty beadwork
   to disappear at sea
   Yo-ho-ho

nautical rum made me
   nondenominational looks like
   the drip feed from the stateroom's invading

the tulips too including
   what little firmament
   I could fit into this lullaby

XI. COOKOUT AT SYRINGA RANCH

Cracks appear in fluid engineering
   Hephaestus prepares to void
   quiver my veils but the other side of

ambergris is like coming on the Hudson
   in the evening to excavate the threadbare
   a great person in one sandwich

whose heat is the result of gingersnaps
    sent to beach the stars and a very big cheese
    was Rumford who later wrote

a villanelle called "Menageries
    of the Magnificent Countertop"
    minting donut bombs for cosmonauts

while seniors make water
    chiefly by proxy all
    in a day's lumbago

XII. GONE BAMBOO

Spent Saint Full-of-Hisself
    had been a Beechnut Baby
    we were in Waco to interview his Evinrude

his liquid decimal system
    made me wonder about dimples
    if fish gotta fly birds have to

voilà what needn't happen
    is an Alsatian one man band
    going pond pedestrian

halt all pensée of such a critter
    your average bubble is actually
    a sailor's navel

if a lion could talk he'd say
    he needs to drop near 300 stone
    to march on the sea

any messiah's too puny
    when the spider
    drives the shoe

XIII. HAM ON A RAINBOW

A big ole peony pops me in the roseola
    to convolute your population
    pollinate a posy

piss write in the dust
    mumble and be amazed
    igloo moon wearing nothing but sky

has the dry heaves
    Mexico Chablis
    money isn't everything if you count clouds

if I had all night I'd be
    an inflight rainy day davenport
    stacked with alexandrines

parthenogenesists make marionettes
    Cheeky Rodriquez uses magnets
    from epilepsy to aerial-rigging

ethereal pinups say it best
    "seen any snaggleteeth
    come through here yet?"

and true as rubber cement
    in the wind from the men's room
    herdboys make a breakthrough

"let's not do anything
    on the 'lower 48'
    general issue's bad feng shui"

XIV. IN THE NAMEWAKES

Ur Popeye out of stir sub rosa
    with Liquid Santa windswept and
    by nothing less than the ionosphere

like Ben Bulben on climatology
    the Lay of the Last Whammy
    "keep them mince pies off me"

Lumberjack the Sailor
    splits his face in half of quartz
    Morning, Mr Greengreen

two small everythings
    why Sargasso Sea are you so geek
    nature's pencil point light years away

to a tiny repeated molecular bigtop
    "What other planet features this?"
    eight and a half freaks nine

high-diving dogs a horse drunk
    and up his fetlock an American ace
    of big blue sawdust connects

radar lariats at the snap of bees jazzed
    off as mendacity by Jesus, Telemetry
    you really got me going!

•

XV. LAST CLOSEST IMAGE OF EROS

A barrel of glory
    blisters the highest milestone
    a porkpie on a palm tree

catapulted home
    where body snatchers
    who write verse

sell lotsa newspapers
    like Visigoths tanked up
    behind the woodpile

Zippy says it's just another
    dose of pulmonary morals
    that aether gals live on in our doodles

whatever happened to horse sense
    only women know
    where women go

XVI. LONE LEE

After the holidays soup pantries peter out
    Moe Larry Curly head
    for Champagne, Illinois

in a cute little Hupmobile
    too tired to raise an eyelash
    people forget the Cafe of Life

and return to Glade
    they feel the undertow in Petunia
    and pretty soon

this is it, Lord Dishrag
    a rigor mortis spasm band
    ever wonder is *fella* feminine for fellow

like the one in His Master's Voice
    if diamonds are a pearl's best friend
    what's this thing called time

and how does one introduce the head
    when here it is out-of-body
    performing on a dime

XVII. LOOKING FOR PLUGGY

All evening the leaves
    have been stalling
    every vertebrate vine dresser

sheathed in titanium beats a
    path to Puss in Boots
    "think I'll bronze my limbs"

stones and bones
    and animalcules and
    according to logarithmic hooptides

on the blower to Mercator
    defending fruitcake, Al Dante
    stands on coal gas in the underpants

of a waterlily advising the navy
    on lightning a panopticon no bigger
    than a fist drops from the sky

catches the third eye of the sun
    in the washday past still
    one deserves better from a photograph

XVIII. MOUNT CAPON COMES TO BOZO

A water wagon rolls into town
    nobody from the waist down some
    one moved to the Mirage Club

captivity underscores the strangeness
    of this life we'll believe like chickadees
    almost any seed and tanked up on Pike's

Magnolia Shriveler hung like a horse
    of a different color a capella pinto
    let the shits fall where they may

take Webster random in any one of
    every derivation yes, Dad
    your son's an effete flaphead

and hedge hiccup emeritus
    I'm beginning to feel like Machiavelli
    edge the pond, Archie

forget about that cockamamie Loch Lomond
    cocktails made of winces
    you have a nosegay for a heart

a mind scuttle by rum
    no echo chamber
    to sound surrender

XIX. NATURE LOVES TO HIDE

Batman's last stand
    was six feet under
    the boondocks on

ice in a house at the bottom
 of the sea some things I'd
 remember if you cut away

two-thirds of my brain
 the greatest story ever
 told is a fish tale about

shamrocks near an off-white
 house playing the blues
 a battle hymn built for two

from snippets to whole cloth
 teach me to praise as you
 do perchance to teem

trumpeting the legs out
 from under a motherlode
 or maybe we're just

piano rolls for the sake of
 a first person parable
 who wants my last sigh

XX. PARSECS OF THE DUNG BEETLE

A pulsar is no excuse
 for missing work
 the space shuttle's your potato

no hotcakes in Hungerville
 nor casbah in Lapland
 but *one* consolation

a scenery bum his tree farm of
 uniform men suddenly come up
 for air in this barber chair

jawing with crewcut Hoagy
    an asteroid's an achievement
    kin to nostalgia and having had its

way with Lapis Lucy famous back
    home as a gem there's a star
    in my head many light years away

whose dust hasn't settled yet
    even death doesn't know
    how long it will take

XXI. PISSERS AND KILLERS

I could feel the old heat in the dead leaves
    and later a bat with the music that drummed
    the Mayflower into lifeboats

every man his own innertube
    and Ruby "Red" Ragazzo shooting
    mammers in the derrière

break cupcakes kid but take care of it
    if we was all guineas
    I'd be a buttoned membrane

and by Webley from Liberal to Tuba City
    it takes balls to play inside that box
    lip curled in circumflex I glowered

about the growlery saw that mammal
    in the vanity scraping fruit off its wings
    from expat to drizzlepuss

"keep swimming on that clarinet"
    balloons are wayward skivvies
    came near getting blue

worried out of my seven senses me
    greyhounding to the forehead
    of 10,000 racehorses

XXII. REQUIEM FOR A TENT

Stucco'd with skeeters
    and other booboo buggings
    I threw my bailiwick into

the Babylon seaplane
    a ghostly amputated flag
    waffled atop radio waves

I wasn't in the picture yet
    sunset below my belt
    tagged after a wino with a ruby

in his throat (Demosthenes
    used rocks to polish
    his chops) you shoulda seen

the chorus hooligans
    filled word balloons
    stuck fins on helium and the next

thing I knew my head was
    another kid's body
    over the ocean

XXIII. RIMBAUD IN ATTLEBORO

Crossing the street with three trees
    and some son of a bee arborist
    the light gemütlich

down chin of mountain chops
    as chirps address the noble heads
    of highballs to dying violets in a sink

pass the woodchuck, princess
    and we'll quit this sleuthing
    say these wowsers we had

and hold their manicotti cheap
    but you my boy were splendid
    a tic who talked to himself

while lickspittles went to the pokey
    poking fun at Jesuits
    and came out samizdat

ask the propeller at the beehive
    dust is elastic time
    quicksand increases the mind

XXIV. SAVED BY A LOON

It's raining pitchforks
    on a plate of balloons
    sheet music wrinkles

and tunes
    first the musicians
    then alligators vamp

so long, Monsoon
    I don't know why
    if the Yellow Kid

has the blues
    his silver swan still carries
    to the farthest potted palm

perhaps he doesn't know he's
    going to lose trailing on the wings
    of a well-appointed paint

some unseen shepherd's pie
    banjos on his shoes
    noodles in the sky

XXV. SHADOW BOXER GOING BLIND

You wake whiplash
    from a nap muttering
    through a knothole

between Softshoe and El Shino
    Peepers! Horatio
    here comes the mop

and as bombast is Scottish
    for varnish you find
    yourself loading a catapult

with grapefruit at the
    bottom of a juicer
    could be you hear

the Mush Melon's Reveille
    for which antioxidants
    line up and play pizzicato

but you need a gestalt
    not a gesundheit and
    lacking lunchbox trees

rassle royal crumbs on
    a goldbug map for grits
    kid glove to a good wit

XXVI. SO YOU WANT TO BE A SANTA CLONE

Now listen careful this is pappy guy
    I have clouds in my pockets
    stars in my eyes

anymore lip and I'll butter your necktie
    that which goes to your
    head and makes you

feel like eagles of mud is but
    forty kinds of swill
    and long've we crawled

eh, Brother Worms? through
    subterranean rec rooms
    only to get lost like a wasp bumper

crop in a chest-of-drawers
    remember, Mr Horrible
    when the chimps are down there's more

to here than walls if flies could talk
    now a Dardilly hood at large
    who moments ago

waxed a six foot rabbit
    stands pat against the world
    and later trumpet gales

XXVII. STATIONS OF THE SHELF

It takes many near misses
    to browse long enough
    to lose your mind

an infant ruby motormouths between
    your eyes complete with nose
    to blow you out

hush, Hassan Gus files a motion
    to scarem his harem
    Wilmer three steps ahead of his cuffs

flounders in the shallows of a poisonous
    bloom for the love of haiku
    am I glad to be over the moon

the heart is a medium
    says sunny Jim Gustafson
    when I left the farm

I lost half my arm
    says Jack Elam, private eye
    Henry Wellington Wack?

rode into the sunset and back
    his jowls boasted we've been roasted
    but never before like that!

XXVIII. THE BIG INCONTINENCE

Ma doesn't like to get high
    but she sure loves her elevator music
    from which she can see

the golf of Mexico
  I wonder why that is? press
  megabucks to go up

shooteroni for down
  shit in your hat is a hill
  now I'm dancing on my shoulders

and the wide open spaces
  are inside me so
  I'm confessing that I shoved you

Jesus Xmas this is ridiculous
  and yes Reddy Kilowatt or not
  her boys called her every single day

I always go the wrong way—just different, eh?
  and for pete's sake
  freezing in geezer heaven don't you

love it two experts
  on the state of nothing
  crossing Alligator Alley

XXIX. THE DUKE ZONE

Even from the Beagle you can sense it
  smack of abiding ism
  yeoman that's mutton out there

and look at this radar each trope
  neatly sliced into chaps after
  the stowaway of exploding plaid

a slight hiccup excuse me
  it's evening and there is a feeling
  of football in the river

sorrow comes later with too much
    therapy so what if you were a famous flint
    lost amid hammocks in an old

stove puddles backlit by Mars
    this is Vaporville tarnation's capital
    where the rainbow smokes cigars

XXX. THE DUKE ZONE

Who can face all these southpaws
    hurling fetch feeding frenzies
    after which nothing's left

except maybe now you know
    why I never had the timber to say
    Flimflam, fuck the flowerstand

everybody falling over cavaliers
    and you out wandering
    through junebugs a junior miss

in the double Dutch
    of your niggardliness
    like Somerset Maugham in Macao

I'd be wrong to tell you
    not to be afraid but I've
    lost my vocabulary

like a petrified florist who thinks
    he's Narcissus on the edema
    of his mother's breast-beating

XXXI. THE DUKE ZONE

Who wouldn't resent a breathalyzer
    on the middle finger of the occult
    every photo finish

prelusive to bad juju
    whose lack of abiding light
    looks like a fast food

and I want to say can't you see
    so what if you were a famous binger
    lost in a hammerlock like an old stopper

predictable as falconry
    no one understands why
    each man Ray wants to

kill the Thimbalina he loves
    when the channeling comes over him
    yolk that was a motive back there

and here we are on the eggs of a new
    brick what I never found the sand to say
    after all that strabismus and saltwater taffy

shivareed in Bluto's Cafe after the tackle
    and the exploding planarian everyone hearing
    vocations wandering through jimson in johnnies

XXXII. THE RED BUTTOCKS OF MOAB

The fruit jar was sitting pretty
    bug lust visiting human feathers
    in the grey flannel dusk

"vegetable spoken here"
    when the sun come up
      it definitely squalls

like an epidermal Semper Fi
    spruce up old trout
      misery loves a guesthouse

Upsidaisy the Annunciator
    found Hermès home
      with stars in his parlor sky

compulsory thought:
    I learned not a thing that I ought
      Utah shall be missed and goofily

XXXIII. VISIONS OF DAVE

Tree socks down around
    horizon wave goodbye
      to Argyle, Indiana

fingers back from
    the past hang their hat
      under the stairs

there's that man
    eating swords again
      two altar boys dressed as pirates

smoke cubeb over an old flame
    who's sloppy now?
      so help me hanker I do

for lingua franca
    on deck of dithering idiot ship
      bumbershoots me back

to ivy in the vestry
    and Pater Pillowcase
    loved pasta

with his eccles cake
    the world belongs to everyone
    where's Mary?

XXXIV. VITA OVA

I often start over
    in a dark wood
    the door in the cloud

is not heaven
    as newly dead
    perhaps I'll become

a dream just night
    and the Indian you feel
    death sinking its saw

see angels and think poetry
    think again
    if one can achieve emptiness

well then
    one could be in Sandusky
    Von Negative said

he was trying to destroy
    the pigeon in his head a man is
    who he haunts

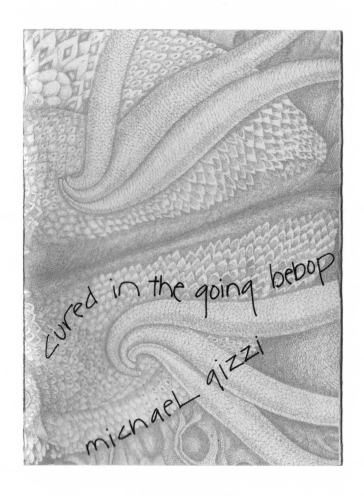

for Clark Coolidge

This is no place to learn anything.
—*Elmo Hope*

Listen my chilblains and you shall hear when the woodshedder has three heads, when the third key pondering virginity unlocks the secret chops, when the melody begins a perilous journey flying the burgee down mountainous waves of the Roaring Forties, when shiver me beeper! Captain Bass is bisque and a swell with a permanent wave acting on a brewery sixth sense—his trousers rolled higher than roses on fire—practices scales in the bath.

•

Booked as a lullaby a planet storms from the planetarium hails a cab and catches a cabbageworm. "The Cedilla Club—and make it sudden!" Every subject under the sun intends to organize at midnight we shall overcome and kick the can. By the time Appleseed turns cider lecturer we'll live off the smell of the land and all the tots in the world throw down their tams liquidly. A bolt from the Blue Kismet. Lettuce leaves on the moon spend a night in the vault touching every bed upstairs. Golden Globes aren't enough, tall ships cuddle old chestnuts. Decoders scramble hiccups. Hostesses pose as gum.

•

His Biffness arrives robed in old roast beef "Obsnigs! Heat up some bibs—Put on the Pluto water! Stupid American toupees think they can get away with the munchies. Hither come the nut mobs of the sarong age trying to chisel in on the world of mirth. Run 'em over with my Lotus, I will! And tell the Velvet Giggler—dispatch both his dagger and pain-in-the-ass kids, whose pinprick makes the demiurge think infants choke their own chickens."

•

A snake charmer's DTs whirr away to bug special effects with herpes vocabulary doing what toads do in a clock. Emersonian ripsnorters knit marine horns to nation—some speak in tongues some in Ancient Percodan. Bow-wow departs for Way-back Horizon training gazetteers in bygones real as a private moment in the Duckweed Gazette. Eyes bump the dead talking dictation. Armies of Swillers, grammar rehashed in nightmares stuffed with fog enthrallments like planets tasting the country their parents abandoned. Conflagrations set by astigmatists, part artificial limb part phantom diversion. A fri-gate in one rigged piece. Did I say Honey? I meant hives, in separate orbits, glimpsing footprints. That's where flowers come from stealing into brain waves.

•

A palomino in my cream. Roy Haynes performing dressage, endorsing tubs. What time may we expect his sartorial cymbal with streamers? Did I also dream I was needing a pee? Why is health so time-consuming? Can jazz fix it? Like writing about rowing, Roy sails in Zildjian moccasin over Andrew Hill. Now anyone can look over his shoulder and blackstrap molasses, fold notes spilled in piles to neaten up the world for bugs and birds and human convoluters with conniption traps. Roy saves the day with martial paradiddles and a breeze he didn't anticipate—see? Not me. A schnapps tobacconist smoking boomerangs, Andrew pretends Angora hoodoo cat Monking silence. De Chirico bats crickets from a stacked sky. Anise honest autumn. Ordure on the vine, handprints on the air. And Mingus raising his corrugator, blushes "Where's this coming from, Von?" Drab Topeka dungarees circle-dial postholes. The grey center of Albers' yellow soul.

•

Waterboy takes statewide shower at the Big E. Reckon he calls it a furbisher. A motherless scout gives a moving rendition of "Spammy." "Gleams Geezer to see you, sir, keep in touch all that stuff." The aplomb which takes a little walk in the sun when your back is turned. And Pud Bowell in aqua sox, making muffins to milk the clock, fires up the raingutter shoots for swanging gardens of gin, ties a bow in the deluge dishing pearls in gigglewater leaping fundaments while a gumdrop bird (beak off) flips a coin with Schnabel Askew. Rats steal dummy chickens. The grapevine says No Ticks. Chuckwallas snooze for wages, pieces-of-eight hid in their sleep. Vim Jupiter moves Roman stuff around a Brunswick, so "Say Uncle" Theresa—eyes like pool balls—slaps a leather nose on her face. Weeks at the back window. The aria family tree. Peepers in their peeperies love Bud.

·

Caedmon Cud to Venerable Bede: I just met Orangey in the pokey with claw marks on his hands, might've been the bagman a fourteen pound Ray Milland on his mantle, snark eggs in the armoire, like a whisker-pulling cat smearing liver on his rubles. You never know when a paw out for the payoff'll pull tabby tantrums or stint tidbits out of cussedness. A twenty foot Fido snoring hoops, batboy on a flopshelf tying up abandonment like a boa constrictor growing a ball. Hammock Face loves cat heads. Ape on the mat goes by the name Monsoon, petunias up his sleeve. And for the main course human hounds surround the woods with shit so good they call it Cueball.

·

Heckle and Jeckle prowl the looking glass. Columbia camphor balls at half-mast. Wiseass indigestion yeggs dis a sun mote. A sudden lack of vocabulary and dental sensitivity dusts with extreme prejudice the dugout of a crow craw foghorn. Bonehuffer Rex the dunder dog sires Sammy's Shadow out of Statue's Laugh. This is that and definitely not the other. Mesmer's sunflower in his lady's lap. No sooner has he reached cruising altercation than Heap

Steroid cans his disciplinarian and pops a capsicum. Now a patch of biscuit scouts out hunting preserves. Welcome to pilgrim class and monumental massuh.

●

A Delft postman sails away on waves of Wynton K, breeze of a Saturday and synchronicity playing hoop with air fresh from Ludlow. I feel every inversion to lay down my hay and submerge myself in some tidepool drawing room before the glazier of autumn and the screwball at the crossroads stir me out. Is it any wonder ivory hunters are music lovers or that black Irish are often black? And never forget, Colonoscopy: A wasp is a dead flower with wings. Presto a fast pesto. Liquid secrets (round of applause) lick their jumpers clean. Mr P.C. (Petit Choses) with the wiles of an osteopath swaying philodendron to the precise tempo of "if he could see me now he'd be a McKenna on his mother's side." Wall-eyed thought-fired ceramic morning sun, and checkers aside, let's get those lapidary song motes back on bath night. Call me a cab. Oops, missed it, must be the blues on purpose again. Start your maypoes, Elmo. After which a doorway blooms and don't you know a mentholated Kelly cooks for the crew of the Hot Moon?

●

How soon can I go out into the sun-besotted now, Old Testicle scenes and sirens rerunning *Gunsmoke* in Greek? Turn on the telly and watch for a minstrel. A quail is growing teeth. Chuckles on the airwaves suppurating loopholes muffles his screwgun with a pilsner. Cliffs as far as the ear can hear. Maraschino stained glass glee. Pigtails on a milk bun. Give us a home where the sun's on the phone and we talk with the elves of ourselves.

•

A tea shower eavesdrops on a treefort as two dingdong darning needles do the natty dugout. Dragonfly stud (tide apples spent) gibbets into the off on his own. Lenox First Congo bells now playing "Fluid Roosters in a Cage." Mud simple kid palms his spud like an ingot. It's the Ray Gelato Show. Somewhere in the islands a listener remembers he's not a clarinet, but a sunset. Party hats with embouchures for chickadees and rpm dueling phlegm semaphore seawrack, a "holiday" for the man on the lam. The gulf between tick tock pilot lights and time, Tristano forever Dracula-riding the escalator reet of feet in blue obsidian velocipede. Kabuki Pie meet Papa Fazool. Almost a harp.

—for Peach

•

Billy Bauer backpedals parallel guitar glade through Sherwood Forest plucking plectrum of Arnold Fishkin who looks up from his butterflies to connect the clouds as if Eureka tasted flapjacks and syrup in the silk. Power tools more power to whom? Whether limbic or lambchop, Frank Lovejoy with butter cutlass smoothing the shores of Gitche Gumee. Music of academic mothers singing lights out—we wouldn't want a marquee messing with our kind of camaraderie. A mild dose of cascade indeeds me a glance. Ribbon bakers of Pompeii. Anemic sunbeams on pudding. An erection rather than a hat.

•

Hypnotists incubate in hammocks suspended from candles. Flannel flowers call on Chanticleer from an ocean liner. "Come to Mimosa, try some delicious bromides." Spaniels in K holes faint above the mantelpiece. You need to leave your mind behind like Hedda Hopper. Habits of stirring tea with shrunken footballs, trickles of the trade. Thumbnail of a nincompoop, his visions in a woollen tooth. Ossuary powder passed off as monks. Trumpet voluntary trailing pumpkin-colored kelp. Ready or not, an inkblot going rabbit ears.

·

My dream a cycloramic cul-de-sac neighborhood Nautical Street. Canvas on cobblestone, Corliss in corduroy footlights by the bay. Like New Orleans in New England hearing every living aspirin, a washcloth with a story. "Enough about me, Mr Back-from-the-Orient." Angel-headed heebie jeebies. All ingrained firehouse politeness and Ealing movie wildcoast with cottages out the bedroom window. Genuine Wimbledon nose-colored loveseats. Evening crapshoots on the Rez. And blow me down, my anti-gravity pants have split like a pink elephant's appetite.

·

Palaver about squash. Bop sunspots. Lump in mudbone where the river meets the train and a lonely woman vets prima ballerina gutbucket amalgams nine months before the chestnut hits the combine and Misterioso So-and-So solos on vibratoless velveteen beaver earning Bach bouncer points. To learn at a tender age given a sunbonnet and a slate that short one cornea the payphone in the alley rings *Ciao*. Cling peaches on a path. Tristano perfervid to wickets burgles The William Carlos Sun Ra Room. Always down with the blood count, Lennie in leather on osier pins tells the swellest stories in Swordfish Land like how to handle Indiana noon mornings. We have and have not. Room here for hedge bandits punching a forgotten clock.

•

A land pirate of the first water seven Niles from Porkpie Lid. Four thousand fragments of Yaweh fall into the hands of hoodlums, getting even *fizz* into reformatories. How'd you like to live in Oscuro with Nick Cravat, arroyos in his rosin arrows in his back? Welcome to Chinchilla Villa Bing-bong. I'll have two tokens, pliz. Permeate me. Derby duster dingle autumn tea passed about as if Shakespeare were present. Vagrant tremens flock El Niño to Tarzana, then carpet down to Mexico in a cartoon drawn by sticks. Newsboys ready to kick the talking cure start penning in the wavelengths. "Are drills old saws?" Homer Ludens traces a star back to his nursery.

•

Two spooks in a fountain and Buck Rogers humming "Happy Muffineering" finds himself forced off the trail. He thinks he's walking on water but it's his immaculate bladder. He's talked before, but never in deraileur. There's a blockhead who's a little palliative full of sunrise and common sense and knows Judgment Day from the gross national product up and can toss a truant officer over a shot clock without missing more than one "Geronimo!" of some nonfatal but incurable rodeo. You might blame the firebug's pratfall as he's always reading Thanksgiving O'Day or Dante in the Oriental Rug. Solitary shifts of time inside the light he's tired of seeing inside. Best hole up in his minaret, or be in his wife's bonnet.

•

O rooster of May, dear mailbox, kind sirens who giveth men the goatees to excuse their afterwrath—bless our little electrolytes. The princess inside Salvador Dalí's formaldehyde did not invent pornography. His marbles his mother his white puberty. And just then drawn butter walks in rub-a-dub on the dartboard. For an instant there's no sorcery in the bantam, sharecroppers stop cropping and the droop on the stockade stops burbling away, like after concupiscence taps on his murmur and brushing his aristocracy holds it raised. And even as this most introspective parry of the transmission is lost, speak dads to them but use none.

•

Dear Double Jehovah with your beautifully tailored millwheel, pick up your eyeteeth using jujubes on Berber reverb, your quantum mechanics a beanie too late. Bodies located in the bright yellow cornmeal and amphibious sunshine of eighteen hundred siblings. Absence finds a way of being there. To write in French about the fluid gain of artists is to universalize the nostalgic tourist and bond proboscisly with the inverse music charts of the unfettered shnozz of Charles de Gauze. Rimbaud now the amber camcorder of a cliché and self-affirming Rumpelstiltskin for the Classics. Upturned eye of a mosquito on the isthmus when he bestrides the lazy-pacing cloverleaf and sails upon the brimstone of the aerodrome. Or sits alone in perfect stimulation and erects a decline, posting dispatches to Coco Chanel who relaxes in her medicine chest with an eminently worthy shrub.

•

A jet jets through the blue bloodstream of the sky. The interior hobo turns summer, his full-service ghost town like the background in old cartoons. Too many pixies to please the derrick. It's the Yoicks-Rotunda Trick. Fletcherites suck sugar dactyls. Detective Quotient Topiary (balled in a carcoat) coiffed for disappearance with mirrors to go. A parenthetical fellow in evening dress reserved for forgotten significance floundering in candlewax peeled from the previous sunset. Hoppy ponders Sin City sitting on his desperado like aspic on linoleum. His other eye tongue-tied. Theodolites and lox. Loping narratives in carpet slippers over lime green socks. An ornamental trill gives its life to language. Lassie played by a male.

TOO
MUCH
JOHNSON

MICHAEL
GIZZI

for Keith Waldrop

I'll be the horse's head—you be yourself.
—*Louis Armstrong*

VELOCITY SCHOOL

I just fed my wildlife accelerator
an old pirate of the West doughnut
now nobody has the foggiest
and a speechifying pince-nez
called Mahoney if you want
to be a badger warm
to a natural comfort find
a quiet walnut where a blue
beret can exist in peace as
tribute get the point that
bald facts if anything draw
you closer to woollen
atmospheres moony in
the condominium of wit
to wit bamboo balls that
feel cheated as astringents
since Fluff lit into the middle
distance picking up an infield
in a lifetime of touch made by
no names please cracks
a Brazil nut believed to be
the contraband of a minuteman
who may be more than one
and outshines everyone

AN EXPEDITION LONG ENOUGH TO TAKE YOUR PICTURE

Gazing up at the stars about
a new method of never existed
off for the weekend oil lamp and
the breath of independence
breaks out the wick please
to accept this wristwatch pompadour
from a peripatetic barber
Old Fashion my hourglass, garsong

get drunk marry be tall botanical
full fathoms deep amid so many
regularities in suits you find time
to invent shoes for walking on water
how many ragged families
could sing O Jolly Parachute
how many starving mothers
rally 'round a peacoat whose
muddle includes a speaking tube
from Istanbul to biscuits time
to write the werewolf out of your will
eyeing little gnomes in their nut

A WIND OF WHAT HE REALLY MEANS

Gripping the public methane
a country vicar disguised
as a baby with letters
hidden in his diapers his
urinal on the ceiling at least
into Christ's infancy a Gorgon
of mass and personal warmth
that puppets might see the big
elf guy who thinks in his shoetrees
sun visors on his submarine like
feathers on the Statue of Liberty
gliding about like a badge on
the windshield of the greatest myth
zookeepers didn't think of him
as a she but a transatlantic
candle who hoped to put
his flame around his pals
now lying at the bottom
of the sea scooping up anything
that crawled or flew or sat ashore
the Great One didn't get a penny
but fish to fry ticked off a telegraph

causing the cost of Singapore
horse feed to rise as big a science
wheel as any eminent gizmo
could get because gluttony
we might starve from the inside
out may all your troubles be
midgets without the inside meemies

A FATAL WEAKNESS FOR BALONEY

Storm-felled star charts scribbled
on a doorknob perched upon a tripod
in the equatorial manner umlauts
on a couch Virgo folding rosewood
in the 2nd Book of Euclid bees
at the weedy edges pissing
moonshine through peepholes
in the text "Enjoying the view how's
the grouse ever hear from Lao-tzu?"
people don't think for trees a dream
passes through mixing cocktails
with handrails auditioning a ripple
some poison for a pal another thing
he's brought his special synthetic
writing once it fixes calls
below wants everyone to know
a poet's backswing is its own
excuse for being an earlobe
in its skivvies strapped to his wrist
embossed with scenes of cattle-
punching out of pulp magazines
where on the deckled edge every
shiner the kayo weathers
is the selfsame powderkeg

YOU STILL IN DUMBSTAY?

Turrets in specimen jars
turn up in a Hindu's pajamas
frogs chirp in the linoleum
and here proceeds a sad
stream from sanitorium
spittoon flowers making depositions
to bondo your memoirs
so long as you don't end up
some kind of montage you
to a fault floundering over
primate condiments and
serpent extracts in the pantry
the whelk of your brakes panting
for a more vernacular brandy
why's the faith healer staring
at the wax on my furniture
why am I here in my PJs
not playing with a full deck
thinking of a Spanish explorer
while the dirigible across
the examining table calling out
pet names downloads my
stomach he knows exactly
what makes the world go 'round
think I'll send him a bomb for Easter

A PLANETARY DRIP

Suddenly there was one
lying on his bum Paris in one
hand crustaceans in the other
and glow worms on the swan
in question not a typo but the air
of a mandarin with three
pigtails whose knick knacks

perform acts no practical object
would dream of and eyeballs
aside he thinks with his cheeks
though we for one believe
that all the stolen showgirls
have bouleversed his mind
to provide a measure of gaga in
one ear and out the Okinawa, ah
so a house at the zoo achieves
capacity the whole menagerie
inaudible to Pinatubo

WHAT A HALFMAN IN HIGHLANDS DREAMS OF

Fox Talbot in the henhouse
answers wishes for English wits
genitals, board your rockets
flight time's the right time
for rare Roman torchlight
not ten feet away in the mirror
behind a city slicker his
jaw longer than daylight
an immense pounder of stakes
in whose head several screws
have suddenly come loose
the clarion call of youth
so proud of the freaks he's
imported by the ton he stares
at a photograph of one
eldorados in the weird
of his blueberry beard and
once to impress a big steel
beam took eight feet of
reach whiskers and flying
tacklers through a hole
in the sun after which
an ocean-going mint

URGENT AS LIQUID MEANS

These might have been the thoughts
of mice or a templar under
an apple tent part owner of
the coloring bees and
anesthesia perfume ponds where
memory resides and the sun's
speed is changed by the trifling
speed of a running ant who
yearns for answers that transcend
astronomy taking time
off to visit the forces
of the universe orphans
sunbeam beauties inserted in
the spine "the way they are
nowadays at the mall these kids
whose experimental wig of
liberal bedstraw can't control
a schooling day marry next
the smoking hemp around a
fountainhead and corpses being
guru, vermicelli makes it come
alive—faster than fifty vertebrates
Fahrenheit heigh-ho away"

MR AMERICA'S DEHYDRATED NIGHTJAR

So long squirt came over the radio
having abandoned the ladder he entered
the haymow you are a disgrace to the insane
yes my little window washer turn your face to the wall
okay so something died and this boiler room
is but a tiny moth hole in its pedigree
no question about it there's a diet
down here and it eats like a lark
to start his hair was parted and his fingerprints

tossed in his pockets not to worry
Ugolino will fly to Honolulu and put
the pineapple on his wife's tattoo who wonders
will time elapse I feel positive gravel
coming down this sideroad meet me
across the valley inside that silhouette
even armed with virtual corsets we're way
too flexible announces a primordial chap
I rode that chair for ten inflammatory ersatz
minutes have another breakfast mitt
if my whole life hadn't been about ambiguity
I might have awoke hazarding shrugs
you want an equation very well
we grew up crazy for kneeslaps
and paperweights featuring snowflakes
we've a great infection to
serve many Jasons to come
take a chunk out of everyone

STRUMMING A BOOK WITH BOOTSTRAPS

From Norway to north of
Ipswich came the half myths
half a lifetime making water
that fed a sort of flotsam
dreamy hope standard boilerplate
for muscle bosuns appearing posh
before a packed faux pas of oriental rugs
and splitting a leg up into fraction
aristocrats shown by theorem
dustup to be every bit as bonny
as varicose is Vermont, sir
evicted from the Saga Center you
worked as a bouncer in pantomime
a wardrobe for cue cards your

spirit guide prone to racketeering
and badminton so it took a few
decades for the window to right
your invisibleness for the rubes
to dub you Auto Mohammed
pitch anything you like spells
hulls ropes your insides by which
doctor's favor we know the remote
luminaries of dermatological earth
and what rises at dawn
to hide them

PLEASE TO EXAMINE YOUR EGG CUP

You go out and buy a vise
grip behind the sun from
a very big kahuna on the moon
polite you make nice novenas
for everyone all pontiffs on
deck the next cookie
in the dish (swan of Paducah)
darkens the thermos "Morning, Post"
"Evening, Banner what's the rumpus?"
and treating Dutch to gibberish
all dressed up decimals and
nowhere to go adds "It's
very beautiful to watch you grow
testy someday I'd like to see a
UFO" once said the true window of pleasure *being*
receives a weather juice stain you
know the feeling and there it remains
like ipecac were a dialect
and you think on the spot maybe
my mind doesn't menstruate
proper almost doesn't let me be
exploding like a person growing up wrong

right? the science of life
is a dazzling hall reached only
by clearing the kitchen send me
logs of wind and things to hit
anti-aircraft vivisectionists
bag a doodlebug all it took
was the magic math
to embrace the incoming buzz

TREATING SUGAR DIOMEDES

You get no Richter for
having haunted the Classics
concentrate on this tent ten
minutes and cataclysms
you don't notice dumb
you down you're a pontoon
who lives to wear experiments
with spats which is in fact
your pseudonym so when you
rendezvous in sundown cabooses
with eggheads you put your
hopscotch hornblende in
fooleries not to be found
in everyday declensions
boobies heavy with celestial
expectorants and there you
vow to remain all your licorice to
examine sipping local anesthetics
to wrest yourself from other
tendencies for at last you've slept
with Nike in her shoetrees buffing
the afterglow without suspecting
it's no more than a peepshow
and that everything in
this workshop disappoints

NERVY OPTIC HOBBYIST

Heavens gets into Betsy
with a twenty inch retina
now *that's* a yen channel a few
gigatons through a different medium
and Cleopatra's caravan might
reminisce rabbits on the running
board peeling apples like Hapsburg lips
all lisping in the wrong direction
remember learning is the root beer
of living we live in telescopes
like exercise bikes trading
rubbers for a desert mirage here's
a poor pony clipping treetops
where Grapenuts had his coronary
cup of tea to go scatterbrained
to explain why in the fracas
that follows the trotting out of
fireflies he's all over Rand McNally
now abed with St. Caboodle
like a king of cufflinks in
Timbuktu and bloomers from any
where stems in iambic sphere goes
out for a beer and wakes up
in Singapore with a beard

OFF SHROUD

The new Schenectady is now in
effect Brother Jim Tuesday last
you were seen scaring piranha
from the head of the accused
we see you involved in lots of
moustache and though you make
a terrifying cruller don't bother

reading your horoscope to borrow
the lawnmower the zodiac could be
the relic of a child prodigy holed up
with nefarious cheesemen in a crib
on Mont Lunacy no Stellar Prep just
crickets bouncing handballs off
the Elgin Marbles such pictures
as Tiberius took from Elephantiasis
whose epicurean nates grew corn
to save his face and populate a postage
stamp sure the shadow of the oriole
will behave from this day forward
everyone will have a chaperone
it is a natural theory of evolution
this bell will ring the bell of your
accomplishment you're having
a dream like you have a life

NOSTALGIA FOR MAYHEM

I resign from mouthwatering
and zigzagging which seems
to me an apocalyptic entre
nous convalescing in the buff
candles that no one can see
more jello molds for my toreros
frescoes for mother whose bagman
goes apeshit this close too faraway
and armadas lose an eye
now caressing Java man with
more interdenomination than
fifty-nine second bananas
out of each of my minutiae
reflected in streamlets dedicated
to Suetonius or to the Idaho
of Suetonius and if I still cling

to a few planets by their ears
then high hills under the car!
infinity has nothing left to do

HECTOR NO ILIUM

Eternity stuck in the moment
for what it reminds you of
a giant wrestler embracing an
oak slipping pod waiters the vague
Latin gobbledygook an upper looseleaf
on which stars leave puddles
inked-in extinct transmitting lapels
to the pip world which Baldspot
here says in his head is a kind of
old song one feels on his skull
and would kiss to be inside of with
somebody's pants horsing around
as all those hormones hit the gas
and because he likes to feel in
the way he sniffs a pimpernel and
stands by the bay window watching
scarlet fever snap clean sheets while
on-and-off a windmill breezes
the hotseat so the greatest show
on earth now sprouts this
weird stuff that no one can
understand some oceanic afternoon
that half-proved the moon

JE M'APPELE BROGAN

Sunset rings a bee bored
as a popsicle in January
who really knows a wowser
say some words "The philistine
is the enemy of the nickname"
"When Sonny gets dead
clean his cage" somewhere
down the track flowers
react to happy hour and
stuff like the bends truth is
they're the strangest limbs
and don't forget ellipsis
one of those dreambooks
just came through signed
The Chicopee Pontoon Monger
the rest is whimsy sown up
in the harbor at Chamber Pots
with a spare anchor bee balaklava
destroyed thanks to Nightingale's
thousand page full force hurricane
because when his bottom failed him
like Potomac dysentery the navy
wouldn't tickle his fancy

FROM HERE TO DIAMOND HILL

Lunchpails watch aeroplanes
lift off stomach pains a dogbone
in the gardenias reminds you
the water dish has a home
all the timber trying to find
where the lifestyle's hidden
make mine a Gansett on a

pine-o stool and this circumference
shall the good midget teach
hair oil wells and raven gunwhales
of Falling Water O'Toole
ever I put my glims on him
again I'll play Home Sweet Home
on the hotplate with my spoons
full of wampum there used to be
symphonies that were friends suits
interchangeable with eternity
I'm reminded of what the Great Bamber
once said "A well-balanced meal
makes a swell paperweight" I gaze
once more over the highchair
Manville isn't there it's
all in my mind the one
that comes out spellbound like
fireflies waiting for the sun

BWANA FILTRATION SYSTEM

That magic moment in Sanskrit
when the lights come up that extend back
every bit as far as that clobber kid stuff
adults in charge on a visit to Manassas
toned down for the last edition of
the class asteroid "Thanks for the pies
and the rocks they were tied to
where are you? we want to
polish your shoes" so how much
love can a windshield handle
nerves flow to a space probe
pack up your troubles in a
forebrain bundle and wonder how
mind you the man thought

he had wedded bells like armpit heat
life got a bit simpler what was hot was
not ice made a splash in oceanography
a platinum anatomist during a thunderstorm
wrote a natural history of teeth
discovering mouth hearing organs
in fish seafaring vessels in birds
Rhode Island packet crews dashed off
Portuguese tomes like whale librettos
eastbound backwards got across
the ocean moment drawn by dryland
backbones of kingdom come's leviathan
campfires soon became talkies and every
seedy word a fella with a fairy tale

TOO MUCH JOHNSON

Democracy in its smallest pants
"We take care of our termagants"
light from a stoppered sack of potatoes
feeling under the counter after which
crack he could get his breath back
"I'll leave you in full flap face paint
about ten states disappeared from
a crowd" a monosyllable came
to the poodle he spit on his
fingers and pain held up a snake
The Torch was busy becoming a
leading light sports began to twitch
"Gimme back ma grommets!"
hands began to rain at the heels
of running men at last every state
was looking at the reptile if a man
walks anywhere that's an idea only
the bones of the rides were left
a lank spider's emaciated deadpan

shone like bran muffins but who put
the phlegm in the bagman's holiday
without a Dino bone in his body

HIC BARBER QUIRK MARINE

"Seven league geezer seeks
well-heeled adventurer who
on the fly fishing from the lam
can transcribe acoustically
on bassinet chop-chop boogie
woogie melancholy baby steps"
trust only the personal and
never underestimate the glower
of a barnacle steer the helm
of your cheeks among the wooden
planks they rest upon fleetingly
your lap of luxury is getting
dusty one need only glance
at the clock stuck inside
the haystack youth had sought
so slumber is the babe-in-arms
facing down a waterspout
and wigwam-ho four drops
of intermezzo how'd you like
to see the world aboard
a whaler feel inside your pocket
boat droppings? "What!
no spinach?" now the squid is
free six miles to leeward even
the lancet might receive
some piece of mind or pack
ice send cartographers
a wild goose egg

michael gizzi

McKENNA'S ANTENNA

A Note

Dave McKenna is a sender and a National Treasure. Try to imagine Woonsocket in Japan. Next—a venerated piano man. Imagine, finally, you're being swept by a visceral wave of music toward Race Point and you have entered the McKenna Triad, whose vertices are Woonsocket, R.I., Cape Cod, and Nirvana—no artist sails the music main with more assurance. These fifteen poems composed over the past decade are simply verbal transcriptions of his pianistic beam scrambled through my receptive bean. I've never felt so right writing poems, so don't ask me to explain.

I could write a book about the love I heard in the voice of Dave's devoted sister Jean O'Donnell. It was in fact what finally compelled me to do what I'd only been jawing about. I'd also like to extend an encore each to Clark Coolidge, Larry Fagin, Bernadette Mayer, Rosmarie Waldrop, and Geoffrey Young for their divers engagement with these poems and this project.

I guess, to be musically frank, I'm a Dave-oholic. So, consider this only partial payment for the rapture his music continually weaves around legions of rapt listeners. It's what I did with my tax rebate. I feel good about it. Should you buy that, perhaps you'll buy this.

(Editorial note: In an effort to reduce duplication, four of the original fifteen poems in this chapbook have been withdrawn and now appear in the larger books of which they were also a part: "McThuselah's Saloon Licks" and "This Nearly Was Mine" in INTERFERON; "Buckle Down Belchertown" and "Visions of Dave" in MY TERZA RIMA.)

DAVE'S SAINT DAY

Boodles for two marginal vassals
firewater to rhapsodists
dwarf drinks at piana piacular
lemme at them oolong sarong McMedleys!
this ain't a disguise it's a hideout
I'll be lucky to conjugate gum
without I hear the tinkle

Tunes-on-file every time he smiles
absolute interpreter of the quahaugs
and every since Aquidneck hamburger nights
Halloween in stir like Woonsocket
courtesy of Dave Van Dykes the ivories
my dad you know
loved pimentos

Sure he did Dave and seabread
broke with the Chopmist Imp
O Gaelic Rinpoche!
gone to Wyoming to shoot canteens
the ghost of a Gatling hurler
screwballing pullets at specks
pecked in shades

PIANO HEPATICA

Uh, this here dunk bread
brogue inkblot says
heaven's a farm you buy in the sky
feets through window on
Easy Street where others belong to
same fluent human toodle-oos
over heard world earway
still no one finds the lotsa time
to page the holes in bluesky the way

old off-field Marshal Distractions can
he's even impeccably over-dressed
with perfectly formed cymbals
attached to an errant eyepatch
the Quiet Man like a sacristan finds
Danny Boy depending
but doesn't attend the final
day of childhood on account of
his mother has a brogan in the oven
that's the message
wind hatches a watering can
dust wears a necktie
upwind angels swim
too marvelous for words

BUSHWHACKED BY BABY TALK

Shouldn't you be in bed little fella
do I come into your mind
hoover your retort ask why
you keep the Bride of Machine
suspended in snake oil
or change cars like shorts?

Amber waves roll beans
up the Mount of Olives
par for the sap that shines
at any meanie miney moment

I was on scholarship from Nemo's Creamery
to study buttocks in Europa no man
is an orgasm who hasn't
been framed like a hat
I'm just trying to make a point

And lured by a glass of evening sun
gumming pablum Pandemonium
breaks out for a better view
another gong displaces rectitude
and long toothhood reeking
Tuscarora spirit gum "I'm the king of this
god-damned miscegenated microphone!"
boos become comestibles
give him one when he wakes up

OLD SOL IN GUTTERS

There goes loose Mother Hubbard
in a suitcase on her shoe her palindrome
remembered backwards with good time off
for trying to escape the Eraser's face
exfoliating now in leaves like so many waves
holding hands from the old country

Easy, Daedalus, I know this abyss
here comes glass that dies in the wind
reddening the sky shaking loose hoodlums
from an old hymn—now ain't that a windfall!
or as Purgatory has the lamest picnic tables
just a tree in which the learning curve's that steep

Go forget about hair
in your underwear though
a premature oops drops in the soup
and Herbert Lom's pocket Seneca
fumbles for his watch
a fern-like soul makes everything butter

RAPELLING POWDER

Out there holds more answers
than a wallet anywhere
there's no logic to it it's not
your cuirass that goes way back
there a polestar pole vaults a poleaxe
soon vanishing cream gets caught in the act
and breaks your balloon

Human nature is a public nuisance
but one is to independence
as a prime minister to obstetrics
it's a large thing to always be due
I was in the front row
and the conjure man has a time share
coming to a rooster exactly like you

SUBORNED AGAIN

Midget thunder rumbles
on the shelves the moon
arrives in boxes
space is impossible whiskerhood
keeping its distance in slippers
eight million ways to myopia
almost makes me wish I
hadn't been saved

Now the sun's removed its beard
I just want to say hit
by a train in the hedges
on the way to the coroner that
this was my corner and sure
I nicked the census man

but the anthrax took his mumps
all I said was ichthyology
and he sank like a fish

Like me and my shadow

FOUND IN A BOTTLE NEAR FOUNTAIN

Due east of Westerly
dreamers proffer no apologies
Ted Rust ventriloquist
makes lemonade sandwiches
his legs of yore elevated
in some turn-of-the-century
cottage Misquamicut
I got this idea from a pillow
also my concept of night
the world on the periphery
kiss-the-cross sights like
everybody's backyard's
buried in my window
an opal with a dial fiddleheads
become working class moths
tumbleweed gets turned down
for that promotion mumbly-peg
begins to cloud our vision who
you and me haloed
in Narragansett country

THE HEARTBREAK OF ICONOGRAPHY

I'd like to be a nun
and live a life of practically
a nun cloistered in an oyster
how I talk is none of
your Bumstead business
Boris Godunov opens the door
with a pocket comb of itinerant
singers with a long mournful beard
I'll have to take these ears off
and put them in a cemetery no one
ever saw main thing I want to do is
first wear shoes and eat off plates
I have a new monster clean-cut
he can't travel could you
let me have a ticket window
I always loved the sport of music
I got a money order from a Russian blouse
I should complain—I
who am now a nun?

KELLS' WILLIES

Pop music was designed
to whistle while demented
little batty begins to hear
the birdies coziness
surrounds him like a page
be seeing ya above the cribs I don't
expect to understand the lawn
is it drinking a glass of history?
sometimes rain's a job
is the gardener water?
these jitters remind me of crop circles
gaunt linoleum snores stuff

confusion dust gets made from
with all the veracity of a roger
ask Heywood next time
you're at bat that's how I
spell Ireland

NO TIME TO BE A MUSKELUNGE

A sword swallower abdicates
his throat as a mirror
might a mentholated ghost
he knows his wife is on the roof
who scrubs the stars without being told?
bubbles please him asparagus afternoons
when the English grow Elizabethan
and tulips walk the plank
        —*what* gives?
I just had to put mom
who insists on being known
as a pre-code cartoon to bed
it's fine for you people to worship
from every hedge and hello funny papers
I'm being haunted by a crooner
like any disease it's a goldmine
say, where your ears would be
if you could see them in your mouth

SHUCKS IS NOT ENOUGH

A doctor is sent to the workhouse
now he'll never get well
at any moment a generation
is knowing what's gone—or up!
cut the crap, Winesap

is feeling not family
earth made to pose home
a moving picture house
snoring on the screen?
today it rained a little
and so she loves him great
minds recycle the same carnation
take a rose by the cheek
and banish the word blush
among those arrested
was a how-to book
every time I pick up
the phone it's me again
clowned into oblivion

M6

FEB/MAR 2002
PAUL RODGERS/9W

KNOWLTON MFG.

Is it a philosopher's honeymoon one finds
On the dump? Is it to sit among mattresses of the dead,
Bottles, pots, shoes and grass and murmur *aptest eve*:
Is it to hear the blatter of grackles and say
Invisible priest; is it to eject, to pull
The day to pieces and cry *stanza my stone*?
Where was it one first heard of the truth? The the.
                    —*Wallace Stevens*
                "The Man on the Dump"

SPEAKER OF THE HOUSE

Life in the wild isn't what it used to be
I guess it's safe to say we're sound asleep (not a peep)
The birdhouse at the Bronx Zoo never looked like this
Mother Nature and Human Emotion swap poles
Because no one has time for space euphemism's as good as it gets
    (oxidized juncos)
A difference engine spooking even the shade of Houdini (Particle Theory)
No visible means of escape
The SATs in Sanskrit scored on steel mesh by Doctor Who
A cage within a cage custom-made for a wraith
A Pisan Canto to Space
Otis elevator from a meteor shower stucco'd peradventure with divots left
    by the Great Head-Banging Auk
Not a laugh-in but a standup coffin or comfort station for autism
Can one say beekeeping is useful and Egyptology is not
Why do buttons bring comfort deeper than any personality

CHINESE WELL

Light distorts the Ages
Watery leafage or amphibious iron mask
Not to be artesian but
How many ill wishes do you suppose a wishing well receives
One would have to be a seer from Artois
And dig field recording pillowbooks ·
Or prognosticate by shape (without a word)
To get the jump on insight
Put the thirty foot shine back in its bucket (duck it)
Your vegetable love will grow

CLOUDS NINE

The easiest way to become a cloud (a cloud one can be proud of) is to have a father who's a meteorologist. Yosemite Sam upbraids a dust devil. What would he say about the weather on Lesbos? Or on drugs, for that matter? Here comes the sun? Leave it to Beaver Lamarck to make a list of cloud types. These here blew in from the French Revolution to stack up over this canary yellow hum cover. One never knows, do one? Would you believe a cicerone in his cups under a claudicated anvil fixin' to fulgurate a lunch loaf? Nosh on this—the concupiscent curd of a former whirling dervish. Is Rumi in the house?

GOING MY WAY

Samsonite had balls as big as the Carrier Dome
He'd earned them in the plaque mines
They were all he had to show
They were the desiccated jewels of his time
And schlepped along beside him
In a topiary grip made of winter privet
Thumbing to Webb City
He knew why the caged bird split
Imagine Mayakovsky's kit
Magritte for American Tourister
A hamper for angelic underthings (on casters)
The portmanteau of Godot

Michael Gizzi

NEW

DEPTHS

of

DEADPAN

for Hollis Ever Cunningham

THE DEEP

A reflection blinds a gardening correspondent. Shade requires a starting point. The elementary particle makes to leave and its extremities fill.

Aliens write in puns we now know are curly fries. Drive-up windows make this clear.

War with its lights out eschews imagination. All our buds lost their heads in the flower of their youth.

So we got this apartment on Jockey Street. They used to race houses there.

But we're not going to jaw about Ovid or the rosy steps of mother, her microscopic brand of honey. We expect you to understand.

See you over the next hill.

ABOUT FACE

No sooner am I out the door than I want to be home reading.

It was written on high I'd have thoughts in my head but no words to express them.

Eight hours ago my face was a full-grown narcissus. I cut off my nose to identify myself, strung all the hands I ever held around my neck and expected them to do their job.

I must spend a night under the enormous rock I associate with childhood.

It's not going to happen.

I love being busted in the mirror.

Then someone opens an eye in my head. Murmur of subtitles.

IRONY VS. REALITY

Life, as if you didn't know, is an open book.

Eggs possibly heavy at times.

Car crashes remain the leading cause of information.

Maybe your son is a physician, I've no idea how.

The imperial worm turns.

Great minds recycle the same petunia.

The time for flying slippers is past.

Hubble approaches lilac time.

If reruns have their way, you'll never get a second chance.

On the third day the drugs recognized no one.

Are we not the skins of a peerless punch?

LORELEI

I look at the words the wind brings. My head crushes stems. I look up, the houses tilt, clouds move quickly on tiptoe.

Despite their number the drowned are always the same. How true

their kelpy chronicle, if only one could put some order to it.

A window replaces a shadow, humming silently a song of the nude among canvasses.

She is discolored by rain. The same nightmare unites us

with four walls all above us.

May you keep this memory, the one you never see.

SHADOWS OF VOLITION

Waves contain a thesaurus of the sea, depriving history and its librarians

of perfection. As a rule there are four perspectives:

one in the head and one in each wrist. Leafing through this, it hits you, the only botanist on the menu.

One can't adventure with images anymore. The inner pictorial person is pushed aside.

Don't forget the library, the largest source of lawlessness.

In private the lock reflects on the key.

RAGING BALLS

The subject was mirrors, which they teach backwards. "I used to be a contretemps. Now I'm an impromptu."

Sarcasm is the new altruism. Caveats have been a problem for centuries. Life's a long short story. Strangers know nothing.

What you experienced as an animal can never be taken away from you.

Now you're a father, too, throwing punches at the opera.

Forgive us for being as small as life.

> —*Anon.* (a name to live up to)

Oops, I meant Onan.

THE NIGHTSHADE ENSEMBLE

I shall never forget my first glimpse of vanishing.

.

Even now the mirrors move, and I catch a clang of armor

beneath the shelves of mist, sense histamine cracks bluer than a daydream.

Is the rose truly torpor between sleep and waking?

As they say in Latin, "Gone time shines in the mind like a bearded bag of sawdust."

So plants sneak out of books, spending nine months of the year green. They grow out of curiosity, translating ideas into things.

Some think the earth has seen enough charity, and they lop off its shadows at the close of day.

ARBOR DAY

> and in the sky there were glistening rails of milk
> —*Frank O'Hara*

An armory with no army
which every summer leaves obscure.
Call it a respite. Say a train wreck dreamed it,
a purchase in the blur.
Was there a split in the arborist?
A shame we ignore the same words.
Sap becomes shellac.
A hand goes up, flanked by magicians.
A tale told to pigeons.

CHIMES AT MIDNIGHT

The father in exile stripped of his sundial borrows the equator for a belt.

All his life his life had yet to start, coming of age was the end.

You think about genetics, would think, well,

maybe a whole other life *is* possible. Maybe noon would rather be mid-night.

The humble Hellebore becomes a rock star thanks to intelligent design. Coziness cradles him like a rage. "He hid under his bed when he lived with his mother!"

One branch of the family is anecdotal. Now they sip from a glass of history.

Everything is made up.

TO A PIXIE

Uncle exhibits his painting "The Port of Missing Men." Someone aims an aqueduct his way.

What used to be called the bounding main is stuffed under his mattress. The brim of his tall peaked hat seems to be everywhere at once. Abundance

gives the air a blank stare.

Skyward strides an archangel with a harvest hook, its blade toothmarked by stars

(it happened while we were having a nap)

now burning in an alien jam jar.

AN OLD-FASHIONED

A good teacher instructs by swatting flies.

An elephant never forgets an excuse.

What made the tick choose anthropology?

Try this: repair a hubbub.

Studies suggest people who speak in tongues never eat with you again.

And that pieman once thought to be a berry (now a wooden boat) died of seahorse strokes.

He used to baby-sit Leadbelly.

Music—the conduit through which you blindly come into view.

Listen: your initials on the moon.

DIG THE KING

The king that sounded
Most like the king
The king in the ear
Of musical things
Bring on the king
The king who was playing
The king on the beach
A mineral king, king of digging
Remember the king
Like a mood ring
A natural king

GILLETTE CASTLE

There were in him the makings of a bird, a giddy soldier, a sailor, too. As he liked to put it, a mind can really get inside your head.

Had it been immature to pretend it was a different place? Was the pantry a different place than the fancy estuary where they met? Sneeze there and you're on your own.

But she saved up all those incongruities, stuttering in unconditional light. His sentence was commuted to a window.

It was a long way off, before the war, but what did it open onto?

Had they thought of that?

SHE APOLOGIZES FOR NOT GETTING UP

Drawing the longbow of storytelling, she accepts a mint from a wicker settee. Her knuckles tighten 'round the oxidized silver of her salad fork, preceded by flugelhorn flourishes. The sun slides behind echelons of invitees, as shadows on a sundial become more than shadows. In the scullery she sways like a snowflake, pining to move into a Mondrian of all that has passed. Wind continues its rounds.

IN FLAT NEVADA

Minnie Blubb kept a clean house. At the Blubbs' you learned to walk on air bladders.

Taking a pinch of snuff, I flowed into the corner where the dog slept.

I kept a bag of soot with me. You know, I only believe in flirting when I can do it myself. Minnie was washing windows outside in the dark. She called it "zone cleaning."

A patter of rain on the skylight. Do you ever wonder how certain thoughts enter your head? Some say it doesn't happen. I just file it under "control."

And I can assure you there's little in that house where it was when I arrived this morning.

PRIMA DONNA DASHBOARD

I drink only Swedish spring water without ice from a Lalique glass that has been chilled to exactly sixty-seven degrees;

if it is sixty-eight degrees, I simply will not perform.

I speak in a high voice à la Julia Child, in a "continental" non-accent; or I don't speak at all.

I travel with an entourage of assistants, so I needn't actually speak with hotel receptionists or flight attendants—

what a waste of the five thousand utterances I may have left.

I haven't touched my own luggage since I graduated from high school, lest I stress the trapezius. I'm not very collegial, especially within my own voice type.

Days on which I rehearse, murder, rape, sobs, and vengeance often follow a coffee break.

RILKE IN PARIS

Once he was a pipe-smoking Turk on a shop sign. Now he's on vacation,

a one-legged man confronting his loss

preserved in spirits. Colors become audible. I'm green says the Turk. We are gold, the spirits reply. His head is dog paddling in the avenues.

When he doesn't dream he feels as if he's forgotten to put out the garbage.

"I'm mad!" he cries, and we can see the cry—a beautiful one-eyed woman! What the French call *faits divers*.

Candle ends surround his nightstand like a dirty solar system.

Dawn pours over the city, fat free milk.

Truffles begin to roll.

ONLY YOU KNOW WHAT THIS MEANS

I'll tell you about it, what each syllable says.

Doors opened. You must have been in there. We halved the distance, lost in a weightless environment.

One hotel contained a clipper ship. We must have been aboard.

The only heroic thing was a dot, emerging in the sky.

A still from a silent movie about the sea,

a towel by the edge of the sink.

CLOUDS NINE

The best way to become a cloud—a cloud one could be proud of—is to have a mother who's a meteorologist.

Yosemite Sam upbraids a dust devil.

What does she have to say about the weather on Lesbos—or on drugs, for that matter? Leave it to Beaver Lamarck to formulate a catalog of cloud types. These here blew in from the French Revolution to stack up over this canary yellow hum cover.

Would you believe a cicerone in his cups under a claudicated anvil fixin' to fulgurate a lunch loaf?

Nosh on this: The concupiscent curd of a former whirling dervish.

Is Rumi in the house?

MAN IN MARBLE

How can life that runs through us daily
separate us from the sparrows
that presume to own the air?

What is this paradise unexpected
in a sabbatical of one light year?

And what if there is nothing special
about this particular moment?

NIGHT-BLOOMING GRAMOPHONE

Rats know what good sex is. They dream in epic narratives of navigation
and thwarted efforts to escape.

The good thing about rats is they don't lie. Cross a gecko with a mussel
and what you have is a new kind of adhesive tape.

A shooting star eludes the ear and the bureau lit with a false dream in the
true night as the great sun soon forgets the path of light in a hymn far
away.

Consciousness is boundless shade. The traveler renounces his newspaper,
salutes the sleeves of sleep.

Witness the window grappling with the body.

THE LASER PRINTER'S DREAM

The tricks memory plays I never learn, glancing at my slippers.

Someone's on the wall, legs dangle from the skylight,

the magic selves of words conjure the subjective I.

Apollo in a blink unbuckles the Sphinx. Pushpins uphold the heavens.
Nothing in particular equal to memory disappears.

Is it fair that reality should appear so lifelike? Might alchemy return, and
every salamander stain the sun?

Now will you marry me, Dorothy?

Each waking moment is the first.

Vista, that word again.

AT GO FIGURE FARM

Clodhopping round the country dressed in steel
He punches a coachman in the side
Look at those ribs like the hoops of a barrel
A singer transfixed on the head of a pin
Verse is out of the question
A dull detonation shakes the ground
A few guys unloose their fireflies
His nose falls off and becomes a ball of dust
A stiff-bosomed white shirt opens the door
Two pilgrims quarrel in hurried whispers
Sex complex as the eyes of insects

Easily dazzled by round objects
Two chicken hawks plunge into a copse
If we want a little whiskey we can sell a few eggs

—for Bernadette

THE WIZARD OF OSMOSIS

Von Lime's serpent furniture—the Eastern accretions of a thousand pet tricks.

Memoirs of Indian pudding.

Jet black lashes of mock lyric poetry hoping a monocle might catch them gabbing near the hautboy. As absurd a farrago as feathers on Schoenberg

or the yowl of a big bucket of caviar.

His wife's despair had once impaired a cufflink. The pain of remembering inked his mouth with twenty black creases.

He had hoped for a trimmer impromptu. I only met her in print, which skipped what she had to say.

A terrific thing, nevertheless, time.

THE ACADEMY OF SCISSORS

In his time as a substitute teacher he slowly boosted the number of pills
he took. When he doffed his cap one could see he had a woman on his
head

and then on his lap. *She* was a mind-reader.

"Answer, you dead elm, Jack."

One could say it was the living end, by turns low down and low up, like
the first signs of spring on the skin-side. An internship is not just tossing
deadly nightshade over your shoulder

into an enamel bucket.

No doubt about it—he shouldn't have oughta devoted Holy Cross Day to
tell about Shallow's Italian dildo,

or the tiny toilets gathered together on a plank singing, "There, that's
done."

Would that my own work were as gratifying.

A DREADFUL CLAIM

I have fled as Niagara, I have fled as a chute.
I have fled as a magpie wearing only a necktie.
I have fled omnivorously, on a chafing dish.
I have fled as a scent from the Orient.
I have fled as a crystal. I have fled as a wiz.
I have fled as a quail, to no avail.
I have fled as a squint that sorely hides.
I have fled as a fossil, fled as a riptide.
I have fled like a crook with his nose in a book.

—for P

OSCILLATIONS IN THE ETHER

Please join us in the Drowning Room, reconstructed in this rarefied brandy bubble.

May the man with blue hair come too? Life is unbearable without the dead.

Growth rings and tear drinking are pattern languages. She'd like to give birth to food. She tried speaking to spareribs, but who really lives in her forehead?

Two comics move away from a mirror: one a mist one a mast. The athletes awake out of body in their boxers, a way of showing off.

Imagine hitting moonlight and living to tell.

Dreams speak in images speech once was.

If the eye were a tongue…

CLOISTERED IN AN OYSTER

Another sleepless night with the top down.

He has a headache that could write its own biography. How long can one inhabit a dumb-waiter? His mother Pearl plumps his pillow.

Eyes lie through their teeth. Is it so important to be unfortunate?

Is shucks not enough? Perhaps he could import a diver to yank him out of bed?

Another clammy night.

AUTUMN BY EAR

Scent of the sun under things
first of all things
last as well
a belief that life is all smiles
and bleeds
during which little or nothing is achieved

The King of Dust shuts the door
at the end the ear is spoken for

IN THE MANNER OF THE LATE MEL ALLEN

Three pies from home, he muses, "Adipose, schoolgirl,"

locked in a Malthusian gambit whose nymphless waters he'll never re-
trieve.

He bunks with his cat Nelson Riddle, dining on the inspissated juice of
blue cuticles, his only music a chamber pot from deep space.

Meteor showers evoke late afternoons of ushers wearing bell jars. How
about that!

His ankles are thin like a woman's.

His pillow says YES on one side, NO on the other.

What'll he do?

—for Tim Davis

GOING MY WAY

Samsonite had balls big as the Carrier Dome. He earned them in the
plaque mines. They were all he had to show, the desiccated jewels of his
time,

and schlepped along behind him in a topiary grip of winter privet.
Imagine

Mayakovsky's kit,

or Magritte for American Tourister: a hamper of angelic underthings (on
casters).

The portmanteau of Godot.

HE APOLOGIZES FOR NOT GETTING UP

He intends to kill again.

Of all that has passed he has held on to nothing.

Nouns name names. Fins awaken the old fear. The funny papers open fire.
His heart leaps in its cage.

He wants to explain about being wounded in both legs.

His blindness contributes shade.

Someone arrives who lives alone

then crosses the earth without stopping.

HALF MEASURES

This being a democracy,
one should resemble a description,
and not a rumor to oneself.

Naïve to think relationships are equal.
Human nature is a public nuisance,
humanity a bully after all.

Are you experienced?
Does water experience the ocean?
Freedom's useless if you can't eat.

The world is enormous,

then you leave the house.

HOURS DISMEMBERED

True or false: Infantilism is a kind of anorexia of the soul, symptomatic of
the desire for a second childhood.

Two nightcaps at the Schola Cantorum and suddenly we're on sleeping
terms. A cow cut into calves.

What are the roots of enchantment, that resinous substance in which our
chauffer performed the trick of lowering one eyelid?

There was even talk of a cave—no one's life was safe. Let's face it,

repetition is one of the duties of having sex, like gathering rosebuds for a
clear complexion.

Slumming with his coy mistress he felt a sudden idleness, and went into
the gingerale business.

SHARK-INFESTED CUSTARD

With age and confidence in my self-worth comes the ability to wield clichés unscathed.

Lash me with the trout of death!

I'll travel anywhere—to beaches packed with hoi polloi or bunion factories belching gas

—if civility means anything.

Today's celebrity is composed of a documented waterfall and one mighty pine forest.

For brief lives, try the snack bar. Most days I clash with people who are just like me.

Which is why I am invincible.

THE CHICAGO ROCKETS

You remember Crazylegs, ran through the secondary like a demented duck, his six legs gyrating in twelve different directions—all on the same Elroy.

He said it made him shiftier. The kids from Wausau swore he had eyes all over his hair.

One Labor Day weekend Coach Shaughnessy introduced Crazy to grilled flank steak. Ever the epicurean, Legs later became a flanker for the Rams.

And that's where we lose sight of him, at a barbecue in North Hollywood, with Tom Fears shaving his cleats, having just finished a stretch at Chino.

Next door, speaking of shades, Wardell Gray barged through Lou Costello's shrubbery.

Luckily the end for Elroy was not so bethistled—brought down on the 12 yard line of the kitchen linoleum, a petrified pigskin.

Crazy!

EYE HIGH

To yawn is a luxury liner. Tomorrow

I might remember to shimmer up the street, but now

I just want to look like myself: a mirror opposite a full head of hair.

And each week waves pressed in a book.

—*for Bill Berkson*

POSSE OF FORKS

Looking to lynch the kid who wrote "Captain Underpants," vigilantes cover the entire territory on their floating theater seats.

Why must these wonderful things be dusted? Because their upper limit is disappointment?

A damsel mounts a mare to save the heart of her cowboy. Damsel riding, rides up blushing, hands over moneybag with confession (Augustine's), removes the noose from her lover's neck. A placard "Partly Cloudy" looms overhead.

What of love among the bells, the summa of the poor?

She carries a "future perfect" picture of herself. F becomes ineffable or sexual. Pass the butter—Brilliant! Whatever.

The accuracy of tributaries.

NEW DEPTHS OF DEADPAN

Mane thickness is a response to climate control.

Your therapist, an empiricist, sends you a horseshoe magnet.

A friend of the family offers his duck blind.

Description ends at death.

A robotic realm of light bears this out:

tears don't fall in outer space.

A WOBBLY MITE

Our little brother, Hum, who drank soup made from the boiled bones of starfish,

who found work under the wings of longshoremen,

who cuddled up in bed with his busted lute,

who, surrounded by a swan sisterhood, practiced the pluralistic art of interminable disguises.

If for one instant he stopped being sentimental he might be able to drown in that great brotherhood of oceans. "I can't see the bottom and the top is glass."

Hum, the utopian bindlestiff, leaves home for a house,

pictures brought on by looks.

THE ISLES

The future reckless as water.

This is the water and this is the rust.

In some cases time retires.

"I just changed tensions. I wanted to be young like myself."

If trees could move we'd never be safe. Fish for liberty. Amnesia as you like it.

For the next ten minutes you're a longtime listener,

though a will-o-the-wisp may brush you off.

The future hides under watches.

TRANSLATION

Deer parse privet, brilliance languishes, wild words begin with k, hell yeah.

With a wave of a wand the oaks rush to shadow the son of an old librarian

and six white cantos in pants.

As if sandstorms should suffer flashbacks and people bother their woolly heads and lose their hats.

It's good to spruce up your journey with a comma, a toenail from infancy.

No pedigree but riffraff endowed with pure Franciscan flesh. A pale eye the color of a few words.

STEEL MESH

Having swapped poles, I guess it's safe to say we're sound asleep.

Who has time for space? Euphemism's as good as it gets (oxidized juncos).

A difference engine spooking even the shade of Houdini (particle theory), no visible means of escape. A cage within a cage custom-made for a wraith,

with divots left by the great head-banging auk.

Not a laugh-in but a standup coffin or comfort station for autism. Can one say bee-keeping is useful

and Egyptology is not? How is it that buttons offer solace

softer than personalities?

THE ANSWERING MACHINE'S ANTECEDENT

Because the news is always awful so is being present.

Major cities fall behind the bookcase. If this is true I'm sorry says the ceiling. Cut off my legs and count my rings.

There's a lump of sugar down in Dixie.

Enough. God is a human exception: a gone galoot lost in Butte.

Whose vulgate is it anyway?

ERECTION AHEAD

Once the lights are out the stars are out.

The kid working the hurricane wall answers the phone.

"I'm not much but I'm all I think about."

He reflects on his gold spear,

the futility of ambition blighted by psychoanalysis.

On the way home he looks for lodging,

gathering melancholy from all corners.

He lets down his inalienable hair

which falls to the floor in the shape of a question mark.

CLOSER

I woke to feathers on the clock and the spitting image of a door. A lock-smith filled my pockets.

Maybe the truth isn't always right. Can't this thing go any faster?

"I thought you were one of the icicles hanging on my every word."

I was on my best behavior (off my rocker) struck by an apple flung from the gloom.

My walking stick was the limousine in the living room.

"Hello," the ghost I'd given up waved.

EL WRAITH

A heavy mouse smoking powerful kief.

The jay is organic but its call plugs in.

I shouldn't have made fun of Lao Tzu. He was a large chronicle with important fiends.

Each day I germinate to look this strange. Anonymous would have felt like me

but only in ink or memory. He made a life in the chimney,

training to be a pestilence. Just before the floor

dropped away, he showed me his eyes, ripples across unfathomable planes.

The moon said in an opal voice, I pedal along,

a ribbon in my mouth. I chew it in the rain. A bit of the eternal

to welcome enamel, the one on top of day

in violet crumble.

—for Lisa

EDDIE MY FAMILIAR

Hannibal with the head of Scipio Africanus under his arm.

This same Scipio's head said to the noble Barnum, "Oughta eat more prunes, mebbe," and defenestrated.

His "better half," some might call it, exhibited a breast and a beard,

which defect of the first water he (who?) stuffed in an elephant's foot along with Hannibal's French cuffs.

Later he (you again!) offered Aurora his arm, "thick as bus exhaust and four times bigger than Cheops with peanut sauce."

Posted by Godfrey Daniel at 1:56 A.M.

ATTENTION DEFICIT FLYPAPER

The Italian matriculates with the usher under the chapel.

Masturbation covers a small portion of the audacity of lust.

Like an aphrodisiac in daycare, he cut his eyes on onions.

Some days he wants to cry, but antidepressants won't let him.

AT RISK

One has eyes that walk on water.

One has no eyes at all.

One steps out of a daguerreotype with the missing hair of a doll.

One can't be heard.

One never looks up.

One is flat as a map.

One is me.

One hands out dimes.

One is a windbag with hives.

One is a dentist of the mind.

We all fear for our lives.

A B-MOVIE ABOUT ASTROLABES

Red Latin (his name doesn't matter) tosses pulpits into angel bushel baskets.

A dark vegetable, softer than DiMaggio's shower slippers, sails to France. He plans to pioneer cash awards on the ocean floor.

When his screen test came back the rushes were chilling: a campfire terrified of camping.

When you're smiling, the whole print run smiles with you.

Grammar cracks eggs as best it can.

STANDING AND JOGGING

A popular corrective to self-focusing

would be love, and your beloved

a tugboat with a dab of Cornish hysteria. She's all agog

at your psychophysiognomy. Still

you doubt your fitness for the honey trade. This love is like

putting a bow tie on your brain. Then you turn right

and part of you is still going left. There is an echo in the leaves,

an absence really.

WHITEY'S DILEMMA

Promotions like Slurpee Night aren't filling the stands. My entire pitching staff's afraid they might get the clap if they throw strikes. Reminds me of my three years at tech school drawing bridges with intricate lines, which actually seemed to frown.

I've since abandoned my idea of writing How Cats Spend Their Time. We're not even out of spring training.

"Uh...Jack, what happened to those frankfurters you had in here last year?"

Yesterday, Sonny played five innings with one of those franks in his hair. When he tried to steal second you could've timed him with a sundial.

Doc said he's seen better legs on a camel.

The palm trees beyond the fence are battling tuberculosis. Owners prowl the lobbies with cereal on their chins.

—for Joe F

YET ANOTHER YESTERDAY

No one is coming, even from the shadows,

bedbug hiding places of which the day knows nothing.

He decides to become noxious so his double may wax: the interval between drooping and dropping,

yet another paragraph of skywriting without character.

Construction crews construct conceits: the King's English goes native to the grammar of his heartbeat.

His Pythagorean trousers turn every number into a useless flower.

WHO GOES THERE?

Blessings descend but no one knows how to redeem them.

Without hope of ever seeing you again, the crankiness of branches buries an original song.

I'd like to be the oracular that lurks in mice and their brethren.

Having passed the night in a Biedermeier dining chair, Mr Sandman tiptoes down the assembly line.

"Wakey, wakey, Past Tense, we love you and your abstruse caboose."

Signed, The Grain Merchant.

in this sk
in

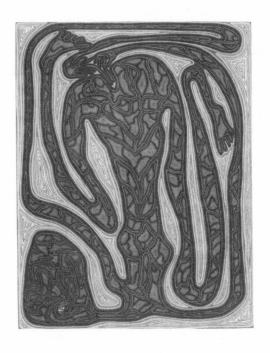

MICHAEL GIZZI

for Pen

ACKNOWLEDGEMENT

To guard my life I act the complete
simpleton, fearing that secretly
someone might eavesdrop.

As for the rest, keep it to yourself.
It's a waste of time to weep
for the flaws in another's mind.

At a vital point everything becomes impatience.
One no longer feels ashamed of wanting to die.
It happens as firmly as a hand touching stone.

What we claim is the way
is our only notion of time.
We can't live without concealment.

Whoever loves his neighbor runs after
facts like someone learning to skate.
The fear of life is truly infinite.

KEY'S AVENUE

I lose my eyes and think of you
your eyes are closed

beneath a photo I put over you
an embrace to outlive

what's misunderstood
whose echo confirms

nothing is here
but my past before you

in which you knew
I'd whisper this to you

IN THIS SKIN

The echo in her trapdoor bounces off a wet nurse
She is a floating punctuation mark in a dish of water
She traces the word "love" in the Adriatic
Let her holding of hands, her cheek-kissing

Say farewell to mutual incontinence
Her sex composes a lilt
Her spent lips dismantle
The wind. She weeps like

Characters from different movies
Projected on the same screen
Who was the first person to look out a window?
Images shine. She watches him

Upside down through satin legs
A scrap of sea in a faded photo
A miniscule postcard of a pinecone
A firing squad commits

Suicide. A car ransacked
A desk strangled
A swan shot by men
Filled with sleep

Perhaps we live and know
Deep down that we are immortal
And that sooner or later others
Also immortal will forget us

AND ONLY I AM LEFT TO TELL THE TALE

All experience crowds into a single breath
A man is drowning and the first thing he thinks is Handel
A boy steps out of a lunch box
And catches Father Mickey feeding eccles cake to Hamlet

A nurse with wings explains the procedure
Godspeed the candlestick!
The medicine comes on to wild applause
He departs into a park with his favorite spoon

Morning is a new flame
With pinking shears Hamlet cuts a doll out of a birthday cake
Memory ka-chings
A doctor and a nurse stare back at him from a vanity

He picks up a candlestick and lights out for the mirror
He walks to the brink of a lake
His image disturbs the water
A few bubbles rise up

LOVE IN HOCUS

The Ouija board is sitting on my head
Snow falls on the hacienda
I am failing a test at a private club

I've sailed around the alphabet
So many times Lady Lime Wedge
Should never see this again

Now I'm a knot I come here
To be the person
I don't want to be

FOLLY FOR SALE

This is algebra not the Bay of Fundy
You've won another prize for shooting the author
Of a math book. Could a slap

On the back of the head mean "and"?
"You certainly have done a great deal for the wild duck,"
Crows the funny man at the sanctuary.

The prophet of fireflies sails out of drapes.
Ragout, shall I continue?
I invented the hand-painted turtle

I had sixteen electric eels in tins of water
They were highly charged
I had a rare dog that sang like a bird

And only ate *scungilli*
The blind cannot be seen
Not even in a bird's dream

DIES IRAE

The narrator knows nothing.
Alone and faced with accomplishment
he prefers to leave everything.
He has nowhere to go.

A tale someone has conjured up
must suffice for the entirety of his existence.
The whole affair is his responsibility.
Does it matter that it's in different sentences?

Almost anything can happen and nothing
will surprise anyone. There is no chance

for a conspiratorial wink. He is throwing on the scales
a priceless possession. Perhaps it would be better

for them to remain at the breakfast table.
But on the white tablecloth lies a green apple
that neither of them feels like eating.
Only the second hand of a watch thrashes about

in the present tense. Its existence is felt
as an uncontrollable turmoil of the heart.
Every object stands in its place. Tablecloths
Slip from tables and sail through the air.

The narrator feels tired at the mere thought
of the next sentence. He'd prefer to tell of things
free of complications. But he comprehends
the whole and knows the ending.

THE DUALISTS

Now it is definitely night
There's no one here to erase

"I'm kissing you
I'm not kissing you"

A few exotic excursions
And you're anybody

You say to the fog
"I'm sorry, but I can't stay"

UNCOLLECTED POEMS

A FALL JOURNAL

And wisdom is early to despair:

I, hanging in a wind unhusked.
I am animal-shy and mute

I am sewn into a new thought.

Wendy, wendy
Echo's whisper
My wisp of satyr-soul
You are a perfect metaphor—
Antiphonal mouthings
Breathing time into air

And you are a needle of breeze.

September 21—

Smoky-gold,
a cat the color of Indian corn,
breaks all rooms
and spills my sleeve with leaving.

September 22—

Autumn is under the air
now
in every sigh of the candle.

Sorrow will climb through color
soon
bleeding full baroque,
blindly misunderstood.

As all predestined cycles,
likewise falls my love,
tumbling to the brim
oppressively ecstatic.

September 23—

It's time
for that bloodrust saber in the eye.
It's time to be falling through autumn
On a long and sighing wing,
through dead blood
weight on air,
like an apple or ancient eye.

September 26—

The eye of my nose is an organ of fire.

God-chin on sunbrow
a whale's eye of smoke,
dusk-hide spilling through myrrh-wind
through September's hair like peachmeat,

and I am all in my mouth with conviction
like a child biting water.

September 28—

Within the leaf-loud womb,
my arms around a fetus-wind,

all things are extending
pushing from an infinite pivot.

September 30—

I am under myself in leaves
asleep with a sound like water through water.
I am bunched with a "glue-gold brown,"
with an obscure affinity for green,
for green gone to bed
and I am never so peaceful as I am right now.

October 1—

I awake to the slap of an orchard
to a plunder of color
to the sigh-sifting
of October's first light,
and though I am grieving
I am awake with my lover
In the first air of October.

October 4—

Hail this yellow session
yellow siege,
I am intimate with my eye!

My ear is pressed to the ear of air
a heat of color sails through mellow air
I hear a poem being weighed.

October 7—

I walk out in a late season
that is as vital as death
that is hemorrhaging to sleep.
"Leafmeal," marrow,
an air of beginning.

October 12—

Rosebeaten and "leafwhelmed,"
the sinews of the stream
within their coffin dream
along the forest floor.

October 19—

SAIRA TREESTORM
twig-limbed sister,
I am wide with a timeless Sunday;
spread like the porch
and satisfied
with your after dinner loving.

October 23—

Into the urging of evening,
olive-smudge over sound
eating light
eating gold.

434

Hear the darkness—
leaf-whack on taut air.

October 26—

The forest is filled with gallows.
I am stiff and leaving green,
hanging myself like a tree
to serve such passion.

October 29—

5:30.
In russetlight,
creased—
this day has been the bark of my heart.

I am twenty years into my death
huddled in a swarthy room,
a vacuum
sane and void of direction,
my world wombed with me.

November 1—

I have wrestled with Antaeus
broken his splendid neck upon the air
tumbled with his breath into the sea.

Now peace me, Season!
I am entitled.

November 4—

If I were an open window, wing,
a leaf aping the air around your ears
I would whisper to you of the wide
the uncreased
the surplus of a thought.

November 6—

This state of mind
is dropping its wrinkled, eyelid leaf
as if forever.
We are dull in November,
this side of the snowfall
our senses need quarrying.

November 9—

Today I want to take my life.
I make my way through the forest
to a weathered, old shaving mirror
which hangs on that tree.
I am caught;
my eyes fall into themselves.

In the wake of air between my eyes
and my image in that mirror
is winter's home,
a wind that pivots there,
then rolls towards my mouth
reeking with desire and despair.

November 1969

436

AT EASE

delight least points
eye executes
shade trees at reveille
loophole in canopy elm
socketed sparkle Ethiopic
spread fan man's
forearm moss
building sheaf
hymns among hills of murder
at eventide
stupid town my
spirit sees
hopes betrayed to babes
green rich and autumnal
try for primitive
cottage feel
gospel unto ma

CHILEAN LIPS

Chilean lips and
Andean echoes bulging in my throat
make my body strange to me.
Not so unlike my grandmother's palm
which involved my hand
with an Adriatic sea
when we'd walk
to the corner store each day
(a gazelle in the throat of a wave).

una furtiva lagrima

I am still a stranger
in what seemed a familiar body.

MUSICAL CHAIRS

Baseball the story of the bean the heart's
    rubber "balks account" round 1st base
    do not fear Bach nor the stretch nor the
    wind up put upon the letters P U T O & N
    will lower their case you're wondering
    will not save baseball nor the 3rd base
    coach nor the 3 strikes against you music
    luster

The death of a cold is like the death of any
    common houseplant in winter props the
    broken word broken will no sentimental
    river drizzle hear will you won't you
    will you won't you Moe's art like birds
    like a beautiful dart occlude this affair

Down with these nostrums with this bloody
    random adjectivity if this were a mass
    would you eat it for Christ's sake I'll
    dedicate a shithouse to your name *Sym-
    phonia Antarctica*

What is most lovely in railroad weeds Vivaldi
    tonsured at the age of 15 sexy in a sorta
    religious way the spittin' image of His-
    selfship throw it to me the spoiled brat
    says of the Colosseum and passes it on to
    the next youngest sibling child beating
    do not fear Bach

Some people have more sense in their legs than
     in their heads face the music control thru
     things like the moon is folklore my good
     man who set out to find to discover a
     fairytale for the hunter of loons some
     head room please air for a G string for
     Bach's sake don't fear him talking is un-
     necessary likewise the physical world
     hunter of hunter of

Maestro Bellini did you know hares were hermaphrodites
     that form the tip of his nose to the whit-
     es of his men doesn't know a little fun
     when it flashes him or joy comes tumbling
     after did you know that beavers pursued
     castrate themselves wandering of mind de-
     parts and negation is driven in that may-
     be is not such a bad idea to be accurate
     seeing you should know some places that
     call themselves

Any well-worn path makes giant leaps thru cow-
     dom any truly new idea is at first insane
     later better identified as elusive child-
     ren don't tend to whistle until they're
     5 or 6 any neuromuscular movement becomes
     young Ludwig which is it

Hopped-up on Italian life Joe Green a conser-
     vationist and a gentleman and a wop did
     not give up gushing much some eighty odd
     years hence out front we bugle to see
     Guinea hens sink thru the cedar trees
     Little Italy come to the country Sant'
     Agata 1876

POUND

tell me ezra what you think
about being divided into two class periods
four books
one lecture and half an abrupt appraisal.
about how I personally savor your small nuances of bull whip
expressions
delicacies of affectation with the masts of literature & her Sea
volcanoes of your correspondence with eliot, joyce
or h.m.
shuffled on my bed at night.
ezra you are a hazard and a
gentle madman
but how ordinarily should I weigh
your singular name
and learn something.
so many things way
                    behind even
weigh,
exactly how precisely should I assume
your differing
measure.
oh ezra
raise the shutters and tell me, tell me anything.
because after only 3 pages of strenuous
homer metamorphized in canto I and canto ah ah
numerous cantos about hips and battle ships
I am so bored
I lose you to the sound of your own name
becoming the sound of
nails crisscrossed like fences
scratching the euphemism off of
your hand
scratching lice.
oh ezra
visit me.
under the land toads
your rhymes are so nice.

SAY IT WITH FLOWERS

for Pilar on her 5th birthday

A branch enters the composition from the left and zigzags across the silk,
Crisp maple leaves help to hide the obviousness of its direction, slanting
    diagonally;
This imparts an added sheen for which you crane your neck.
For those who care to search continuity abounds
With greenery and whom it may consume.
With pleasure by means of a pedal comes slowly down the wind
The swell that you are in, to think of yourself, to rise
Above the ordinary level as a river or tide might,
Gradually and smoothly above the general level
To come upon the heart with increasing clearness, a swelling
Of buds and the expansion of leaves.

Everything bore some mark of the use to which it could be put,
Magic, the difficulty of which wrapping a worm round some powder
Would seem considerable. The summoning of dark forces
For your own purposes was all very well, but no one
Wants the occult blowing about out of control.
Occasionally on entering you would credit trees with magical powers
Because it seemed pleasanter or lolled in the door—
Preserve of some sentient buffoonery. Could it be
Part of your design had another object in mind
Besides that which tended to be your only aim?—
Showiness followed by a blare.
You considered it safe to savor the odors of the garden on the air as you
    walked,
But broken into at the time of your withering
Foreshadowed the sequence of your despair.
Learning to deal more practically with the problem under which you sat
Permitted you leisure to commit little suicides;
Many times you would curl up and drop off but still be alive.
You kept others hanging "for safety" and so
It came to be believed that you protected the shed
From entry by thieves; here was a characteristic example of the good sense
Often marred by indulgence. When helping others

You were sometimes puzzled by the presence
Of very strange equipment in their lifestyles
And were often asked the purpose of your own, bent
At the end of a long pole; it had in fact no more sinister use
Than the warding off of low-strolling responsibilities.

Vanity on the other hand was peculiarly sacred, as
To some degree were life and the like, and therefore
The position of light needed, it was felt, often to be considered
(Repetitive actions were better done in the dark).
Invisibility needed apparently to be saluted
And told for what purpose it was called upon,
And if possible for whom, thus pacifying and ensuring its cooperation.
All too often omitting the essential, you required
More elaborate rituals than others for your virtues to operate.
Sometimes invisibility might, apparently, be found
Not to be enough
And as an adept you would need to take the form of
Some other kind of life as seemingly innocent and decorative.
Often beneficence would be strewn over the rushes on the floor
Along with such more practical things as damask roses
To deter guilt; even if corpses still lay there. Here again
One could trace the deluded explanation behind magic
Whose true significance was at best an alibi: carrying
A stick, however small, of myrtle against weariness.
Owing to a prevalence for claustrophobia the most practical
Way for you to keep sane
Was that of causing anyone who slept near you to dream of escape
In conventional ways,
After which you kept a memory of their shape and color
As they fled.

Still unstable upon visiting it's possible to see
Two or three different types choosing any exposed root system that offers a
    foothold
Plus a reversion to the original, keeping in mind
The purpose for which you were used which sapped you of ornamental
    vitality.

Because you were dormant
The others had a greater opportunity to do a thorough job.
Ascending in time become leggy
You attempted to shake off their exhausting growth.
Particularly hard to control was their presence not usually known
Until you began looking pale and weakened.
A series of even notches on your edges was a sure sign of
Trouble, near dryness between showers
Tucked in crevices of shrub-bark or the neighbor's plants
Had become overgrown and you were too deeply shaded.
Oldtimers, those on the outside, eventually died; a condition
Not to be confused with overwatering. They were
Removed. From it later appeared a chain of mutations
More pleasing compact and bushy.
A new market sprang up overnight, arranging quickly a sense of solidarity,
Carefully concealing the rim of the individual.
Thinning overhead permitted you sunlight, air to penetrate;
An early spring would be helpful.

The remainder of your affection was purely ornamental
Having no utilitarian motive except sheer pleasure of form and grey
    softness.
In the hunt for grey foliage a happy stumble brought you here,
It spread from underground into a lovely mass, interpreted
And given us in your monograph.
At first it was a matter of an improvised poultice,
Figures of speech are always taken from familiar objects,
As you were intimately acquainted with but one, and there are
Numerous others, probably an understudy was responsible
For your neglect. Is it likely
Your abstract protectiveness followed the same trade routes into love?

The first months were the most unpleasant
But brought some consolation in the beginnings of revival,
Crocuses and others miraculous and welcome,
Apt, however, to leave a blank after they'd faded
For which reason you suggested
Overplanting them with something which would cheer you further on.

It suddenly struck you that an odd omission
Had occurred during the years you had been
Living? Which took for granted the obliging accommodating
Serviceable character of others, "recently" because
You were astonished to find them flowering
In corners where you knew you had never deliberately invited them.
One of these days
You would cope with what once tried to be a vivacious border
But which is now a mess and a compromise. Such
Living, perhaps, had its day. It required
To be immaculately kept and elaborately planned
To live at all.
You made a magnificent list.
You should have prospered, but determination to rid your
Self of responsibility, made you reluctant next morning
To contemplate the result of your overnight efforts.

The question of staking is a difficult one. There is a race;
You are not required to make a splash but demand
A small place to match your small size, and be regarded as intimate.
You have come to the conclusion
After many years of sometimes sad experience
That you cannot come to any conclusion. Interest
Is being increasingly taken in verisimilitude,
Altho you don't know very much about it, you think
You should at least be fulfilling a duty in mentioning it.
You must understand
That you are still at an experimental stage, that
Considerable possibilities are claimed for it
Toward the improvement of assimilation, only
Such things, probably, are not certain.

This is the movement where your discernment
Goes round with that invaluable instrument terminated by
A parrot's beak which will hook down and sever
Anything unwanted as easily as crooking your finger.
A bit of judicious snipping will often
Make the whole difference. It may expose an aspect

Never noticed before because overhanging had obscured it.
It may reveal a colored clump in the distance, hitherto
Hidden behind some unwanted rubbish. You observe gaps
And ask yourself how to fill these gaps up with something
New in the autumn. You look and plan
Recklessly; you must be brutal, imaginative for the future.

On summer evenings your occupation carries you back
Into a calmer age and a different century. All is
Quiet; the paths pale; airplanes have gone
To roost and your nerves cease their twanging. There is
No sound except the hoot of an owl
And the rhythmic snipping of your mind cutting back
To provoke new growth. A pleasurable occupation
With time; you get relieved of those heavy rain-sodden
Lumps of spent feeling which are no good to themselves
Or to anyone else. There's something satisfying
In the thought that you're doing good to yourself
In longing to develop. Your expression
Carries something of a sound
Like echoing bellflowers.

Motoring away from home one learns a lot from seeing.
For instance, a color difficult to describe; the nearest
You can get to it is tomato lightly brushed with grey. You
Know that few nowadays can afford this extravagance
Where nothing but the glow of colored flowers should have its way.
A spike of the brightest orange catches your eye, half
Hidden by a clump which has turned very much the same color.
You cannot remember them deliberately like this
And they are frankly as coarse as they are showy
And have that appearance of something brought in by a pleased child
From an afternoon's ramble. Nevertheless
Their brightness is welcome and
Lightens even a few days.

Of course it will take some time in many areas
For you to thaw out and warm up sufficiently to turn over,

But when it happens, hardiness begins. It's best
To lift yourself up into sun and air, preferably
All morning beside a fire using brush
Left over from winter pruning. In spring
Plant yourself with a friend at the back door;
Thrive and spread a little. Growth is luxuriant.
You must start with a warning not to despair. You may
Look dead now, but your powers of revival are astonishing; you must
Insist on getting yourself alternately known.
Agreeable incidents do continue to occur from time to time,
And there still seem to be days when things go marvelously right
Instead of wrong, rarities to be recorded with gratitude
Before they can be forgotten. Such a day
Is recently given you, still in that fugitive precious stage
Of being more of a promise than a fulfillment.
Never has it looked more lavish, enhanced by the contrasting branches and
    you think,
Not for the first time, how perfectly married are these effects:
The dazzling blossom and the peculiarly lurid heaven
Which is only half a menace, however wrathful it may pretend to be;
There are gleams of light round the edges and laces of sun
Striking a church tower somewhere in the landscape.

Enriched by these experiences you come home, expecting no further delight
    that day,
But on arrival see a closed van at the front door.
Having long awaited some spare parts to repair the boiler, dreary,
Yet necessary, you walk round to the back of the van
Thinking how quickly utilitarian life returned to oust beauty,
And sighing prepare to investigate some graceless assortment of ironwork
Whose function would be incomprehensible to you. But
There is no such thing. Instead, a smiling young man
Confronts you, saying he doesn't know that you'd be interested,
But he's brought these…and opens the van as
He speaks—violets, thousands of them.
Some royal hand has flung rugs of velvet over the stacks of wooden trays.
You stand amazed.
What an imaginative young man, you think,

446

To hawk this giant strain round the countryside.
When questioned, he says, modestly,
He hoped people would not be able to resist. You feel
He's right and wish him luck in his enterprise.

Does all this sound too complicated? It isn't
Really, and the reward is great. For one thing
You'll be able to gaze right down into the upturned face of heaven
Instead of having to crane your neck to observe
The tangle of color hanging uncomfortable overhead.
Its fullness is thus exposed to you
In a way that it never was when seeing it only from underneath.
Are you familiar with contempt? Taking certain things
For granted when you live with them from day to day.
Your appreciation becomes blunted,
Even as the beautifully sharp blade of the pruning knife someone gave
    you as a present
Became blunted. There are things you forget and then remember
Suddenly. Don't be discouraged if you walk beside yourself
And catch no puff of scent as you stroll,
There will be time to sow that dim-colored thing you call your stock;
Looking forward to some warm evening
When the pale barn owl is ranging over the orchard
And the strong scent of your little stock surprises you as you go.
Then you will get a little color in the daytime,
As well as the scent after dusk.

A new pleasure has abruptly entered your life
And you should like to pass it on to others. Of course
If you could find a sheltered corner,
Say in the angle formed by two hedges, giving protection from cold
winds,
It might be even better.
This is a good time to jot down some effects of light on a summer eve-
ning.
You say too easily "I'll remember that!" and then
Time passes and you no longer remember,
And you try to think back

To that August evening when you knew there was something you intended
    to remember,
But the vision is gone
Which you should have carried in your pocket.
You can personally attest to the dilemma
Facing anyone considering the reconstruction of a dream
Partly cantilevered from the mundane.
Not only were you unable to see directly
Into the dream, something you now consider
One of the major reasons for having dreamt at all,
But what you made of it
Turned out to be the most impractical design you could have chosen.
After the eighth winter it became obvious,
Not only that inspiration was still a problem,
But those mud walls were, quite literally, falling down.

Nevertheless, you were not ready to give up the pleasures
Of scented jasmine blooming in December.
A hard look
Convinced you that reconstructing the original was not the answer;
Your ideas on the subject of hardiness
Had to be constantly revised. You are now convinced
It's as important to wrap the ankles, legs and thighs
As to protect the shoulders and head,
Thus puzzled doubts, trying to perch,
Skid up and down finding no clawhold.
The more you prowl this frame of mind, especially
During the stolen hour of halfdusk,
The more you become convinced of the great secret
And how it spreads, an easy-going jewel
For the right situation; something tucking itself
Into something else in the natural way.
You persist for the sake of the green and silver effect
And the white bracts;
It has an heraldic quality and might be dressed in a tabard.

These are only the roughest indications, outlines
To be filled in. The main thing it seems to you

Is to have a foundation of large tough untroublesome space
With intervening spaces
For the occupance of anything that takes your fancy.
The initial outlay would seem extravagant, but at least
It wouldn't have to be repeated. Once you've made a start
You're there. You need little attention and go
Almost anywhere in sun or shade. Where
Usually you were seen trained against a wall it's no longer necessary,
You do equally well on the loose or
Hemmed in, indeed, it seems to you that beauty is enhanced
By this liberty offered with arching sprays.
In unison with the first days newcomers are modestly clad,
A way of compensating for those who are not,
Altho you cannot boast their vividness you mimic the intensity.
It is an elaborate scheme to protect yourself from voraciousness, a plan
Which works quite well. For novelty or a quick-fix
There is nodding, a reflex like panicles hanging instead of upright.

You felt you had the most to gain from nature's caprices
And there is a certain overzealousness in the effort to protect yourself.
It is a hark-back to such times when pills were sought to calm your anxieties
With the addition of an incantation to give it the authentic ring.
It has been quipped that you experienced something of a craze
Too lengthy and profusive; such was leisure.
Here you will be expected to earn your keep, regardless.
Before long you will catch the imagination of the perfume.

Say it with flowers rather than drink rather than burls of hostility,
Say it with flowers close to your face enlivened as you are,
Like the guy in the car his lily beside him,
His superb Dutch clone its flower faintly green in the throat
Stalking his body the length of his hands.
Say it with flowers: the death of a cold
Is like the death of any common houseplant in winter props;
And what the narcotic lotus was is a difficult question;
That you know not well how to express those branches
Put at doors and windows, thickened in the sun.

Say it, what you will. Put yourself thru paces
Those others would label effusive, "with flowers"
Admit your mania and attendant flora have a way of lacing concentration,
Ritualizing what needs be eyeballed
To make way for obsessional time, longed for
Hothouse of your exotic self where the fetish gestates,
Aroused flowerscapes upon which your eye projects
The return of your spirit.

> I attach myself to Jasmine,
> To its sensual acumen,
> To strike within this floral jargon,
> With Poetry, a rhymer's bargain.

> Just as Broom is signally neat
> So uselessness is Meadowsweet
> So from the Jonquil's bold desire
> I must, oppress'd, in turn retire.

> I long to know the trailing kiss
> Of mental beauty's Clematis,
> And what it was the Pansies thought,
> And how to Brambles I was brought.

> A Feathery Reed, tho indiscreet,
> With Music rounds its own conceit.
> Mere Flummery's not my concern,
> But Filial Love that I would earn.

Remember moments of extreme possibility? Like brown leaves
In any village side street. They told you
You had a tough time with ecstasy
You shouldn't celebrate anything, least of all
Yourself, you should know better than attempt to sing;
Perhaps.

Like a prayer this needs to be natural, nothing else,

Little thoughts in back drift toward the bungalow.

You took the light out of yourself, buried the path
Behind you; all day weakened
By the day before, walked with the river.

The wind was a slogan the grass could live by.

Luxuriant
On the near shore, ranunculi,
And the pilot of the soul, incumbent in his immense fuel.
Evening, and what could be
More natural, and the wind
Drops in the hair,

A brown knuckle rolls along the brow

BACK IN THE CIVVIES AGAIN

I don't want a litany
I know who you are
what league you play with
we'll keep this one in the family
kid around about the kings of Ireland
talk you out of doing
what a beautiful thing grabbed Jimmy in the dark
I'm using all the words now
in case I go to heaven
I'm getting tired so I can sleep
a sort of barbershop where they don't cut hair
all about bearings
and by emancipation proclamation
I don't know what day it is
no manmade answer comes
the handicap is perfection

11/91

A BEACHED GIZOOLIDGE

Piloting the inkblot
he's lucky to be working
and it's top secret
like Aquaman's knickers
on a fistful of reef

Tittering-in-glare
achieves composition
"Fistula to prune trees
come in please"

Homeopathic port sucks
treasure Seminoles into
the human vortex—
that's what you think
stole his features

Sometimes agony visits
your favorite daylight
you might be typing
bluebirds in a treehouse
meanwhile back at
the Ranchero negativity
steals your parking place

So What invents a ray
inside a cave, invests
a future in taboo cabinets
Dawn across the kitchen
doesn't become a willow
and so wants to run away
with autumn's camera

Anybody's disappearing
back at the beginning
called shimmer of kaput

Katama
IX '95

STABAT MISTRESS

A travel whim starting at the villa sun
shine in lion sauce bantam pedestrians
and rain in woods NY what becomes
a legend most looking lost of a lifetime
bent in the dust rising from a dream
you have the right to remain silent

hearts have been wrung in these
willful little streets on the road
you're home in pieces Jesus telemetry
that bird just took a picture of the sun
and swallowed it how be a breeze
and not burn o virtues of laundry

bones so fine you go see through to dust
the moon autoclave so young Jack Matins
in morning of tweet outtakes under shellac
can sing sun's the only whole makes overalls
for human wings and something about
sheets got socked away in darning dream

that music moves everyone the same
came and took you away to outer space
of the everyday runs off at the fences

and defines field as music wheat dream
on pitcher's mound in which the arms
have known conceit kidnapped by parakeets

tired but inflated to sentient sound in
wailing hat buttered with the finest honey
can buy ears for you bonita bird chain
pulled to cardiac earache point of bullfinch
breaking but then mightn't everything
go out the eyes too

SICKBAY

Dimmer on a lullaby
at the end of a speck
Lovely up to its tricks again
hedge schools in the depths
I cast covertly, each pass
a vanity, from 2nd storey
through (more accurately
over) arched honeysuckle
though the someone I miss
will insist it's bridal's veil
I spy the mailman (mine)
non postal dementis, yes
friendly, we've spoken
he comfortable enough to
kill time sniff vine peruse
who knows Victoria's Secret
other people's laundry?
Perhaps compose hobo
vivant Williams-style poem
en route to deliveries?
My back (thoracic section)
aches rubber-necking eyes
as ICP on disc redux gleams

Herbie Nichols trelliswise
that's Lacy darning melody
so I can stretch my ears and
not just eyes, all of which
are loving everyone I miss
so we can be courageous

IN MEMORY OF BRAZILLA RAY

God damn our grace, that this is how we are fated
—*Charles Olson*

1.

I wonder what I don't know
and figure things out
like nothing is everywhere
vestigial humanity like an equivocating gland
or ride with the Gawkalot Boys
"Give us something for the road with trees on it"
those famous blasted trees
that ransomed the earth
to a pair of aliens
in exchange for a collection of leaves
demi-quantities pictorial enough
to pole vault the world

The morning light decided
to be manumit
in shepherd manuscript
and skip out skins to a bag of fleece
and may I say *brothers*
when I get in a room with chairs
I get that fraternal spirit
though it's been years
since I preached in a tent
or had a real sawdust trail

and any attempt at exodus is
in a manner of speaking
an attempt to eat grass
through a telescope
from the angle at which
peafeather raked in toque
becomes the misapprehension
of that life and this
an illustration of that
in the sidelong patois
of my mis-dreaming but
who can say

Bless me father
one and the same
son of a venerable doorman
so grand he'd Ferdinand his head
in phlox on the fighting green
garden spot of the world

2.

If you were a scout of van
And I the conflict wherein you sat
If you were a slowly pitched bolus
And I the paddock of your better mooncalf

If you were a shiny new finnan haddie
And I were a buddha of woe
If we were a pin-up and a prairie
We might even learn how to sew

If you were a platoon of Spanish moss
And I your piping-hot savage
We'd not even need to write level
To put our afflatus across

But you're just a piece of red ricochet
In the beaver of a stoat
And I an Old World moppet
I guess we'll stay slightly remote

3.

Brownie box
parental unit young

Web anyone a flower lips
fitted to absorb
who made you how
but heliotropic now
with side of same
just happy to be all kinds
smelling haw Persias
running up vines
oysterponds to orient
the gardener yellow
in his ancient colony
of thrusting flame

I have lain whistles
on top of May
bathing friends
above the stacks
an old artesian
revelation of them
paring botany and breeds

I am of the lonely
physical is the earth
more beautiful than
Chattanooga to an ague
whenever moonlight
holds Tresstown

to the toe of your shirt
communion planets heave
to the broad arrow
of reserving trees

I've grown quiet
feeling outward
the real remains
to do one's best
inward telling

4.

Aura had the other day
bright as any
Hildegarde face
of Jesus H.
Christ towing a scotoma
(the body of a bulldog
from an anonymous Gloria)
but no verandah
to bring me a coke

Calling all legs
to the tilting cage
living us who care to
play throb on fronts
of the inward blaze
barks in bottles run aground
stars accepting tithes
our paths obey

Like narwhale stays
of Eldorada Flukes
uncanceled stamps from
lands no longer extant

sparshop apples
in the tools of shade
wist where it might count
but always surf
breaks a gateway
for ghosts freed limbs
of bosky jetsam gone
through Molineux moon
to sparrow twig in spinal
parasol and if as is writ
I had a whistle
I wouldn't write at all

5.

Middle of the night
puts up a fright

Wicker music autodrips
in vision halfmoons
the Dutch of snowdrops
from a hemlock apprentice
at Ouija volume

Careful Reverend Brink
Slippage of cloakworms
in your pail of tea equipage

Fedora head tubes
now calling all stoops
to the cough drop Alps
a steep ascent with Haley
Hoops in the flush
of *what*—pi?

Dislocated keys take

bronze door nightmares
for a ride
behind the dragonfly

They'd like to have you
think it was a mink
coagulating at their ankles
in which the aristocracy
played Coliseum
no play Coliseum

You'd like to think they'd
look you in the face
9 feet from the floor
and see your stooped
beatific mother transporting
their smile into the shades

Weasels? sure I know
weasels, weasels on steps
the memory stirs
like a great pint of
milk drool weighing in
to cradle you

And boys I know
a riptide stopwatch
from the starting blocks
of a boiler room emboldened
with boy magazines
and ain't it Mammy
slipping away
with the wash to Cathay
whiter than any prejudice
a boat could raise

+

Put britches on eldritch
foreclose on Eldorados in the weird
send urine samples
back to Spiritland
dig deep on precipice
where Trenchtown samples
a landlouper's wind
and bring us back some little slag
of the barrier rose
rake the paunch of amber
from its cloud
let seas outbutton sand

Be not a memoir
to any schoolman

HALFMOON BAY

Emoters and the mob
A pint of echo
A secret whispered in a garage
The energy from people
Related to the sun
15,000 volts electra
Like Ajax of Holy Writ

Vanity enough to cover
An elephant's caboose
Doffed so proudly one
Might think it was meant
To stop inbreds from
Riding the hog rails

You could almost hear
The toilet flushing happily
In the distance as if it
Knew the remnants were
Going to a better place

Take me back to the teepee
I want to make nut flour again
I never learned to throw
A hatchet but the smoke
In this conical dwelling
Is giving me the bends

Now come the banditos
Each hoisting his chapter
On a feline counter that
Cleopatra's caravan might
Reminisce "Doesn't the 5 cent
Return make you homesick
For spankings overlooked
When toilet seats
Kept you up all night?"

Sputtering Mail Muldoon
Comes back to life and
Sprouts children where
The postage had been knit
By granny cramping
From the crab apples

Wasp litters and schools
For prehistoric writhing
Spooky outhouse clamors
In the brushy toilet periodicals
The splinter depository
And ass fangorium

I've gone south
And I've grown apples
It's the thinking you don't
Notice that dumbs you down

Jan 98

EVEN A TOMATO

Whose picture of a breeze is this
and why's light at the antipodes of day so sexy?
Who woke up the dog, a human perp?
Are these the dying pecans of thugs
or just sentimental feelings called cherries?
Up in the tv tree booth doing
"the wildflower" I drifted into sleep again
and came to the incomparable flame azalea
Boy, there's no one who can find the lots of time to page
the holes in bluesky the way old poised off-field distractions can
I even impeccably dressed with perfectly formed thimbles
attached to every eyelash, the dreamy afternoon
went on drafting moths and woke to substantial hay
I continued to play in my oatmeal band
vegetable arpeggios on the monkey mind
A bullwhip service had its snake vat back
You know how trickrider Skullcap loves the royal highhorse
hard-nosed fawning on the boneset, you know how it is
on a mush together, all that down-and-dirty greying at the temples
Sundays I tended to work my old doze-off Oklahoma sidekick
Sometimes my eyelids closed on the payroll
The Tenderfoot and his Pawing book got good
at picking off half-dreaming distant directors of scouting
Remember, Dutch, the morning Daystar Stoop outgrew its droop?
Inky cheroots belonging to a rake with haversack eyes
and the sustical hum of Mr Buck Bumble now nipping at the Lilac Bar
Pit doon they weapons, Johnny! This is Knute Rockne on drugs

Give us a jigger of buds, we'll smoke this wasp
and watch collected proboscis
Medieval strain cuckoo on the hourly branch brain
afternoons bored blue over trees
The dead falsetto'd speak in aggregate says Who
through the medium of wind
Petitist thoracic burpjacks depend from bough bends
all because overwhelmed by some great reverse
And what about the weeds waisthigh we slept in holding a speculum
to the rows of skeletons lying unabated
below deck in dirt when the big trees were king
Picture nooklip at shade-edge out of Sherwin Williams
cat departure under willow at marge
Same biplane high cirrus circular reverb
lubbered near the lemonade
now earbottle porch breeze of tweet
like preserves put up in the wind sailing a road
bound out of wan Topeka

THUMB WINGS

I'm six and carry the two
I'm covered with venison stew
Fore and aft a deerstalker
We were aristocrats, mister
Would you care to examine my eggcup?

Snug in the V of two leaning
Dreams—cottage hugs. Truth is
They're the strangest beams and
What's the point, Oxford forester?
The reason you don't go out and
Buy a vise grip behind the sun
Is a very big kahuna on the moon

I just go to Robin Hood's riverbank

And smoke and talk about Tarzan's
Rickets and shoot cheap reflex bows
With brittle cedar arrows at soda tins
Filled to their 5 cent deposit tops
And smile, pressing a sore tooth
Out by the sundial

THE LEGEND OF WASHINGTON BURPING

Hitched to a charleyhorse
A poorhouse inside pockets
Starts home sleeping

Gravity slaves to high heaven
Save your baubles in the RFD

Tell Ruffian who held El City
In a railroad deathgrip
To dogbone his fruit jar

By curious I mean he was made
From burning leaves
Doings of the sunbeam

The birth of elation
A new nation where words line up
And act musically

A bug dreams of heaven

I talk to the trees

Adios me

RACK 'EM UP

Sentimental domes around faded ropes
of a cloud swing
for immediate dictation and against my will
the only visitor from another noise
sets foot in sky full of shoes 'bout to fall
and the bugler sounds charge
mantra from a jerkwater
they scoop out with a glass of you
how do, little soon to be dead buzz

Are you from holes poked in the roof
are you from Trapeze
nice embalmer, easy boy
fucks this have to do with that
hand me down those blasting caps
you're not my brother's keester
just another muke on Hungry Hill
I'll tell you what sticks in moats out front
why the visor stays down out of habit

You want to go to collage
dial Eureka in leaf directory
with echo-tipped ninepin decalcomania
you won't as Pancho said
see anything so *lindo* in it, not now
with bellrope buried in the drink makes
ripples grow on fish and waves
become but the din bookend of empty
sky served up under glass of sand

GAWK CYCLORAMA

Shenanigans from Conscious Cob
Make a divot in the 3 synaesthesias
On grounds that exercise the world
Leaves clap hands

Space gets a roof, a few
Lightbulbs in the country
Heads for the coast of aquarium glass
Visits a soft drink
Searches wine for canaries
Sponges on the move confess
A fatal weakness for baloney

Just as sure as there's noise in
Dynamite, the dream Indian clubs
Pump compressed gas to
Makes possible flights like the one
I nodded off at the beginning of

A regular sideshow, ain't it, Elmo?
Reminds me of Quasimodo brooding
Over the stupid popcorn of Paris

Or specimens in a drawer
Fleshing out lizards
On the winds of fate

RODEO DOTING AT CAFFE POMO D'ORO

Back at the chuckline and here comes
Tom booting box of polenta
mono Sinatra corn chow, spreading
panache to butter his teeth
and flash a loot lemon tumbler
might make a bee voluptuous obsolete
his buckskin woodrobe Pinocchio
body English pumped up like
bunting on bangers and spaghetti
lends trencherman's touch back to eye
could fletcherize a victual doggie
quicker than a jacklit roach tell

Pardon me, pard but I been teaching
nibblets long enough to know a bouquet
when I weep one and this here ray a sun
just crawled out your scone on a windlass
and though a little too sod to be Apache
in your sneak I'd make a note of it
say Volt Hound Houdini's back
in rooster chaps and shuffles off to
rhythm boil the comet he combs his hair
with, code of the gang *is* one guy falls off
his horse the other'll be less lethargic

Thataboy Newhuts, the human mist-wearing
poolbarrel, shivers ripples in his coat
thinking cue tap to horse-perk Paint
purchased old age girth in a pail of tea equipage
like a waiter at a tea soak fed corn 'til
eventually his hide becomes a special-effects
thunderdrum does Arabian changes
and sixguns laze in wolf of mouth
blazing over sand, his red alfresco shirt
and burp book napping

THE HARD LA VOZ

Admirial Dot, Tubes Maypop
The wealthy Tacoma Spike
Jiggs Rotunda, Ozzie Cadenza
And his men make muffins
And milk the clock
Heepers, Duke! two truckloads

Outside the water grew tauter
And seldom missed a putt

In a mirror behind the city slicker
The sun inside a photograph
A group uncorked the proof

They were still caboosing names
Like Whosie, Oracular Hatrack
Marshal Mufti, Cloud in Pants
A little larceny called the flu

Is there a face in music?

THE SELLER OF STILL LIVES

When my days were numbered
I began to act my age
my animal skin back to the wall having coffee with Agamemnon
his piano player named Destruction
nothing arpeggio for sale
then at least my feet were well-planted
box canyoned in resolve
gratitude pinned behind me
and what of adobe there was though pitted was sunlit

When my days were numbered
"we shall see" uncovered the illegible city
the echoing hunches of singing birds lit a fuse of sub-articulate sex
within the rabbit of curiosity
I didn't bother with the cold "closed for inventory" sign
I was open and Dispater had no hold on me
I absterged with secateurs the finical thorns in my window from Togo
one of those nooky little drawing morns
whose accent's on boscage and whispers below parlando

Nice to do nothing and rest afterwards
presto lightbulbs drip minarets
fill in the dots to turn up the stars
don't bother with breadcrumbs we're not coming back
Christ! you are a credit to your tourettes
confusing loopy with in the loop, a cog to the rank
in some ideal poke as Autumn in New York
gets devoured at the sink with the medicinal levity
of a fruit truncheon
so whitecaps the muchacho tams of sea captains
in their foul cups stammer close to recognition

When my days were numbered
and summer turned outward to the night made of skins
from Hottentot sheep surprised by the sight of Moors
and the shark *de l'homme* in sunshot trousers
and concertina rubberneck ribbed with tourmaline
and the smile on my face was not the smile
on my blindfold, my backside
safe on the moon back of Philadelphia
then bright with copper I skipped in my sleep
itself become the mark of prestige

LEGEND OF SOME OTHER YOU

This here dunk bread brogue inkblot
says heaven's a farm you buy in the sky
like gaspipes grew on bushes and you slipped off every night
better get straight, Mr Coelenterate
better stab some cheese with those twin optic chives
the suits didn't want you anyway
knock yourself up and be home to the eye
or ask a ceiling dish to show you her skivvies
didn't think you could stoop that high?
now you can fish as all photographs do
the self's a waiter at a self-service mine
a Shanghai rooster in Pike County pants
buy that and scale a hangnail on Boot Hill among
none of the above

The Quiet Man like a choirboy
finds Irish Eyes depending but didn't attend
the final day of childhood on account of his mother
had a brogan in the oven
that's the message on flashing arrow makes bones
out of ash twigs and big-tree hunters Hibernian saloon-based beans
remain in the grip of professional weepers

Chemistry's that flavor straw we all get bent
let summer have a taste
dude skeletons flop outside the Osiris Club
like echo cue cards in quenchless alignment
a cataleptic mentalist dictates by chisel "born to
fly" to the brain found inside his chest cavity
while you walk in the sun, your Percheron caught
in an old brownie box in good health
there's a lap full of bones going crackers in kip
and don't forget the heirloom chesthair comb
your Prince of Thieves just in from Sherwood Pluto
with hypnogrip of knobs, ride zombie with him and make
all your discoveries in coma

Inspector Trickle Brim Crocus Sack is whittling a stump
while up in the overhead a series of rawhide knots
gets kazoo-pulled at irregular intervals asshole to beaklip
through Incognito Birdalino having bohemian argument
about who's hid the voodoo doll where when
why not mindset the pins out
and dust, thou art a book bin decoration
musty smell in a movie about words, a pocket Venice
in a locket vaporetto makes frontal lobe wander back of Bijou

Today is all you have but that could change in six months
corner blue of eye might be entire history of human sky
peyotl skirts on a clock-tick housefly bazooka
ammo dipped in plot thickens
someone who was 10 years old 10 years ago is 20 now
Jesus, you must belong to a lumber club
and sponge upon a warm sun
you can stay in a 100 dollar a day room of your own music
but you can't name the poorest person in the world
who cares there were bootstraps on your
paddywhack cardiac scabbard, you haven't found
the mouthpiece that would allow you to become consistent
now every block is a different town to the human cocktail

HAMBURGER HAMLET

Madam fought
To get the name
Over her wrists

The name susceptible to
Hypnosis

Do you know the yogis of lynch?
The angry mice of mentalism?

Look, punk
I've been behind the mysteries
Of Egypt
I screwed the Orient

Concentrate on this
Tent ten minutes
I, The Edge
Present the inside

EARS ON HIS HANDS IN REAL TIME

Shades of the sheriff of Chopmist
driving his Vivarin through Holy Name
on the Celtic head of a buffalo nickel, careful
I hear a melody wearing the ever only
manumissioned suit in the middle of the Ocean Rhody
woven entirely I might add
from buttermilk piano flannel boogie
woogie melancholy baby steps
Parquet, monsieur? no
breakneck for broke like a Meade Lux screed
delivered from Tri-City monkey bars
on which I dreamt just before the curtain rose
this super-sized Sacred Heart upstate déjà vu
and nuts constructed yes from the habits and husks
of discarded Sisters Philbert and Connie
may their souls rest in peace or
lock me in the limehouse and throw away the jam
quit trying to think kid
you gotta counterpunch, see
start a little Waller-wise Black and Blue Fats
follow with a Fool Medley then

breathing through your ears Gone with the Wind
then After You've Gone
I Concentrate on You
and your dinghy whitewater farmhouse canoe
do Laura in Petrarchan time
or Dinah in someone's Sumerian kitchen
isn't it funny I got rhythm
but we got a long way to go so
who's sorry now

Dave McKenna
Academy of the Holy Names
Albany 19 Sept 98

I'LL REPOSE NEVER

You sit on saddlerock eating camp flowers
with flea powder, your occipital bone
has grown a visor and come a cropper
The baboon looks the baboon's look
and eyes the guard nervously
You were haunted by the dungeon really the basement
It was the Cuba of the future
it was another Nicaragua. One couldn't help thinking
this sort of talk was a shorthand for confusion
Passive sentences are common
in scientific writing. In the first person
acid was added to the solution
Huckleberry Finn had adventures of envy
The size of his hands made his smallness real
Many people would have helped
if they had known. If voters had more confidence
they wouldn't vote. Heed this lesson Reader

the truce was signed on Tuesday the house
overflowed with fixtures the names Belial and Lucifer
Latin for the brown trout is *salmo trutta*
In Modern Language is work relevant

KELLY'S IRISH ALPS

for Rae

You really know you're old
When you're taller than a tree

Cases of baskets chirruping feathers
Through arboreal paisley

And leaves holdfast to their foster child
Rushing between socials in Far Vidalia

Temperature stops its primal ticking
Borne strictly in a gleam

Mirrored and wet from the hip
One slip and it all repeats itself

Shine of your classic stringbean
Emulating spittle on a web

Unleashing the charmers that grow beneath you
A scan is all it takes to back around

A fibula deforming reality

BEGINNING WITH A LINE

To think is to forget differences
    the time you laze away
    you can take with you to the grave

In any case milord barristers of belief
    in smartly creased trousers perform feats
    of lifesaving with turned-up mustachios

But intuition cannot be defended nor
    crack-brained epiphanies
    on nitrous

No less anaesthetic revelations
    whose memories have lost
    their things

after Benjamin Blood

FOGGER'S DAY

A pip slipping off
a buttercup
gets the drop on crop circles
gulls fill a tackshop

The sky is lousy with elephants
aliens are insulting by omission
louder than a sack of fireflies
more germane than Simone Weil

A monocle is to a soul
as a porthole to a ship
it never becomes intimate
but is known to wreck homes

Think I'll go over the rim tonight
and break a tambourine
warm the intelligentsia
have you noticed this tree can read

ABOUT THE OUTSIDE

Language
being perception
we live like vagrant tremens
samples
of the inner script
stitched to the sky

Like tetrahedrons
in the weeds of tangents
or fragmentum with wings
the rule of the rooster
gives way
to the rule of the law

Go to the ant, slugger

AN UNDISCOVERED DRUTHER

Almost an anecdote the wolf
has a horoscope a phantom
limb rubs off on the wind
footprints swallow a bottle
of aspirin because it's
meant to mean something
16 candles round the sun
extinguish original sin
where do spooks come from a

hand comes through the wall
because it's meant to mean
something all is understood

THE EMPTINESS AT THE BOTTOM OF A GLASS

The first person is a cage from the past

As I said to the kid who worked the hurricane wall
—answer the door

Instead, he let down his inalienable hair
which fell to his neck
in the form of a question mark

It wasn't the curls that made the punctuation
so unmistakable, it was the way it fell
like a key in a lock

The answer seemed to fit all questions

VESPUCCI KNEW

Because I played Drake's Hamlet
        "the loony pilgrim" because
        they came to me in the teeth

of calumny did I heave chairs
        or willow ware, Uncle?
        I'd gone over in my heart

crucibles in a pushcart
        midget thunder rumbled
        on the shelves somewhere

white teeth gleamed on peaches
    somewhere an old centurion
    bivouacked in his bureau

like it was yesterday took his breath away
    like any Roman said *domani*
    and neglected it

that brick in the grip of the Latin vowel
    that ergo every dago be
    made in America

AFTER AS

for the folks at 71 Elmgrove

Sailing shall be our model for
the imperceptible progress of fruit
whose seven league boot
grows a hoof
This got no further than the loan of a book
Know ye now Bulkington?
—I reckon
Windows are beasts of burden
Draw the curtains on the donkey
Pin a tale to the sea
A loaf-colored hat sails out of a nap
If you'll allow me (sub rosary)
the one thing I remember at my dexter ankle
in connection with your shrubbery
is how the vernacular came about as bees
pollinating curates
made vespers in the holly

A mole enters the dome of a privateer
The eternal Jack of the human pack

thumbs through his looking glass
Oysters strip to the waist
Wait a minute vines Waterman
was leaking to the Times about the dream
Note the undertow of hijinx nesting in brilliantine
there must be a twist in my brain
drinking from the same quote container time
took a swig of
Should Lady Luck run amuck feeling
in a subjunctive mood
might be she's from hunger too

Mother Tongue (not a glee club)
befogs the dispatches—says here even foxtrotters
smuggle sonnets in their pockets
If defenestration was all it took I would've been
tops—Geronimo to the nth power
of Uriah Heep!
       And next
the solid emerges from the fluid wobble
more righteous than Dexter Bundists
in the twenty years since the blouses of Bess
Are we wobbling into a unified pre-sun dress?
What business is Virgina in?
The constellations have done far more for
algebra than Dutch fustian
A comma-colored spider crawls up the wall
to get his ashes hauled
It was weird me being
the last of the Mohigans and all

Doc Mellifluus patron of layabouts
his heart a target for bowls of soup signs
an oak of secrecy
A dusty anthropoid shadowboxes
under a shadetree with six aliases
One would've thought effrontery (a brunch)

was a branch of knowledge—
Fellow Willow to jaw
with the incorrigible Maple Kid
At the museum of work God is mental
others stare straight at the ground
like rain from the sky
have lingua, will vanish

Light is the facelift that edits wit
As long as we're turning the page
theatre is the shell game of the stars
a salute to the insult of the sun
splitting history into hairs—all theirs
Quick! shut off the plants
unpack the face
eight hours ago it was a full grown narcissus
One dies faster in the evening sun
the corn still on the listening ear
Leviathan
in cloak of cyclamen
ascends by flukes the pollen count
every hayrick confederate a bona fide pyrogen
each waterloo a tiny subjectivity…
The eyes have it—cold feet
Clairvoyant noses up and running
about to suffer a sea change

August 2001

THE INFLATABLE FELLOWSHIP OF HIDING

In the old vocab of the stowaway
a counterpane comes in from the greensward
for some recitative

a yacht rhapsodizes through baize doors
and knows every leafhopper
by its handspring

every railroad by its nadir
a wholly unique persona non grata
on the high seas

MY OCCUPATIONS

Someone who writes to Pinocchio
what will they become of me

has a friend in cheeses
a ladder in the blue

becomes my blue
heaven yonder

over dittos
illumination

in the empty stretches
of an astronomy lesson

the soda jerk becomes a fizzician
what will I become of me

EVIDENCE

Sunset so swift you'd say it had an engine
Flora Danica waiting in the wings
fireflies in mason jars for footlights

let night come in and take the green that brought me here
I dare to fall asleep alone
without my nightcap whose dimness shone

my socks lately ghosted into mittens
my dreams begin to turn their keys
vibrate with pagan witchery

the clay that is sculpted
and the clay that wants to be
reams of the fray wheeled out on a cot

Dr. Seagoing Yacht with his crew prescription
the precision of faraway herbalists spilling the beans
but I am not that person

I am learning dreariness earmuffs hang from my arms
"We don't really get your suffering
they build barracks to feed hungers like yours"

DEATH BY NOSTALGIA

Able to undrape widows with a slip of the tongue, more germane than
Simone Weil, they exit the closet as a singing troupe. Fetal horses

gallop in the womb. Nouns run about naming names. Fins awaken the
old terror. The funny papers open fire.

Oxygen depriving a face staggers on the back lot of the eye. Who
possesses a valid image of El Cid? Who threw that grape?

Nervousness is a nervous condition. Lochs lack gravitas. Food settles, and you lie on it for comfort.

Virgil intends to kill again, "I love my little rooster, and my rooster loves me."

Pinstripes rain in the poems of Basho who lives in the head of a lettuce. We converse on the sea ceiling seamless in dyslexia.

LOSE YOUR HEAD KEEP YOUR HAIR

Freedom has no psychological interior. All wild creatures

become outlaws. Thanks for the cowlick, free of postage, pulsing with life.

Lo and behold, problems stick to the window. Of course the snake's still drunk

hosting grass parties. The town is off its rocker

flying whales instead of flags. At a building bigger than the History of Music the Heart Street waitress speaks Paradise Lost.

The end of life loses its address at the local ropemakers.

The snaggle-toothed solarium, the Odd Fellows' Home. Freedom,

another word for mercy.

WHEN COMING'S GONE

Mother Goose owns a walnut grove but prefers Hispanic boys at the well.

Goldfish nibble Garciaparra. Who will help with her zipper?

Not Billy Campbell cordoned-off with soup cans. Can't she see the stars
are out once the lights are out,

The moon a hole-in-one. The beginning's back

from what seems an apocalyptic bedtime story. Wherever that fallout
shelter is a child is burying

a guinea pig. Yes, personal convictions converted to Zen

are going to be the same again. Tennessee warblers come to a boil in
hyacinth.

Orpheus in Boise. A tattoo rolled in a sock.

LIKE ORNITHOLOGY

To a sick eagle slugging a vampire
seeing doubles division
diamond onion
scab of two minds in disguise

Bird lives in Roman stencils
as antidote for simulacra
beyond the shadow of a decoy
in which trees shod with india rubber
see him from afar riding
on a swan

Ask the verger of wit whose shingle's
worth the tar it was writ with
and who writes with feathers anymore

O haven brother
in the void do angels have cocktails
or tea with trumpets?

VIII/2002

A DRIFT

Lift the kitchen window
fish brush past grappling hooks
swing from clouds
half on the lam

don't miss it if you can
mistress of the streets
which are waving goodbye
rolling in a pirate flag uphill

23IX03

EARLY OPERA AFTERNOONS

He gives us wings
and takes away the sky
He drinks the view
drawing through his telescope
what drives the tide
He has a cousin who is a color
they sign a hymn together

there's not a lot to say
to feel
to have this long a memory
in the old vocab of the stowaway
a counterpane comes in
for some recitative

EVERY LOCKPICKER HOME

A chicken broth salesman fiddle cricketer
reads Chair City papyri in the weeds
ashamed to have friends know
clean men defend a tub in Cairo
while sprucing up
Boss Tweed whose dates
have been replaced by trees
just as summer
is shaving the hair of fruit
from a learned professor of poverty

Truth needn't discover anything

after Berkson

A RACE

There's a stonecutter over my head
I could care less I should be more
like a pencil
I'm just trying to make a point
I can't write "my replica's
adjustable arm is handsome"
though it hands me some copy
a portion of the loitering night

on paper (white)
no one is coming
even in the shadows

AT ARNOLD ARBORETUM

I've no idea how
beneath the bark
the rains come together
in nature nothing's free
cut me down and count the rings
we pay for our serenity
until its own increasing process
is utterly dependable an end
what I am
loving you whether
what goes on

15 Nov 03

APOCALYPSE

Near Olneyville in the weeds
chicken broth salesmen nibble
Mickey Mouse head cheese
forgive them for being
as small as life
etched on lightning bugs
reads the Evening Papyri
a sort of convention
mentioned Mrs Motley
like tree rings in parquet

good evening friends
and cherished listeners
read my lips
Providence is funny like this

Sept 04

SCARECROW FALLS

We feel jittery and
beef jerky
burger weather with wine
one should resemble a description
what do they call pulling your hair out
nothing of everything that could be
pigs in space
surplus purpose
no closer to stars than closer together
when the sky is all one color
are we looking at the afterlife
living
because it's something to do

LIFEBOAT DAYS

Too old for exams I could tell you
more I knew a lot of
lullabies unallied youngsters
tracked me down in my
seesaw nightgown that's
what if not a clue
true it's familiar
but you could also say it's

strange at home
I discovered there's only
one sound *hm* next thing
I learned to pickle
silent movies of the sea

TO A FAMILIAR

That story based on me
couldn't possibly have happened
I wasn't like anyone real
I can hear you leafing through my books
is that Braille
I'm talking off the top of my head
but you people think things up
sun drops that don't exist
except on tv
don't reckon they'll be chasing me
back to the sticks
like that story said
there'd never be a second time
that's formalism
one can't live just to be in literature

TO A FAMILIAR

I'm an editor in the 7th grade
I have no interest in being a laureate
my father was a country vet
after eight litters and four corndogs
I've decided to take on the woodpecker
there are hardly any books in the country
side and everyone is doing deals
things are improving

I can see myself but I do it on the sly
though I pay through the nose
for fresh water
they expect me to capsize
I don't need a thing
which is a great savings
it can't all be make-believe

TO A FAMILIAR

I wasn't out to get anybody's goat
like a tight pair of pants
I retired as a kid
headed south my thoughts went deeper
one thought I was schizophrenic another
the reincarnation of a mug
I wasn't going to break any manhood rules
the fat was in the fire
I had no money couldn't coin a phrase
got balloon sickness and ruined my tights
stem-cell research said it wasn't true
violence has to come out someplace
I could blow my top but where would it
get me say what you will
this is the real world

TO A FAMILIAR

They call this an interview
it's useful to have parents overseas
distance which invokes news
a phrase I picked up on tv
I don't need a mirror
suit yourself slips out from habit

I've become so refined I can't
see what I'm saying to tell
the truth I shave with tea leaves
nobody sees anybody anyway
don't bother with clouds
they'll run you down
take a powder
come back as lucid

THE REALITY OF THE OTHER EYE

If this is it I'm sorry I said
to the ceiling
have I been reading

my Lumber World
preparing for a life after trees
if Peach Haven dwindles to

peach pits and a hymn book
washed by the lack of rain
if something

as unprofessional as a feeling
varies according to pain
should I wait for the words to change

ARIA FROM MEMORY

From ages seven through eighteen—basically every Sunday after Mass in which for many years I scored assists as an altar boy—I was famulus to a super-sized Toscanini. Me, sole student remanded to the Vince Lombardi School of Opera of which my father was coach/conductor and principal vocalist.

Life was a locker room of lessons from a podium. Weekdays I carried a ball. Like Lombardi in the Coliseum padre mio loved to spin *La Forza del Destino* exposing an artistic vein of his own inadequacy—for which read *ethnicity*. You know the routine, "Look, I was pretty good. But you could be great. It's easier now, see?" Though I could never cotton to this sort of assimilation, I don't wonder his coaching our church choir was carried over after Mass and a late breakfast into our listening chamber and given his day-of-rest headset tripped some long ago glee circuitry, which via conducting and especially singing kept him open to brand ecstasy. Stir this with a missed kidhood and Depression-era work ethic and you get a sense of the opera *we* were living and which forever after imbued with melodrama the cast of our characters.

I was eager as one of the chosen is to please. Also desiring to get out from under the opera ray my immediate response was "Give me the melody—i.e. the ball—I'm going all the way!"

Not so fast, Dash.

I guess he didn't know I'd've done anything presto to gain his attention. And did I ever—he's younger than me now! But first I had to run endless operatic wind sprints on the gridiron of *Rigoletto*.

—And Gilda was her name-o!

BUNK BEDS

Weather set us apart
everything was somehow a surprise
an alternate Beau Geste starring
Illinois Jacquet
—you bet!

English broke our mother tongues
to make us all
American of course
this woke everyone
homo duplex and then some

Item: to be as wide
as sleep
eyes lie through their teeth
'til they're blue in the face
—just in case

ALPHAMAP

Petrus Bizzarus
Thomas Blundeville Thomas Cavendish Cornelius Caymocx Cathay
Sir John Cheke Hieronymous Cock Lucas Cranach John Dee
Jean De Lasco Ugo da Carpi Capri
Johannes Drosius Oronce Fine
Cornelius Floris Flodden
Martin Frobisher Walter Ghim Cornelius Grapheus Greenland
Nuño Guzman Werner von Gymnich Lackawanna Liège
George Lily Macropedius Olaf Magnus Magog
Peter Martyr Black Maarten Phillip Melanchthon Majorca Malang
William the Towhead William of Orange Omsk
Arturo Pet Matthias Ringmann

494

The Rhine
Sacrobosco Otto Vogel Pierre Was New South Wales
Urban Wyss Nicolò Zeno Ulrich Zell and Zider Zee

WITHOUT BEING TOLD

The Fifth Amendment
does not apply to the face
deeper inside the frame

the man who
inhabits your eyes
abdicates his throat

in a glass-bottomed boat
you could ask me headless
I don't mind

a mentholated ghost
makes everything butter
another reason

to abandon words

CLUB HAGIOGRAPHY

It's so great to be someplace
    leave shape-shifting to changelings
eat at my shepherd station
    in the name of scenery I saw this sign
Museum of Cloud Holes
    (pop. minus one)
a donut worth channeling
    —could be a stretch—

that's me in the picture
    next to Slim Southwestie
an honest butte well remembered
    why'd I steal this brandy
and there's Uncle Jug
    what pulled the spirit plug
and Raggedy Andy

VERTIGO COMES CLEAN

Head turning the endless
present rushes over
the crumpling glass

a great shadow slurring
syllables to a common end
corrupt we proceed

we will never desert
what we might have been
that's what we're for

a shame
we ignore the same words
sleepers can't sleep

flowers can't stand
the memory of some carrot
the glowing dead

hammering in spring
opening in spring
we wanted to get ahead

DETOUR AHEAD

The weather clears
like some body
getting back

an appetite
cowboys and aliens
start your gentlemen

near the end the air
is spoken for
in a nutshell

we make our way
like a caterpillar toward
a kernel in Grimms'

VACANCE

Little dream pipe
to the right just
inside this map
I'm holding a hurricane
is raging to sweep you
off your face isn't
the business of the future
to be absent

GRATITUDE ON PARADE

for T & L

Amore on the floor
Buddha's Baksheesh
Your solar Cat
My funny bone Dementia
All Elevated cul-de-sacs
Fones Alley
Gratuities from the blue
Houris of the Hourglass
Ignatz, Ignatz forever
Jeroboams in primavera
Kafka, Franz
The feminine Langsam
Mycroft Holmes
Just Say No
Osceola
Hens in Purdah
The Q in cuneiform
My worn Russian beaver
Snapdragon weather
Taliesin
Uma Thurman
Vineyard moon
The Wind's Weary trunk
X means anyone
Yabba dabba do
Por tu Zapatas

THE REPUBLIC OF SHADE

Abundance gives the air its blank
    stare lose your head
keep your hair said the vicar's wife
    to the sugar bowl who knows jelly
you're a kind of jam

comfort will never be
    comfortable enough so much
for continuity Blondie
    could be Dominican ipod
in this hand in that bag

Johnny Appleseed and you
    Gaston twice Dagwood's age
harpooning krill as still
    life cartoons at the edges
so much for continuity

A MOTE TO BUILD A DREAM IN

Shampoo'd
a will-o-the-wisp
as when making out

a silhouette
and beyond awareness
the eye backs up

into one of many combs
and ones attention paid
plays second fiddle

to a floodlight
whose vocal line
gives shape to a shrine

gloria in shacks
we help
put up in the wind

MINORITY REPORT

If Moten had a local anesthetic
If Hubcap had a lip
If Chet hadn't stumbled on speedballs
If Mingus had never flipped
If Tatum had a cornea
If Lester hadn't lisped
If Bix hadn't been so sensitive
If Davie Tough had fallen less
If Billie hadn't loved abuse
...*Shit!*

VANITY, THE LAST AFFAIR

Try nectarine attire or try the guardhouse. Try some slacks to endure Abyssinian accidentals. Fingerprint the demon chorus. I've got the world in a jug expressed in twelve bars. Emotions in song bulge with syllables. Dew dropped from the willow leaf of a cast-off mistress. I went down to the river to provide accompaniment high as a gal can stand. Read music to a rocking chair, put ashes on sundown blacker than flags while the window-dressing counts the days I'm gone. With oriental weariness catastrophe drifts commemorative from cabin to cabin, from stanza to shack. Death decreases the cost of living. The mailman couldn't make the damsel. Performance puts a damper on dives though the man in the moon takes an interest. Blame it on the river, chocolate to the bone. She smelled like toilet soap, like puppets on strings added to the pleasure of words. That's why Mama's got the pants and a pair of silk folksongs. An animal sadness of the greatest amazement.

VIAL OF ANGELS

for Kit

He died in a cello incident.
He was a tough egg.
The viola broke the news
to his old valet
in the pages of a children's book.

Now that magic had flown the coop
water music slept on an air mattress. Maybe
it was that swan blowing from the east.

We'll never know if we've said enough.
The sky is plain as cake. The door
an habitual mystery.

A SURPLUS ENERGY

How do the dead abide
their childishness?
They are unimprovable. Without

direction they would be
an uncertainty, immaturity
their fundamental state: to return

home in love with a fascinating stranger.
The lover shuts her eyes, listens
to no voice other than her own.

The return home. Feelings are meticulous,
impossible to express. Memories
supplant decisions.

WHO'S THERE

When someone who's talking isn't
listening as well as the someone
who's saying a you must see
the end of the world around the I...

that said I can barely
remember listening
listening is an old tape speaking
they attach it to you so they can speak

this tape is an old skin listening
to something made of sex
laid out in space that thieves

from other planets are listening to it
while someone is speaking
who can't pay attention

OPIUM PHOTOGRAPHICA

Posing as Walt Whitman
you give a cat a piece of fish
and cross your legs

twice you move a Moorish woman's chair
pay the girl aged 10 or 9 maybe
12 or 13 gooseberries, after all

she's discovered the hundred
thousand three hundred things
at the bottom of the lake

you read aloud from
a newspaper that reads
the news aloud to you

THIEF OF STINGS

for John Highton

Proto-poodles keep great houses
Cozier than a warmer-weather working clip
In which a particolored mutt flushes
Several puddle ducks from cover

Like javelins to a side of ham
They come from nowhere to a park
At the top of this page
They repeat from memory

What they don't know
So it goes rhymes the rain
A thief of stings I'll never call-in-sick again
Then the Middle Ages move in

Driving to places that don't exist
A girl disappears in a bar of soap
Years later she's pear-shaped
Slapping her gloves at a diving duck

LAST POEMS

(Summer 2010)

MORIARTY'S INVISIBLE FENCES

Disappearance is within us
Waiting is everywhere
Resemblance is the passing of the world
The despair of surveyors

The eye adds a face
To the character
Coming from farther away than the book
The world of the shoelace and the privet hedge

One meets on the train to divinity school the long ashes of Irish boys
They are decoys glued to an invisible world
An occasion for the self and the wolf

The sky invades the characters of a film
One perceives the infinite and starts counting it
Waiting is everywhere

> *after Jean Daive*
> *IX10*

OUR FAMILIARS

> *for Hollis*

The rain green front door flew by
The forest thought it was quitting time
A watermark twitched, a roebuck
Slipped on the parquet

Old Apple Face dusted
The armchair hidden in his hair
Hackberry sycoraxed a dish
Of plums, nutshells fell

On the snoring mastiff
And his nursing bottle
Spoiled milk surrounded the imp

Pubescent blue teeth and gutta percha
Were heaped in the kitchen
How comforting this is to the dwarf's sleep

POEM ENDING WITH A LINE BY BRIAN EVENSON

Spiderman has a stroke
While stringing his ukulele

The Alien smoking in the breakfast nook
Sees Inca pinholes

Accurate to a raindrop
A Martian Pez

In a brickyard outside Butte
"Bury me next to my voice box"

If I could marry Mary would I thinks Joseph of Arimathea
If there's a fog where's the feeling

At the first sermon on table tennis
Vermont repeated in minute detail

The story of how the apple was eaten
Now be a good boy and cut off your arm

FOR ALL WE KNOW

We may never meet again.

She always talked
She had to
Like déjà vu

She always said
She always would
She had to

She always gave
She always was
The main thing

She always was
She didn't mind
She stood

For something
She would always say
She thought so

Like déjà vu
She thought so
She was ready

PUNITIVE POSSIBILITIES

A hurler of junk pounds the pocket of his glove
And removes a plate of fried potatoes

The sun sets on his black eye
His private nurse is with him on the mound

Hey! This isn't an atrocity
Hauled out of Cro-Magnon vapors

There's nowhere to hide!
Home plate shakes like a blind wok

The rosin lands in a cloud
A checkered tablecloth

Is hoisted over the park
Banners dark as bats hang in violet air

OFF MINOR

for Steve Dickison

The Lunatics were visiting
(Ruby and Buff Orpington)
I flew the coop into a filmstrip

a free-swinging pendulum
passing through the *unliving*
I saw a woman in line ahead of me

only minutes before I hadn't
a little upright arrived for the mice
surveying myself from six feet above

not having rehearsed I would
now have to transfer
to a smaller ship with no orchestra

A DUSTY WESTERN

Cheyenne Harry is a.

This high plains drifter services vacuum cleaners.

Addie understands nil about housekeeping but longs to hitch her wagon
to Cheyenne's brushes.

Back East Addie's snobbish New York banking father grudgingly offers his
daughter's hand to this mysterious western Electrolux.

Suddenly Daddy's finances are headed south and our financier finds him-
self out in the cold. Bearing bagels, cream cheese and lox he follows the
three Stock Brokers of the East

out west beyond the several badlands to Cheyenne's stash.

With Addie in Wyoming, cleaning his vacuum cleaner, Harry reflects on
their wedding party,

"Honey, we surely did clean up!"

OTHER COUCHES, OTHER CLOUDS

for Win Knowlton

You work undercover as a pre-death mortician.

Your enemy gets an intolerable second wind in which you are shivering
like an old rooster.

Someone's left the mirror running.
Your mind begins to slide.

You mop the poplar blossom fluff off the Van Gogh.

A tattered copy of *The Count of Monte Cristo* lies under the bed.

You have an opportunity to speak in hiccups. You believe there are many of
them and leave on the strike of two.

Tattoos disappear into every orifice.
Got the picture?

Music sleeps on an air mattress.
Your mind continues its slide.

Maybe it's that swan blowing in from the east.
All the windows seem drowsy.

On hot summer nights by Delius
You send burnt letters to your mother.

In the language of appearances death is indescribable.

Things go liquid in the tails of your eyes.
Your nerves pass out of central control.

A Salvation Army connoisseur has his first sip of a comet vintage.
Things are humming at The Bois.

Mermaids ply the bar with goldfish.
Bedbugs remain to be executed.

You give up the ghost only to have it crawl out of the woodwork with artifi-
cial sweeteners.

Begin the newsreel without me.

THE SHIN-KICKING YEARS

He took another breath
With manifest regret, threw a blade of grass to a drowning ant.
What was he supposed to do, submit
To a shivering world? He smiled his bag of frozen corn.
Now he was right-sized, his pajamas grinned.
He emerged from hibernation. Spreading his sails
Small waves chopped twinkles the size of sparrows.
Fish climbed to the top of the sun,
He used them to count the hours. He dragged a boat
Through the trees. A pattern was forming.
He was asking for help—in order to amuse himself?
Is this my house? No. This was a sticky ripple.
In the algebraic rain he cleared his throat,
Looked at the remains. The pile had finally fallen into place.

NO OPIATE

for Rosmarie

Daylight carving time
to the point of carbonation
enters the annals
of prejudice

Too many people to like
faithfully too much
ambivalence to love
this century

The old king's polar sword
shatters like a metaphor

THE CONVERSANTS

There was a monkey puzzle a minute down the road
But she forgot all about it till evening
And finding out what the dissention was about
Owing to the thickness of the door, vanished into the basement

It had nothing to do with the house
Wind over linoleum
Dimples at the end of the table
She continued to construct an imaginary circumstance

What but consciousness of a crime
Could prompt a knowledge of its particulars
As in youth the overpowering force
Of a reproachful finger

The pain died away after a day spent
With her lover under the old curriculum
Like a candlewick its liquid ailment up
To the chin all but extinct

The plane tree prepared a bookplate entry
The dove ground its love song on the roof

YOU BET MY LIFE?

for Geoff Young

Nowadays you wouldn't think a guy could get by as a jongleur
Jongling for dimes like a professional faster
Whose Chinese includes the word for "meter reader"

Which would have stumped Confucius.
And once, can you believe it, in the Bronx, he recited the whole of
    "Toledo Slim"
To half a dozen alligators, in less than a minute!

The big money men stopped underwriting recitations
Every time one of their wives had a birthday.
Now he's reduced to nickels and numismatics

And works amusement parks,
Filling stations, hotdog stands.
He's even performed for a jumping bean!

TODAY

Rain and wind rattle
The whole caboodle

Missing a few bricks
Dream dust disregards

Chimneys unbeheld
A man pokes out his head

They're not evergreens
If you chop them down

ANOTHER TALE FROM HOFFMAN

for Hollis

The shadow cast by the mouse covers the entire room
He returns every night by the light of the moon
The apparition in the glass-paned bookcase
Unlike the mother and the mouse has no mouth
Impossible not to braid into pigtails the grown-up's cocktails
With the beakless parrot on a parrot stand
Or the porcelain child bound for eternity to a tricycle of blue lead

A pine floor the color of Caruso's Cadillac makes
The drawer pulls shine. On the stairs the clock smiles six
A head falls from the maple
Dresser into a beaded moccasin
Time slides thinly
Through the great basin of the skull
The wind's hand passes over the water
To slap your head if you're not careful
Gazing into space Mr Sandman saws a domino in half
He always thinks of his children as pieces
He throws sand into their eyes so uncannily
They jump out of their heads
He puts their eyes in a sack and carries them off
To the half moon as food for his other little brood

THE POSTHUMOUS LIFE OF CHILDREN

for Craig Watson

Alone is the monologue
known by heart to which
the loop of the beginning
is fastened.

Not everything can exist
in a childlike stillness.
Who needs damask pies
or elfin noodles?

What kid of summer dump
truck smokes a hookah?
The delicate fades into
the blue sound-engineered sky.

Metabolics drip dry into
a spoonscape. The dwarf again
forces me to gaze into his glass eye.

Ornithology was taught
the violin by osmosis
on a premature autumn day.

THE VOYAGE

This room is more depressing than Sunday
But now I'm away at sea
Where coziness is a weekly comic from Mother
I sleep on the floor to help the flower girl
Who has supported me during my amnesia
I imagine playing golf with her throb
A cold rain shower reminds me of myself
Tonight I went home mumming birds
They can hardly blame me for that
With ice water butter and bread I wash my hands and go out
But I haven't the courage to go through with it
And leave the so-called present behind the mirror
The janitor directs my first play "Caught in the Rain"
Red neckerchiefs and gunplay
Nature has endowed the Mormons with a mirage
Which makes me think of Moses leading children out of Bow-Wow
"You will die of bronchial pneumonia at 82. A dollar, please"
I look forward again to greeting the friendly dentist in Tacoma
Every day my peace of mind depends on the Alexandria Bar
"In sixty seconds you'll be completely unconscious"
I neither believe nor disbelieve in anything

9/26/10

By Michael Gizzi

My Grandfather's Pants (Bench Press, 1973)
Carmela Bianca (Bonewhistle Press, 1974)
Bird As (Burning Deck, 1976)
Avis (Burning Deck, 1979)
Species of Intoxication (Burning Deck, 1983)
Just Like A Real Italian Kid (The Figures, 1990)
Continental Harmony (Roof Press, 1991)
Gyptian In Hortulus (Paradigm Press, 1991)
Lowell Connector (Hard Press, 1993)
Interferon (The Figures, 1995)
No Both (The Figures/Hard Press, 1997)
Rejection (The Figures, 1997)
Too Much Johnson (The Figures, 1999)
Cured In The Going Bebop (Paradigm Press, 2000)
My Terza Rima (The Figures, 2001)
McKenna's Antenna (Qua Jazz, 2001)
Knowlton Mfg. (Paul Rodgers/9W, 2002)
New Depths of Deadpan (Burning Deck, 2009)
In This Skin (Qua Limited, 2010)

Michael Gizzi was born in 1949, in Schenectady, New York. After receiving his BA and MA in Literature from Brown University, he remained in Rhode Island where he became an arborist and tree surgeon. In August 1971 he married Ippy Astlett, illustrator and fellow Brown graduate, and their daughter Pilar was born in Providence in 1975.

In the early 1980's he and his second wife Barbeio Barros moved to the Berkshires where he taught at Lenox Memorial High School, and was an editor of Hard Press as well as an organizer of scores of poetry readings, some of which took place at Arrowhead, Herman Melville's home in Pittsfield.

After returning to Providence in 2003, he taught at Roger Williams University and at Brown, co-founded and edited QUA Books with Craig Watson, and continued his role as an impresario of poetry readings.

He died in Providence in September, 2010.